T0147079

A Faith that Stands

Daily Devotional or Small-Group Study with
Multigenerational Insights for Your Faith Journey

TAMMY THURMAN

WESTBOW
PRESS®
A DIVISION OF THOMAS NELSON
& ZONDERVAN

WestBow Press books may be ordered through booksellers or by contacting:

WestBow Press
A Division of Thomas Nelson & Zondervan
1663 Liberty Drive
Bloomington, IN 47403
www.westbowpress.com
844-714-3454

ISBN: 978-1-6642-6582-0 (sc)
ISBN: 978-1-6642-6581-3 (hc)
ISBN: 978-1-6642-6583-7 (e)

Library of Congress Control Number: 2022908326

Print information available on the last page.

WestBow Press rev. date: 10/27/2022

Testimonials

Knowing Mark and Tammy as we do, the release of this book fills us with joy. We have watched them both exhibit "A Faith That Stands" in both good times and bad. Everything they do represents a heart of worship as they love God and others. Their faith has been tested, but in their deep relationship with Christ, they stand firm.

—Chuck and Sue Lamson, Mentors and Prayer Partners

Tammy has a heart for people in all walks of life with a remarkable ability to see the best in everyone, while at the same time challenging them to grow in their walk with the Lord.

—Rachel Schepp, Executive Director at Care Net Pregnancy Center of Milwaukee

Life is a journey. Along the way we can either pass on the lessons we learn in life to others or keep them to ourselves. Tammy is a vibrant, kingdom minded Christian who freely invests in others. "A Faith That Stands" is more than a devotional. It's an invitation to a daily journey of personal growth and spiritual maturity.

—Jerry Brooks, Lead Pastor of Discover Church in Oak Creek, WI

Tammy's love, boldness, and passion for God's Word radiate from her to others. Her transparency about her own faith has been such an encouragement to me.

—Mel Boeck, Bible Study Teacher Buddy with Tammy

Tammy loves people of every age and exudes a genuine heart for her community. My prayer is that God would use this devotional to connect individuals to Jesus by helping them see what God's Word has for them. She and her extended family offer hope that everyone who pursues Jesus can have an unwavering "Faith That Stands."

—Sarah Kopf, Administrative Assistant at Care Net Pregnancy Center of Milwaukee

We have been blessed by Tammy and Mark's Spirit-led leadership. Living like they lead, congregations have been inspired and empowered to grow closer to God. Their devotion to prayer is on these pages. Enjoy as they come alongside you on your own faith journey. We are thankful to God that our paths have crossed.

—Tony and Susan Weinhold, Prayer Partners

Dad

Dedication

Although my dad is now in heaven, he will always be an example to me of God's amazing ability to transform a person at any age. I witnessed this complete change in my dad firsthand, as in my growing-up years, I was very afraid of him. His anger consumed our home, and I was overwhelmed with anxiety and resentment. As the years went by, through much faith and prayer, my dad came to know and follow Jesus. His choice changed everything for our whole family.

I'll never forget, then married with two small children, sitting at the kitchen table when I received a phone call. It was my dad, wanting to take my sister Wendy and me out for lunch to a very nice restaurant over the holiday when we'd both be in town. Something was different in his voice, and I eagerly anticipated what he might be up to.

I remember the white linen tablecloths, the floral dress I wore, and the corsages he gave to us. He proceeded to confess with tears that he had terribly messed up as a father and that he was deeply sorry. No, he couldn't take back all the years of mistrust and hurt, but he wanted us to know that he loved us and wanted a relationship with us. We cried, laughed, rejoiced, and forgave.

That Father's Day, I wrote my dad a song that prayed a blessing over him. He cried, saying he didn't deserve a daughter writing a song for him like that. But I told him that his journey had taught me the most valuable lesson about God: no one is too old or wayward to be changed from the inside out through Jesus. If God doesn't give up on people, neither will I.

Therefore, I gratefully dedicate this book to my dad, Dale Dellmore, for through forgiveness my relationship with him was restored. God is faithful. And someday I know I will see my dad in heaven, where we will worship together at the feet of Jesus (with bagpipes ... ha).

Contents

Preface

A Faith That Stands was birthed out of a time of personal loss when Scripture alone was my healing balm. Inspired by the well-known poem, "Do it Anyway" by Dr. Kent Keith (more famously credited by Mother Teresa), I began to focus on what is important in this life, revisiting my purpose through Christ. As I recounted the many ways that God had been faithful to me, I found myself pouring into so much Scripture that I had to write about and tell others how it had healed me. Only Jesus could have taken me on the journey of forgiving those in my life who had hurt me deeply. There is power and victory in the name of Jesus!

God's faithfulness is also evident in the lives of my extended family, recognizing that faith stands through the heartbreaks and disasters life brings. My desire for this book was to include as many extended family members as possible who desired to write some of their own devotions from their own walks with the Lord. Our different roads give us unique perspectives, but God is the same God.

With twelve monthly themes, *A Faith That Stands* can be used for a daily devotional with questions on the seventh day of each week or a small group study with some friends. The important thing is to read the Scripture passages. Make every effort not to gloss over them or skip them for the story alone. The Scripture is much more important than the story.

The goal for every Christian is to be able to stand firm in our faith, applying Scripture to our everyday life, resulting in a faith that stands the test of time. May we be **bold** to share our testimonies with others and encourage those around us to run the race with perseverance and humility. God is faithful. Always.

Acknowledgments

I want to thank my amazing husband, Mark, for having a faith that doesn't waver, being my cheerleader, and supporting me in all my creative endeavors. I love partnering with you in ministry and am privileged to share my life with you!

I also want to thank my extended family for being a family that loves one another well. I cherish and respect all of you and appreciate your guidance, encouragement, and friendship through the years. A family that follows Jesus creates a strong tie that can never be broken. This is our legacy.

—Tammy

Introduction

Before you begin, I encourage you to seek God with all your heart, soul, mind, and strength. My prayer is for you to find a renewed and unwavering hope and joy as you pursue your faith journey with Jesus.

There are twelve monthly themes with weekly subgroups containing six devotional readings and a day of application questions to tie the week together. Whether you use this for personal or family use or utilize it to spur on further discussion with a small group, please read all the Scripture.

A Faith That Stands is applicable for men, women, teenagers, and older children. A bio page at the end highlights the twelve different authors in this book, all part of our extended family. Every writer has a unique perspective, writing from various points of life. We write about stories from our own personal walks with the Lord, creating a journal of sorts where each devotional is signed with the person who wrote it.

For more resources, please visit my personal website at Keys2Faith.org. Download recordings and sheet music arrangements for piano, instrumental, original worship, children's choir musicals, Bible studies, and more. All proceeds from the website go to support world and local missions.

MONTH 1

In This World, We Will Feel Disappointed, Hurt, or Betrayed by Others

A FAITH THAT STANDS
Produces Forgiveness

Forgiveness: How Do I Begin?
Matthew 6:14–15

One of the hardest things to do in life is to forgive someone who has wronged us deeply, someone who has taken something from us, perhaps our innocence, freedom, marriage, childhood, job, or loved ones. The initial thoughts of forgiving someone who has inflicted physical or emotional pain on us is heart-wrenching. Yet Jesus commands us to forgive one another. Where do we start? Emotional hurt can be paralyzing, leaving us unable to detect the hardening in our hearts toward the very thing that will bring the most healing to our soul. Forgiveness is a process, and the first step is to be willing. "If you forgive those who sin against you, your heavenly Father will forgive you. But if you *refuse* to forgive others, your Father will not forgive your sins" (Matthew 6:14–15 NLT).

Ouch! Amid severe turmoil, I have read this passage only to feel chastised to the core. Disillusionment in trying to be righteous after being so wronged left me feeling alone in my pain. But those feelings did not represent God's true character. God has always wanted freedom for me from the pain that had entrapped me. This is His will for you and me! Our responsibility is this, to be willing to allow God to take us through the forgiveness process.

Do you see the word *refuse* in verse 15? In my experience, refusing to take the first step toward forgiveness and ultimately my own healing is what has left me unable to move forward. I've longed for justice for my offender. But this longing has kept me in a place of bondage, revisiting my hurt and replaying events and conversations repeatedly. Fortunately God has patiently shown me that forgiving others is not for their sake; it is for mine. It is giving me the gift of a peace that passes all understanding and, ultimately, forgiveness for my own sin.

If there is someone you need to forgive but the task seems too great, I encourage you to begin by praying today for God to instill a spirit of willingness. God is asking you to allow the process to start, and He does not leave you to do this on your own. Ask Him for help. Taking this first step will be key to reaching true freedom and peace in Christ.

–Tammy

Stones of Pain
Romans 12:19; 1 Peter 3:9

Forgiveness is a painstaking process that can take time, hard emotional work, and diligence to complete. Not too long ago, I began the process of forgiving someone who had deeply wronged me. I needed to have something tangible that I could touch so I could see my progress. I filled a basket with what I called "stones of pain."

Stones of pain visually helped me through the process of letting go of my bitterness and resentment. In writing the names of people who had hurt me on stones and placing these stones in a basket, I was able to explore a pathway to forgiveness. Each day I took a stone, held it in my hand, and prayed that God would soften my heart. Out loud I named very specific offenses one at a time. Some days I could only scratch the surface of hurt, taking up to weeks or months to release much of what I was feeling. But breaking down the hurt was key so that I could continue the process. "Dear friends, never take revenge. Leave that to the righteous anger of God. For the Scriptures say, 'I will take revenge; I will pay them back,' says the Lord" (Romans 12:19 NLT).

With each stone I held, I confessed my anger and spirit of revenge toward that person. I prayed for my own healing and the ability to allow God to be God by leaving the injustices with Him. This took time.

I repeated the same process, putting each stone back in the basket until I was able to pray for that individual with sincerity and purpose. I could remove the stone from the basket, celebrating the God-given victory over something that had plagued me for so long.

If you are struggling with forgiveness and need something tangible to begin the process, I encourage you to make some stones of pain. Forgiving others is non-negotiable to God, and still He promises to give us victory if we leave justice with Him. In the end, we can replace our stones of pain with stones of victory and celebrate how faithful and merciful God is.

—Tammy

Ask for God's Help
Psalm 121:1–8

If you've ever been around a three-year-old, you may have experienced the "I can do it myself" phase they go through. As a parent, I remember my own preschoolers exercising their independence in this way. They wanted so badly to do things on their own, a key step toward their maturity and growth.

However, this mindset can do us a disservice as we get older, creating a sense of self-sufficiency that leads to handling many of life's trials, grief, and temptations on our own. This can set us on a dangerous path when it comes to forgiving others, and I have personally learned that I cannot forgive on my own.

> I look up to the mountains—does my help come from there? My help comes from the Lord, who made heaven and earth! He will not let you stumble; the one who watches over you will not slumber. (Psalm 121:1–3 NLT)

God is not bothered when we come to Him for help. He doesn't sleep, and He is constantly watching over us. Sometimes we forget that the same God who formed each of our lives in the most secret place is completely aware of our shortcomings, fears, struggles, and pain.

Being independent from God is not a good thing. He did not design us that way, and He fully expects us to ask Him for help. Remember, when we make Him Lord over our lives, the Holy Spirit dwells in us and is working in us to make us more like Christ, dependent on the Father.

When you are tempted to say "I can do it myself," identify the reason why. If it is because you are procrastinating or being self-sufficient, then maybe it is time to take a step back, look to the heavens, and tell God that you need His help to be more dependent on *Him* and move forward.

Seeking God's help is a sign of strength, for in our weakness, He is strong! God is constantly watching over you as your protective shade and wants you to come to Him for everything! He loves you so much.

—Tammy

Let Love Invade the Holes
Luke 6:26–31; Ephesians 4:30–32

It's impossible to pour water into a glass that is already full of something else. Naturally, the water will just run down the sides and be wasted, unable to be consumed. To drink the water, you'd have to dump the other liquid out first and then replace it with the water. Forgiveness is much like this process. Our cups are filled with hurt, anger, betrayal, hate, and rejection that keep us in a state in which we are then unable to drink anything else, no matter how good our intentions are. We need to empty our cups, but how?

Think of the liquid in our cups as acid, eating away at our insides, disguising itself as water but proving more destructive and deadlier. The acid is toxic, but we don't know what to do with it.

> Get rid of all bitterness, rage, anger, harsh words, and slander, as well as all types of evil behavior. Instead, be kind to each other, tenderhearted, forgiving one another, just as God through Christ has forgiven you. (Ephesians 4:31–32 NLT)

Paul instructs us to get rid of the things that keep us from forgiving:

1. Pour out stubbornness. Our will to hold on to our hurt only damages us. We need to let it go so we can go to the next step.
2. Pour out pride. Our human nature wants to win. We want others to side with us and to focus on others' faults before our own.
3. Pour out revenge. God is just. We need to trust Him because every person is accountable to God, and we can rest in His timetable.
4. Pour out bitterness. Sweetness cannot coexist with bitterness.

Acid makes holes. You will have scars. But now you will have space for all the sweet things God wants to fill your cup with: peace, joy, the ability to forgive, faith, and a renewed hope for the future. Most importantly, let love invade the holes!

—Tammy

Pray for Those Who Persecute You

Matthew 5:43–45; 1 John 2:9

Are we meant to be friends with everyone? I mean, if we forgive and reconcile with one another, does God intend for friendship to be the outcome?

> You have heard the law that says, "Love your neighbor" and hate your enemy. But I say, love your enemies! Pray for those who persecute you! In that way, you will be acting as true children of your Father in heaven. For he gives his sunlight to both the evil and the good, and he sends rain on the just and the unjust alike. (Matthew 5:43–45 NLT)

In this passage, Matthew stresses the kind of love we are to have for each other, agape love, unconditional and full of compassion. The opposite of love is hate, and God makes it very clear in 1 John 2:9 that if we hate someone, we are living in the darkness.

I have been guilty of hate. In those times, I have had to come to God on my knees to help me to know what to pray. Sometimes the feelings of anger are so strong and deep-seated, I just need to sit in His presence.

The more I talk with God, the closer I get to something that could resemble love. This constant communication with God has enabled me to surrender my hate and, in turn, love that person through the eyes of Christ. Through this process, I have never felt that God expected me to be friends with that person, only to love them through God's eyes and forgive them. Is it difficult? Yes, especially when we have been betrayed by someone we trusted. The crux of the matter is, do we want to be separated from God? Hate is sin, and sin separates us from God (Isaiah 59:2).

When I pray for those who persecute me, there is something that begins to happen in my soul: mercy, forgiveness, and freedom. May I seek to let God penetrate the wounds of my heart and soften it toward those who have hurt me so deeply.

—Tammy

Never Stop Praying
1 Thessalonians 5:16-18

Have you ever had a difficult boss? Based on the law of averages, if you have had more than one job in your lifetime, you probably have had a bad boss at least to some degree. If you are fortunate enough to have had all great bosses, then think about all the neighbors you have throughout your life. Did one of them ever just rub you the wrong way?

I have been very fortunate to have had some wonderful bosses who have mentored me quite well through the years even after our work relationship had ended. But sadly I have friends who have had some bad bosses. Some have been less than competent, but the ones that have been toughest to deal with were mean-spirited or untrustworthy.

When we deal with bosses or neighbors that fit this description, our interactions with that person often flow over to our relationships with others. We can become bitter inside as well as on the outside. We can gossip about that person. We can begin to wallow in our circumstances, which then permeate every part of our life.

In his first letter to the Thessalonians, Paul concludes with some final advice, "See that no one pays back evil for evil, but always try to do good to each other and to all people. Always be joyful. Never stop praying. Be thankful in all circumstances, for this is God's will for you who belong to Christ Jesus" (1 Thessalonians 5:15–18 NLT).

God has wired me to be joyful and thankful. That is a blessing. But when I read these verses again, I did not jump over verse 17 this time. As I reflected on that part, I realized in some of my toughest relationships how often I neglected the words to never stop praying.

My natural bent is to try to jump right in and fix things often without first taking time to pray and seek God's will. In those times when relationships don't get healed as quickly as I would like, God may want me to be patient, but still to never stop praying.

As we work to forgive our bad bosses or neighbors, remember to always be joyful, to never stop praying, and to be thankful in all circumstances. This is God's will for those who belong to Him.

-Mark

Week 1 Reflections

1. After reviewing the Scriptures for each day, name three passages that jumped out at you.
2. How can you practically apply these verses to your life today and this week?
3. Has someone hurt you recently or in the past that you have *refused* to forgive? Some of the signs of unforgiveness might be talking negatively about someone, constantly thinking about the pain, jealousy toward someone, or sweeping the hurt completely under the carpet.
4. What first step are you willing to take toward forgiving? This could even be forgiving yourself.
5. What is your first response to the idea of praying for those people who have hurt you?
6. How does God want to help you get to this point of praying for those who have wronged you, if you haven't already?
7. What is the danger for all of us if we choose *not* to forgive?
8. Write out a prayer to God that earnestly seeks His help in the area of forgiveness.

So Right We're Wrong
1 Kings 8:46–51; Proverbs 3:7

Have you ever had someone give you an insincere apology? Perhaps the apology was wrapped with a condescending tone or with the implication that you were the one with the problem for being so easily hurt.

False apologies don't do anything for anyone. They are insincere and disingenuous. However, if I am honest with myself, I have been guilty of this very thing to be in control of a situation. Perhaps you have as well? The words "I'm sorry" didn't come from humility; rather they came from a place of pride that shamed the other person into feeling bad about something that *you* did.

Sadly there have been many times when I have unintentionally hurt someone with my words or actions and have had to go back and apologize. I've learned that, despite what my motives were, I had hurt the other person, period. The lesson here for me was that intentional or not, I needed to own responsibility for what came out of my mouth. I needed to humble myself, own my words and actions, and be open to discussion if there were ever going to be reconciliation of any kind.

When my son Matt was in fifth grade, I had a discussion with him about his difficulty to say "I'm sorry" for anything. (Yes, the apple didn't fall far!) From an insightful ten-year-old, he said that if he apologized, he was letting his brother or someone else have victory over him. He didn't want to lose or look wrong! Out of the mouths of babes.

I often say, "People can be so right that they are wrong!" If we are not careful, we can be "wise in our own eyes" (Proverbs 3:7 NIV), deeply in need of a little more humility. The Lord has instructed us to consider others better than ourselves, being people who can sincerely apologize and be above reproach in the eyes of Christ. Let us humble ourselves before God so we can prevent ourselves from being so right we're wrong.

—Tammy

Our Attitude

Philippians 2:1–11; Hebrews 4:12

Do you ever wake up with a sour attitude, already struggling with little sleep, which then allows negative thoughts to creep into your psyche? Your trigger is only a moment away, ready to ignite into a burst of emotions responding to a critical coworker, a teenager challenging your authority, or a toddler's exhausting temper tantrum. Sometimes a bad attitude seems to come out of nowhere and will attack every good intention you have to start the day off right. Sigh. Take a deep breath and take heart! There is hope for our attitudes!

Paul teaches us, "You must have the same attitude that Christ Jesus had" (Philippians 2:5 NLT). There is so much pressure here in this verse! What do we do? Muster up good feelings and put on a happy face while we are seething inside? Or do we set a plan of attack so we can be proactive instead of reactive? In searching for answers, I reflected on the word *attitude*. I sought the Lord and what He has to say about shaping our dispositions, outlooks, and attitudes.

We learn from both Philippians 2:1–11 and Hebrews 4:12 that we can have an action plan. Simply outlined, we are instructed to do the following:

1. Stop and be still. Focus on Jesus.
2. Humble ourselves before God, even with our body posture, by kneeling, raising our hands, and closing our eyes.
3. Confess our fatigue, sour attitudes, and innermost thoughts to God, being transparently honest with Him. He knows our thoughts anyway, so we don't need to avoid embarrassment.
4. Ask God to replace the bad attitude with peace, joy, and humility.
5. Meditate on His Word, perhaps these two passages of Scripture.

We must be proactive! By asking the Holy Spirit to help us, we can have victory over our bad attitudes. He promises to give us the ability to fully surrender those bad attitudes to Him, and He promises to renew our thoughts and hearts. What bad attitudes might you need to commit to Him today?

—Tammy

It's Not Fair!

Jonah 3–4

There is a common Sunday school Bible story that many children learn about involving a prophet named Jonah, a city named Nineveh, and a giant whale. Some of us are familiar with this story, yet for some, this may be a first read.

Jonah was from the northern kingdom of Israel in the eighth century BC. God chose him to be His messenger, and he was asked to go to the city of Nineveh to inform them of God's impeding wrath. Nineveh was a terrible place, where pagan worship, violence, and evil made their home. Jonah did not think it very fair that God would ask him to go tell a godless group of people a message from the Almighty, so he responded in blatant disobedience. Jonah ran from God and ended up on a boat trying to escape. However, he didn't get very far because God knew exactly where he was. In His mercy, God sent a storm that wreaked havoc on the boat, causing Jonah to confess his disobedience to the boat crew and allowing them to throw him overboard. The storm stopped, and God sent a huge fish to swallow Jonah (Jonah 1:16), where he would stay for three days and three nights until Jonah chose to obey. Meanwhile, because God is always working in the lives of people, the crew was brought to faith and salvation by witnessing the power of the Lord in calming the storm (Jonah 1:17).

I relate to Jonah in that life doesn't always seem fair. I've been guilty of believing that people who have made bad life choices don't deserve God's mercy and grace like I do. I rationalize that my good decisions have led me to where I am. Sadly, I lose sight of the fact that before I knew Jesus, my life was in shambles on a road to nowhere. Do you see how hypocrisy and sinful nature can set in?

When we are tempted to think we have the upper hand with God, let us remember that we are all human and His mercy and grace are for everyone! God could have easily chosen someone else to deliver His message to Nineveh, someone with humility who was easier to reason with. But the lesson here is clear: God's mercy, grace, and compassion are for everyone, and He desires for us to humbly demonstrate those things to others as well!

—Tammy

Humility

Luke 1; Philippians 2:5–11

Mary, the mother of Jesus, was only thirteen or fourteen when she became engaged to Joseph. When the angel Gabriel appeared to Mary to tell her about the child she would conceive, he said, "Don't be afraid, Mary, for you have found favor with God!" (Luke 1:30 NLT).

I don't know about you, but if I had been Mary and the angel came directly to me, telling me that I had favor with God, I would be scared. However, twenty minutes later, I would probably let it go to my head that God chose me above all other women! Contrarily, the humility Mary displays, especially as a young teenage girl, is extraordinary. In Luke 1:46–55, Mary sings a song of praise to God, exemplifying her gratefulness and humility in acknowledging all that God has done for her.

I desire that kind of humility, a humility that remains constant even when God blesses me richly and shows His favor upon me. We read in Philippians that though Jesus was God, "He did not consider equality with God something to be used for His own advantage" (Philippians 2:5–11 NIV). Amazingly Jesus was God in the flesh but did not even seek equality with God! He humbled Himself, taking on the nature of a slave and then dying a criminal's death for all of humankind.

Pure humility comes from the heart, not the head. Humans are smart and can display false humility by taking on actions that mimic humility but have ulterior motives to elevate themselves in one way or another. Some questions that have helped me to identify false humility in my life are:

1. Am I able to apologize to others sincerely, meaning that my actions will back up my words?
2. Does my ego prevent me from facing conflict or people who disagree with me?
3. Am I secretly jealous of others?

Like we see in Mary, humility is not just a trait. Humility is woven into the fabric of our character by the Holy Spirit Himself. Mary was not perfect, but in her humility and love for the Lord, she found favor with God. In turn, God knew He could trust her to remain faithful and humble, giving birth to the Savior of the world.

—Tammy

Skipping Steps
Philippians 2:12–18

In the spring of 1994, I graduated with my master's degree in piano performance from Cincinnati Conservatory. As part of my program, I had to do two full recitals: one solo piano recital fully memorized and then a piano trio consisting of a violist and clarinetist. Usually these recitals would occur a year apart, but since I fast-tracked my degree to marry my husband and move to Connecticut, I had to do them three weeks apart!

Practicing for a recital can be a grueling task if you don't have a plan of attack. Hours of practice can be wasted by skipping steps in taking the tempo too fast too early or not solidifying consistent fingerings. If steps are skipped, the result can be a train wreck in the recital—forgotten notes, sloppy sections, and overall lacking in musicality and execution.

> Therefore, my dear friends, as you have always obeyed—not only in my presence, but now much more in my absence—continue to work out your salvation with fear and trembling. (Philippians 2:12 NIV)

Paul is wisely instructing us to pay attention to the details regarding the working out of our salvation. He cautions us not to skip steps, believing we have arrived in any area of godly character, only to realize under pressure that we have a long way to go. It takes time for God's Word to marinate in our soul. We need to be patient with ourselves, not skipping valuable steps. These steps include daily practice, prayer, and attention to areas in our lives that God wants to purify and align with Him.

Sometimes we'd like to reach the finish line on a fast track. That would certainly be less tedious and wouldn't try our patience as much! However, we'd miss the "fear and trembling" part of working out our salvation. We would miss the hard work that sometimes takes tears, sweat, and energy. Skipping over those steps would prolong our ability to grow as God intended!

—Tammy

There Is Healing in an Apology
James 5:16

"Confess your sins to each other and pray for each other so that you may be healed. The earnest prayer of a righteous person has great power and produces wonderful results" (James 5:16 NLT).

Sibling rivalry is horrible, to say the least. My sister Wendy and I did not like each other very much growing up. Wendy was tall, so when we fought, she would use her physical strength, but I would fight back with words. My toxic tongue could cut her to her core. The sad thing was that neither one of us could apologize to the other. We were trapped. The never-ending cycle of differences, jealousies, and frustrations continued.

Far into adulthood, Wendy and I couldn't get past the dissention between us that had festered for years. We didn't have much in common (or so we thought), but mostly the lingering hurts never allowed a deeper relationship. A crisis point came in our relationship when she and I did not speak to each other for a year and a half. Although the silence was painful, we felt wronged and misunderstood by the other. And neither one made the first move to apologize.

Finally a breakthrough came when I received a long letter in the mail from Wendy, explaining in a very thoughtful way what her perspective was on our decades of conflict. Interestingly, I learned in her letter that my words had affected her far more deeply than the instances when she physically hit me. The reality was that I never carried those punches with me. My words, however, stung the very depths of her soul.

I, in turn, wrote a letter back. After a few letters, the ice was broken so that we could finally talk to one another without anger or a snide tone. Wendy and I sincerely apologized to each other, realizing how we each had hurt one another through the years. We also recognized that we were never going to be able to fix the past or address every issue.

Reconciliation came when we agreed to start with a fresh slate, beginning that very day to move forward. There was no more looking back. We confessed to each other and committed to forgive and move on. Seven years have passed, and we are closer than we have ever been! I have gained a precious friend in my sister. God is good, and there is healing in an apology!

—Tammy

Week 2 Reflections

1. After reviewing the Scriptures for each day, name three to four passages that jumped out at you.
2. How can you practically apply these verses to your life today and this week?
3. Have you ever been so right you are wrong? If so, how?
4. What does God's Word tell us about our attitude?
5. When have you experienced a time when you felt like Jonah, that is, God was asking you to do something that you didn't think was fair?
6. When God showed His favor upon Mary, what was her immediate response? Did that change? Reflect on your own humility and how that compares (or contrasts) to Mary.
7. What are some next steps for you to continue the journey of working out your salvation as Paul describes in Philippians 2:12?
8. Is it hard for you to say "I'm sorry"? Be honest. Why or why not?
9. What does God desire overall in your walk with Him today?

How to Love Well

Proverbs 25:21–22; 1 John 4:7–12

All people are loveable, right? People are always kind, considerate, generous, selfless, grateful beings who listen to others and keep their promises, correct? Oh, how I wish this were true. It sure would make this command in 1 John 4:7 to love others a lot easier for the entire human race!

Loving others is not always that easy. All of us have had (or will have) someone in our life that we consider hard to love, perhaps a wayward son or daughter who has drained us, challenged us, or gone against everything we have stood for? Or maybe an ex-husband who was unfaithful and now denies his children their child support? Maybe a friend in school who gossips about you and taints your reputation or a neighbor who has built a fence over your property line? Whomever we struggle loving, it's important for us to talk about love in the way God instructs us to. What is the first step to loving the unlovable?

> "Instead, if your enemies are hungry, feed them. If they are thirsty, give them something to drink. In doing this, you will heap burning coals of shame on their heads. Don't let evil conquer you, but conquer evil by doing good." (Romans 12:20–21 NLT)

When I want to demonstrate love to someone who I have conflict with, I have learned to list my record of wrongs toward that person and read this list aloud to God. Furthermore, I've learned to write out characteristics of Jesus (merciful, compassionate, forgiving, etc.), praying that I might be an imitator of Christ in these ways. As Paul points out, "heaping coals on the individual's head" allows us to conquer evil instead of allowing evil to conquer us. Through His Spirit I can gain God's perspective on those who hurt me and look for ways to bless them instead of retaliating against them.

In my experience, the person does not always change. But I do. I change what I can change, especially in being obedient to the Lord. Then my conscience is clear, and I am then able to love well through God's love, grace, and forgiveness.

—Tammy

False Harmony?

Proverbs 27:17; Ephesians 4:25, 5:10–11

In taking a conflict assessment test, I found out that I am a person who runs toward conflict rather than avoiding it. While this is good in many ways, I have often struggled with thinking I was not a peace-maker, therefore not pleasing God. This has bothered me a lot. Consequently, I have searched God's Word for truth in what constitutes peace in God's eyes. In doing so, I have come to understand that biblical peace is not the absence of conflict. Rather, it is acting to restore a broken situation with the goal of having wholeness in the end.

> So, stop telling lies. Let us tell our neighbors the truth, for we are all parts of the same body. (Ephesians 4:25 NLT)

> Carefully determine what pleases the Lord. Take no part in the worthless deeds of evil and darkness; instead, expose them. (Ephesians 5:10–11 NLT)

Too often conflicts or disagreements are swept under the rug, all in the name of peace. But peace is not false harmony. It is not pretending that there aren't any problems or concerns. God's desire is for us to grow together toward a common goal of reconciliation, perhaps agreeing to disagree, but also encouraging communication and transparency. "As iron sharpens iron, so a friend sharpens a friend" (Proverbs 27:17 NLT).

Peace is achieved when we do our part to speak truth in love and change what is in our power to change. If we have done that and reconciliation has not taken place, we may need to accept that we have done all that we can and part ways. And that's ok.

In my personal experience, false harmony is living a lie, seemingly peaceful on the outside, but having dangers lurking on the inside. Don't get fooled by false harmony. Always strive for truth, reconciliation, and forgiveness. I believe this is what true biblical peace looks like.

—Tammy

Forgiving Family
Matthew 18:21–35

The relationship between my brother and me hasn't always been easy. Growing up there were certainly good times, but there were also bad times. I recognize that forgiving family is a sensitive topic for many people. For some, family life was (or is) full of love, overall happiness, minimal stress, and good parental instruction. For others, family life was (or is) full of constant anger, drug abuse, alcohol use, unfaithfulness, and lots of stress. Still others would identify somewhere in between. Regardless of family history, from long ago or current, forgiving family is difficult. No doubt about it.

I grew up in a home that was very safe and loving, having two great Christian parents leading the way. I also had two brothers—one human and one cat. The cat was easy. He just slept a lot and ate food. No exciting news there. My human brother was a different story. While we certainly had plenty of moments where we got along and played well together, we also had plenty of differences. Being opposites, there was lots of strife.

Like many siblings, we struggled with verbal and physical fights, lying, and tattling. Our parents were constantly teaching us, encouraging us to make amends, and training us to become men, real men who know how to use their words to build instead of tear down. They pointed out and celebrated our differences, helping the other one to see the good in the other. But despite their efforts, I went off to college with a shaky relationship with my brother. I didn't think we would ever be close ... ever.

Today, my brother and I share a great relationship that continues to grow. How? For me, I had to start with me. I needed to settle my issues before I could come to him and reconcile. I had to own my part where my glaring faults affected him. Matt and I matured throughout our time in college, and our numerous conversations with each other slowly led us to forgive. We made amends. We asked for forgiveness and gave it freely.

Jesus instructed His disciples to forgive seven times seventy, with the point being to never stop forgiving. Family can be tough, but the reward is priceless if we are willing to communicate and do the work. Through this process, we become more like Christ, and that to me is worth more than gold.

-Scott

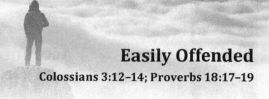

Easily Offended

Colossians 3:12–14; Proverbs 18:17–19

Do you agree or disagree with this statement?

> I am offended when people disagree with me, raise children differently than me, question my style of leadership, politically disagree with me, or approach and solve conflict differently from how I do.

Agree or disagree? Read the statement again and think about it for a minute. If you answered "agree" to any part, don't frown! We are sensitive beings with histories and elements in our personalities that can make us a little more susceptible to offense. God desires for us to overcome this temptation, and He has given us His Word to speak to us.

> Since God chose you to be the holy people he loves, you must clothe yourselves with tenderhearted mercy, kindness, humility, gentleness, and patience. Make allowance for each other's faults and forgive anyone who offends you. Remember, the Lord forgave you, so you must forgive others … (Colossians 3:12–14 NLT)

> The one who states his case first seems right, until the other comes and examines him … A brother offended is more unyielding than a strong city, and quarreling is like the bars of a castle. (Proverbs 18:17–19 NLT)

Yikes! When we are offended, we are more unyielding than a strong city! Life is full of experiences that could make us vulnerable to feeling offended. When our significance, our need to feel important, or our ways are challenged, we can easily take things personally that probably were never meant to be personal.

Disagreements with others are inevitable. This is normal about human behavior and life! Even in the body of Christ, people will hurt and offend us, but God wants to sever that root of being so easily offended so we can overlook others' offenses with love and mercy.

—Tammy

Accountability—Forgiveness

Hebrews 3:7–15; Colossians 3:13–14

Recently I have been reacquainted with a past peer of mine. In our catching up, he shared in a way that allowed our conversation to move to the spiritual. During this conversation, he confided in me that he had many questions related to faith that he did not know where to begin. I asked him to write them all down, and we would tackle them together in our next call. His list included many challenging questions such as "How can one religion be right and others wrong?", "How do you balance science and religion?", and "Why would someone create hell?"

But the one question that stood out so differently to me was, "Is it healthy to forgive and not hold others accountable?" As he and I dug into this question, we realized together that we can and should have both forgiveness and accountability.

There are many valid reasons to hold someone accountable. We may want to hold them accountable in a hope of bringing about a positive change that can bring about restoration in a physical aspect or a relationship. We might even use accountability as a way of protecting others in some situations.

But a key point is there are two ways to focus on accountability, bad and good. The bad way is lording our personal righteousness over the other person. In this approach, we are possibly seeking to create shame for someone as payback or a way to hurt the person to teach them a lesson. This approach is a never-ending downward spiral. Godly accountability, however, is borne out of love. When we truly seek to hold someone accountable in a way that shows them grace and loving firmness, we are moving the situation to a point where positive change can take place.

Accountability with humility and love must begin by forgiving. As Christians, we are reminded in Colossians 3:13–14 that the Lord forgave us and so then we must forgive others. It is through this forgiveness on our part and approaching the other person in love that we will be in a position to hold someone accountable. My parents, spouse, and friends have been the ones who have done that for me, and they did so with humility, forgiveness, and love. I want to do the same.

-Mark

My Shame

Romans 8:1–4; Psalm 34:4–5; Isaiah 50:7

As a perfectionist, I tend to obsess about things I do wrong. The guilt, the pain, and the replaying of events and conversations have kept me stuck at very distinct times, consuming my being in every way. Even when I have read this verse, "So now there is no condemnation for those who belong to Christ Jesus" (Romans 8:1 NLT), it has been hard to accept for fear of messing up again. Why doesn't God condemn me? When will I learn? Why do I deserve His grace? "I prayed to the Lord, and he answered me. He freed me from all my fears. Those who look to him for help will be radiant with joy; no shadow of shame will darken their faces" (Psalm 34:4–5 NLT).

There is a significant promise in these verses that when we confess our sin and seek His help, He will free us from the fears and shame that bind us. He will make us radiant with joy! We must keep going and not dwell on the past. The past is over, done, no longer accessible. All we can do is move forward with a blank slate and a fresh perspective. We will fall down, cry, and grieve, but then we must stand and walk again with our head held high, leaning on the Holy Spirit. "Because the Sovereign Lord helps me, I will not be disgraced. Therefore, I have set my face like a stone, determined to do his will. And I know that I will not be put to shame" (Isaiah 50:7 NLT).

Do you see the promise here in this verse? If we are determined to do His will, He knows our heart, and He will not put us to shame. Yes, we will sin, but as we repent, He will forgive us every single time. We never need to earn His love and grace, no matter how badly we've messed things up. It sounds too easy, right? But forgiveness is right there for the taking, our sins forgotten and wiped clean with our confession. Because of that, I know that the verses in Romans 8:1–4 are true and that there is no more shame and no condemnation in Christ Jesus!

—Tammy

Week 3 Reflections

1. After reviewing the Scriptures for each day, name three to four passages that jumped out at you.
2. How can you practically apply these verses to your life today and this week?
3. Who do you need to love well by God's standards today? What is your plan to achieve this?
4. Describe false harmony. Describe godly peace.
5. Family can be the most challenging to forgive. Who in your family do you need to forgive? Why?
6. Do you find yourself easily offended at times? If yes, what does God desire you to do with that temptation?
7. We all need accountability through the process of forgiving someone. This can take time. Who is someone that can be an accountability partner for you? Who can you help be an accountability partner to?
8. Shame can hang over us like a cloud. Do you carry shame around with you for past sins or mistakes? What does God say about that? What do you need to do?
9. What does God desire overall in your walk with Him today?

Search My Heart
Psalm 7:10–17; Matthew 5:43–45

Life can be very unfair. Globally speaking, we see millions of people living in poverty, residing in homes of dirt floors with no plumbing, electricity, or even clean water. Meanwhile professional athletes are signing contracts for hundreds of millions of dollars to play recreational sports, signing endorsements to promote products that are luxuries in many areas of the world. Is that fair and just?

I have known individuals who have lost a child or spouse to death at the hand of a drunk driver. Loving couples who have longed for a child have never seen pregnancy, yet according to the World Health Organization (WHO), 40 to 50 million abortions occur yearly. How do we cope with injustice so that it doesn't infect our very beings with bitterness and grief?

Sadly we seldom see fairness and justice played out here on earth. With all the turmoil going on in our world, our faith can get rattled. We can easily become embittered and skeptical, wondering if God is going to act on our behalf. Yet, even through the tragedies and injustices around us, God is actively at work. He is aware. He is not turning His head away. God is for us. But that is not always how we feel. For this reason, our greatest need may be to recognize our feelings toward God, and put steps in place to forgive Him.

Psalm 7:10–17 teaches us that God is our shield, He is an honest judge, and He will sharpen His arrows for those who do not repent. This tells us that He is fully aware of what is going on in this world, your world, and my world. We cannot fix what is God's to fix (or not fix). When sin entered this world, troubles were inevitable. But God is a patient God, full of mercy and grace, giving all of us the chance to repent from our wicked ways and to walk in the light of salvation.

We all need Jesus. When we don't understand the whys of life, we can rest in the Lord, knowing that as we ask God to search our hearts, we can ask also ask Him for healing, peace of mind, and love and compassion toward those who so desperately need Him.

When we are tempted to waste another day to negative thinking, may God search our hearts and reveal to us where we need to have more grace, more patience, and more trust and to let God be God.

–Tammy

Action Over Thoughts

James 2:14–26

James 2 is clear: faith needs to be acted upon. When God calls us to something, if we aren't careful, we can be tempted to get discouraged and give up before He has carried out His plan!

In 2009 I started making money from a small side business. I created websites and eventually mobile apps as well. My first couple of apps had some success in the App Store. It was exciting! In 2013 my wife, Ashley, and I brainstormed ways to spread the gospel using this technology. Eventually I spent time creating a mobile app called "Mood Verse." The idea was simple: tell the app what kind of a mood you are in (angry, happy, jealous, etc.) and the app would suggest an encouraging scripture. I earnestly launched the app publicly, with high hopes.

Unfortunately, the app launch was not successful … at all. In fact, almost nobody downloaded it,– by far my least successful app by any measure. It was extremely disappointing. Why wouldn't God want me to try and spread Scripture using my skills? I didn't understand.

I could have given up. I could have abandoned my side business altogether. But I chose to stick with it. I chose positive action over negative thoughts. I kept on making websites, developing mobile apps, and immersing myself in software development.

Then in November 2015, something interesting happened. I received an email from a tech recruiter about a potential project. The recruiter was reaching out to me almost exclusively because of Mood Verse, as the project needed a specific type of mobile app developer with a faith-based mindset. The app framework and the Scripture element of Mood Verse attracted his attention.

I took the job! The project was successful, and I have partnered with this client on many more website and mobile app projects. My skills have been challenged, I've earned more money, and these projects reach more people with the gospel than anything I had done before. All of this from my least successful app! Had I given up earlier because of my discouragement, I would have missed what God had planned. He is faithful! When He calls you, He will see it through to completion.

–John

Sin Affects Our Physical Health

Psalm 38:1–8

Sin can be toxic to our health. What I don't mean is that sin makes us sick or if we're sick, that means we've sinned. What I do mean is when we know that we have deliberately gone against God, we can often experience what David did in Psalm 38 with broken health and exhaustion.

> O Lord, don't rebuke me in your anger or discipline me in your rage!
> Your arrows have struck deep, and your blows are crushing me.
> Because of your anger, my whole body is sick;
> my health is broken because of my sins.
> My guilt overwhelms me—it is a burden too heavy to bear.
> My wounds fester and stink because of my foolish sins. I am bent
> over and racked with pain.
> All day long I walk around filled with grief.
> A raging fever burns within me, and my health is broken.
> I am exhausted and completely crushed. My groans come from an
> anguished heart. (Psalm 38:1–8 NLT)

These ailments (and others) can be red flags indicating sin in our life. Many sins we can identify right away, such as lying, bad language, murder, and sexual sin. Other sins, such as pride, lust, or bitterness from unforgiveness, are harder to discern and to admit, often dismissed in our minds as faults or mistakes. We may even think, *I'll deal with that later!*

Holding on to our sin without confessing it affects us. We begin to see bitterness, defensiveness, embarrassment, and denial creep into our daily lives, causing us not to spend time with God. We also may experience headaches, backaches, indigestion, and other physical ailments that may get worse when sin festers.

Sin and God cannot co-exist. The question is, are we willing to identify those sins in our life and confess them, knowing that God already knows what they are? We can't hide, so let us not procrastinate! There is so much freedom in God's forgiveness.

—Tammy

Spiritual Freedom
Galatians 5:13

As a teenager, I couldn't wait to graduate and go to college where I could spread my wings and make my own decisions. Independence and freedom were calling to me, and I counted down the days.

Freedom, however, can come at a cost for many who walked the same shoes as mine. Soon into my freshman year of college, I received news that an individual I knew in high school was killed after being thrown from the back of a pickup truck on a joy ride while drinking with friends. In an instant, his much-desired freedom cost him his life.

Years later another individual I knew was feeling trapped by trying to be a good girl under her parents' roof. Consequently, she decided to go to a party to experience the thrill of her coveted freedom. A just-once experience led her to an unwanted pregnancy, giving up a child she loved, and a disease she would carry with her for the rest of her life.

I tell you these situations only to explain that although we often want freedom to experience life on our terms, even for a just-once experience, our freedom can lead us down a destructive path. Sometimes we make wrong choices in response to feeling that God's terms are limiting, restricting us from having fun. As a Christian, we might feel like we are missing out, longing to feel a part of what the world has to offer. But the longer I have been on my Christian journey, the more I have learned that God's spiritual boundaries protect us by giving us joy, freedom, and happiness that the world cannot offer. He isn't trying to squelch our fun. He is saving us from a lifetime of heartache and consequences.

> For you have been called to live in freedom, my brothers and sisters.
> But don't use your freedom to satisfy your sinful nature. Instead, use
> your freedom to serve one another in love. (Galatians 5:13 NLT)

When I read this verse, I am reminded again that my sin also affects other people, not just me. The best way I can love and serve God is by staying on course, using my spiritual freedom to glorify Him!

—Tammy

Never Too Far Gone!
Hosea 6:1–3

Cooking and baking are not my specialty. However, in the first five years of marriage with two young sons, I wanted to begin making meals that the boys would someday think of as home in years to come. I experimented with new recipes and made note of the things they loved. One evening I pulled out my recipe box, chose a recipe to try, and began the preparation. I didn't have a few of the ingredients that the recipe called for, but I thought I could substitute with other things. Halfway through, I accidentally omitted an ingredient and then measured the next ingredient wrong! Wow! This certainly wasn't what I had intended. What should have gone into the oven as a neat and tidy dish ended up being all thrown together on the stovetop because it was too far gone from what it was supposed to be. I was disappointed in myself, but in the end, the meal was edible. To my pleasant surprise, the altered recipe became one of the boys' favorite dishes when they were kids. Who knew?

We are very much like that botched recipe and sometimes need to be reminded that we are never too far gone. We may take detours that end nowhere or substitute God's plans for our own. We may even skip some important steps that God had directed us to take. However, our amazing Father is able to take our mess and make it into something better than we imagined.

> Come, let us return to the Lord. He has torn us to pieces; now he will heal us. He has injured us; now he will bandage our wounds. In just a short time he will restore us, so that we may live in his presence. Oh, that we might know the Lord! Let us press on to know him … (Hosea 6:1–3 NLT)

We are never too far gone! There will always be consequences for our sin and doing our own thing. However, whatever mess we may find ourselves in, the time is now to repent, forgive ourselves, and allow God to bandage our wounds. The recipe God may have initially intended for us may be long gone. But if we give Him our mess, He promises to create a new dish, and that is the hope we must hold on to!

–Tammy

Tell of the Victory

Acts 12

King Herod Agrippa I was only fifty-four years old when he was struck by God, eaten by worms, and died! Eaten by worms? What in the world?

Our Scripture reading today is Acts 12. In this chapter, an interesting story unfolds and teaches us that when God helps us in our time of need and gives us victory, we are to let others know what He did and to never take the credit. In this case, we are never to accept worship from other people without giving God complete praise!

The chapter begins with Agrippa killing James, John's brother, because the Jews did not like the Christians. James was one of Jesus' disciples! Following James' execution, King Agrippa then arrested Peter (another disciple) and put him in prison, probably to await the same fate the next day. Miraculously that night, an angel of the Lord appeared to Peter, woke him, broke his shackles, and led him back to his family. Peter told them what God had done for him in helping him escape and gave praise and thanks to God.

Contrary to Peter, Herod was not so wise. Not long after James was martyred and Peter's arrest and escape, we learn that Herod was angry with the people of Tyre and Sidon. They depended on him for food, so they sent a group of people to Herod to reason with him.

> When the day arrived, Herod put on his royal robes, sat on his throne, and made a speech to them The people gave him a great ovation, shouting, "It's the voice of a god, not of a man!" (Acts 12:20–22 NLT)

The people were worshiping King Agrippa! But instead of redirecting their worship to God and God alone, he accepted their worship for himself. Oops! Big mistake. The next part is not pretty. An angel of the Lord struck Herod with illness, and he was eaten by worms and died.

So, there it is the wrath of God in action. The lesson for all of us is clear: We are never to boast about ourselves, yet rather in God. When we see Him working in our lives, we should tell others about what He has done and offer our worship to Him alone!

—Tammy

Week 4 Reflections

1. After reviewing the Scriptures for each day, name three to four passages that jumped out at you.
2. How can you practically apply these verses to your life today and this week?
3. Ask God to search your heart today. Write down any thoughts that He is revealing to you that He would like you to confess or talk with Him about.
4. Have you ever been tempted to give up too soon? Why or why not? What promises can we trust from God?
5. Sin affects our physical health. Have you ever experienced that? Explain.
6. We are never too far gone, but there are times when our mistakes seem to have ruined us. Can you relate to this either in a personal way or someone you know? What does God want to do?
7. God gave us free choice. Sometimes our spiritual freedom can be taken advantage of. When do you take advantage of the freedom you have in Christ?
8. God wants all the glory when it comes to living our lives. Take a moment and boast in the Lord. Write down all that God has done for you. Tell someone of His victory!
9. What does God desire overall in your walk with Him today?

MONTH 2

When Pressures Are High,
Our Responses Are Not
Always As They Should Be

A FAITH THAT STANDS
Produces Grace and Kindness

Taming the Tongue
James 3:1–12

When my boys were in high school, they loved to play video games. On rare occasions, they would ask me to play a game, and I'd agree. To my predicted chagrin, I would quickly die and be out of lives within a few minutes, often desiring a game of redemption for a chance to win. They would reset the game, and I'd start over with fresh lives, the previous game forever forgotten.

Oh, how I wish life could be that way in all circumstances! Yet, when it comes to matters of the tongue, there are consequences for our words that we can't just reset and start over, pretending nothing was ever said. The old saying is wise, "Think before you speak."

Words and the way in which we communicate are so important. I have learned and will continue to learn until life's end that I need the Holy Spirit's help every minute of every day to tame the wild tongue in me, even the tone of my voice and the way I communicate with my face. I recently learned that, according to his book *Silent Messages* (1971), psychology professor Albert Mehrabian at the University of California, Los Angeles, taught that basic communication takes place through three channels: verbal words (7 percent), tone of voice and inflection (38 percent), and body language (55 percent).

Given these percentages, part of taming the tongue should also include our body language and the tone in which we speak to people. Often we focus on the content of what we say, but not always on the how it is presented. Do we sound accusatory, prideful, disrespectful, harsh, or condescending? Do we look disinterested with folded arms, have a sneer on our face, or roll our eyes? Try saying this sentence eight different ways, each time emphasizing a different word: *I didn't say you could drive the car.* Depending on which word you accent, you get eight different interpretations.

Our words, our tone, and our body language have the power to bless or to curse. May we strive to not be wild horses in need of taming, but rather allow the Holy Spirit to guide our words.

—Tammy

Who Left the Door Open?

Proverbs 21:23

Our home backs up to a pond and a tree line, making a perfect haven for insects of many kinds. In the spring and summer, we open our windows and doors to get a beautiful breeze. Soon the mayflies, mosquitoes, wasps, ladybugs, and spiders find their way inside, and the tedious task of getting rid of them begins!

I often think of the human mouth as an open door. However, when my mouth is left open, I'm not as much worried about what comes in as much as what can come out of it! Proverbs 21:23 (NLT) says it straightforward, "Watch your tongue and keep your mouth shut, and you will stay out of trouble." Perhaps a little duct tape might help?

But is that what God wants, for us to put duct tape over our mouths? Of course not. That would probably be too easy! In addition, it would also squelch the good, kind, and encouraging things that come out of the same door! So what do we do?

The verse says it all, "watch your tongue," which simply means to guard, to attend, to police, and to be vigilant about. We can only do this through the Holy Spirit living in us. For those of us who don't struggle with talking too much or saying brash or bold things, be thankful! However, even though some personalities find it easier to do well in this area without the Holy Spirit's help, there are times when keeping our mouths shut is not what the Holy Spirit wants. Sometimes He wants us to speak truth, to be bold, to defend the weak around us, and to offer a word of encouragement to someone. In the end, we all need to be watching our mouths.

Obedience to the Holy Spirit is key when applying this verse. We don't want to leave our doors open when the Holy Spirit prompts us to shut them. On the other hand, if He prompts us to speak up, we'd better obey as well. Being self-aware in this area is huge. When our guards are down and our tongues get the best of us, we repent and move forward. But when we watch our tongues, they can be our greatest strength and healing balm of kindness.

—Tammy

The Weapon of Woe
James 3:1–12; Ephesians 4:29

I was driving home during a summer heat storm late in the evening. As I pulled into our neighborhood, I was bombarded with a very strong smell of smoke, not like a campfire or charcoal grill, but an unusual pungent odor. I went inside the house to tell Mark about it, but we both agreed that someone was probably burning leaves. About twenty minutes later, our boys got texts from neighborhood friends that the house down the street was ablaze and that several neighbors were running down the street to see it. Fortunately, the family was not at home. Unfortunately, the house burned down to the ground in a matter of minutes, startling everyone who had just witnessed this tragedy.

The fire department said later that the fire had been started by heat lightning that had caused an electrical surge, probably starting in the basement. The odor I smelled was probably the sweltering fire in the basement before it let loose on the main floors. Likewise in James 3, it compares our tongues to a flame of fire, corrupting our whole body.

> But a tiny spark can set a great forest on fire. And among all the parts of the body, the tongue is a flame of fire. It is a whole world of wickedness, corrupting your entire body. It can set your whole life on fire, for it is set on fire by hell itself. (James 3:5–6 NLT)

James goes on to say that no human can tame the tongue. The same tongue that praises is the same tongue that curses and destroys. For such a little muscle in our bodies, it sure can cause a lot of problems!

God wants to get a hold of our tongues in every way. While growing up, my tongue was my greatest weapon when I felt trapped, mistreated, disrespected, or defeated. I used to say, "I nailed them to the floor!" and be proud of it. Now, I'm horrified at the damage my tongue has done in the past and can do without help from the Holy Spirit. I want my tongue to create words that are consistent with the Spirit that dwells within me. May I continuously offer up my tongue as an item to be tamed and controlled by God so it will not become a weapon of woe.

—Tammy

Destruction at Its Best
Psalm 5:8–10; Luke 6:27–36

I had been managing my departments with great success. All our metrics were moving in the right direction and at a pace that was clearly at the top of all my peers. My boss was a great mentor, and it was clear that he was preparing me to take his role at some point in the future. I was also fortunate to have a great relationship with each of my peers. My career was moving nicely and about to take on an even greater trajectory. So when my boss told me officially that he was moving on making the change, it seemed only a matter of time to me and my peers that I would be moving into his role.

Then the news came out. My boss would not be replaced by myself but by someone not in our organization. He had decades of experience and probably was a safer choice. What really hurt is that they also brought in an additional layer between our boss and my peers and myself. My experience did not win the day.

Many will have experienced a situation like this themselves or at least seen this played out to someone in their organization. It can have implications for the group, but also it can have a deep impact on the person directly. It can get bad enough that you find yourself frustrated with your boss; possibly worse, your boss can become frustrated with you! The trust and support needed in a working relationship can sour quickly.

Around this time, I remember coming upon Psalm 5. Here David shares about the lies coming from his enemies. With David, his life was often lived in the extremes. His enemies were great and numerous and wanted to destroy him. In my case, I did not feel a concern for my physical life; however, I did feel as though someone else was winning and no one was looking out for my career.

As I prayed, I was reminded that Jesus tells us to "love your enemies! Do good to those who hate you" (Luke 6:27 NLT). This command is not necessarily about having an affection for them, but rather making a conscious decision to show them kindness in the same way that Jesus showed all of us.

−Mark

35

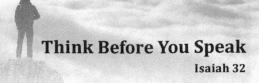

Think Before You Speak
Isaiah 32

When I was ten, my parents started the process of getting a divorce. Both of my parents began dating other people, but my mom started dating someone we had known our entire lives, my dad's second cousin, whom we called "Uncle Paul." Uncle Paul was so kind to us, and I saw how well he treated my mom. When we learned a few months later that my dad had been suddenly killed, I began to see Uncle Paul as my new father figure.

Fast-forward a few years, I was in high school. My mom had married Uncle Paul, and both of my siblings had gone to college, so it was just me at home with my mom and stepdad. Uncle Paul always picked me up from school, ensured I got to soccer practice, and made dinner every night. Uncle Paul, though, liked things clean. I'd joke around with him that I didn't want our house to look too clean because it needed to look "lived in." One day he really got on me about cleaning up after myself, and I, the hormonal teenage girl, got so upset at him.

He's not the boss of me; he's not even my real dad, I thought to myself. It was such a small issue, but I was infuriated. I distinctly remember walking down the stairs and toward the kitchen, thinking of all the things I'd say to make him know how upset I was. I'd tell him he's not my dad and never will be and that he can't tell me what to do, only my mom can.

Then as if God himself were there watching, I stopped in my tracks. I thought of how hurt Uncle Paul would be. I thought about how long it would take for us to get along again. I thought about how upset and hurt my mom would be if I would ever say anything like that to him. I turned around and went upstairs. I never said any of it. "And the effect of righteousness will be peace" (Isaiah 32:17 ESV).

I chose peace that day, and everything remained normal. Since then, he cried at my high school graduation and walked me down the aisle at my wedding. I thank the Lord for the conviction of His Word that kept my mouth shut that day. A Greek proverb I've held onto is, "One minute of patience, ten years of peace." The next time you are angry beyond measure, take one minute, and you may save ten years of regret.

—Hannah

Just Be Kind

Micah 6:8; Proverbs 11:17

My mother used to tell me, "Be kind to everyone because you don't know what they are facing today." Years later a teacher used to say, "An act of kindness doesn't hurt you, and it is never wasted." And my favorite reminder to be kind, "Don't be kind because of who they are, but be kind because of who you are."

The Bible says a lot about kindness. Kindness is an outward fruit or behavior that results from allowing the Holy Spirit to dwell inside of us. Two Old Testament Scriptures point us to being kind:

> He has told you, O man, what is good; and what does the Lord require of you, but to do justice, and to love kindness, and to walk humbly with your God? (Micah 6:8 NLT)

> A man who is kind benefits himself, but a cruel man hurts himself. (Proverbs 11:17 NLT)

Being kind is something that was pounded into me over and over as a kid. One might think I should have been an expert by the time I was a teenager or adult! But I'm not. Showing kindness is easy when others are reasonable and being others-centered. But showing kindness to the one who isn't kind challenges me.

I had a friend years ago reveal something to me that I will never forget. She told me that I was nice 85 percent of the time, but then I had a mean streak that could cut like a knife through someone's soul.

Wow. I was humbled before God that day and sought to make a change in my behavior. I could have easily dismissed what she said because, after all, she told me that I was mean only 15 percent of the time! But 15 percent is 15 percent too much, and I decided to take this up with my Savior. I began to ask my friends to hold me accountable, and I purposely sought opportunities to be kind. After all, I had also been hurting myself.

Father, please help me to be kind. This seems so simple, but You know how hard it can be. I confess and ask You to purify my motives. Amen.

—Tammy

Week 5 Reflections

1. After reviewing the Scriptures for each day, name three to four passages that jumped out at you this week.
2. How can you practically apply these verses to your life today and the upcoming week?
3. Body language is 55 percent of how we communicate. What does your body language reflect about your thoughts and feelings?
4. When is your tongue most likely used to "set a fire"?
5. It's not always what we say, but how we say something that hurts someone else. When are you most tempted to use a condescending or accusatory tone?
6. We don't always think before we speak. What are some guidelines you can implement for yourself to help you think before you speak?
7. Who is your enemy? Why does God instruct us to love our enemies? What does that accomplish?
8. Do you have a mean streak? What is God saying to you about how to get rid of that?
9. What might God be nudging you to do in regard to being bold and speaking up for Him?

Always Be Prepared
Galatians 6:2; 1 Peter 3:10–16

I woke up at five thirty, showered, ate, drank my coffee, spent twenty minutes with the Lord, and brushed my teeth. I packed my lunch, got in my car, and stopped to get gas and drop some shirts off at the dry cleaners. I was in a hurry, as Mondays are always a little rushed. "I hope I don't run into anybody I know" is what I was thinking, aware I had no time for small talk. After making a quick stop at the grocery store to pick up flowers and a card for a coworker, I was now running a few minutes late. Meanwhile, in my rush, I was unaware of the cashier at the grocery store with tears in her eyes, hoping I wouldn't notice. I didn't notice. I wasn't even looking.

Knowing Jesus and following Him has been the best decision I ever made. The joy I find in serving God is tremendously fulfilling. But if I am not careful, I can fall into the trap of filling every minute of every day, not allowing the needs right before my eyes to even register. In my busyness, I am oblivious to hurting people around me because I don't even pay attention!

For me, God revealed this to be a sin in my life. I love people, and God has developed that love in me to offer encouragement to those I come into contact with. If I'm too busy and too distracted, God cannot use me in this way. I can testify today that God has removed the blinders so I can see more clearly the opportunities when they arise to show kindness, encouragement, or even a prayer. I've learned to allow extra time in my day for the unexpected.

To go one step further, when we love others as Christ loves us, people will notice. They may even comment about our faith or show appreciation for our concern. At those times, God wants us to be ready to explain our hope as a believer in Jesus in a kind and respectful way. Preparation is key to being intentional about our faith.

What is your testimony? What has God done for you? What spurs you on to be kind to others? Knowing those answers is important. Otherwise, golden opportunities might be missed. Today, ask God to give you the eyes to see the people around you as well as a prepared answer to the hope you have in Jesus.

—Tammy

The 10 Percent
Job 1:1–20

Life can throw some devastating things our way. Sometimes, they are a direct result of our actions, but other times, there doesn't appear to be any link to our actions and what happens in our lives. We know that hardship will come while we live here on earth, so what can we do?

The story of Job is an amazing look at someone who went through some of the highest mountaintop experiences, yet some of the lowest valley experiences. Charles Swindoll said, "Life is 10 percent what happens to you and 90 percent how you react to it." Today I want to focus on the 10 percent portion, using Job as our example.

Even before life comes at us, we can do things to prepare ourselves for the 10 percent. While the Bible tells us that Job was the richest man in the entire region, I believe the most critical attribute was that Job was blameless, a man of complete integrity. When a statement as bold as this is made, it immediately grabs my attention. I want to know more about Job's faith, knowing that I fall short of this even as I currently strain for it.

Another key attribute we see in Job 1:5 was that Job fully practiced his duty as the family patriarch to be his family's religious leader. This verse ends by telling us that this was Job's regular practice. So even though Job had an enormous empire to manage and a large family to attend to, he still had the regular practice to purify his children, offering burnt offerings for each of them and honoring the Lord.

In my life, there have been many times when practicing and preparation come into play. As a kid playing sports, I would often practice certain drills and plays so I would be ready for any game situation. At work during strategy sessions, my team will often utilize tools that will allow us to prepare for various outcomes in the business. But what about my spiritual preparation?

As a CEO, I want to be like Job, putting much more effort into my spiritual preparation than managing my business. The 10 percent that life throws at me will be hard at times, but I want to be spiritually prepared for everything, and I want to be blameless in the Lord's sight.

–Mark

The 90 Percent
Job 1:21; 2 Corinthians 6:3–10

We previously shared Charles Swindoll's quote, "Life is 10 percent of what happens to you and 90 percent how you react to it." Today we are going to focus on the 90 percent aspect of this quote.

In our story of Job, we learned that while life is going to have its challenges, there are things we can do to prepare ourselves for these difficult times. As Charles Swindoll points out, the next step is 90 percent of the battle. Let's first take a quick look at how Job responded.

We know the story based on our previous reading how Job had enormous wealth and a large family, but through a course of many actions, Satan took all of that away. We see the amazing reaction that Job had after all this news came crashing down. First, he tore his robe in grief and shaved his head. For many of us, that would be a similar start for us, but then our next step might lead to pity, anger, retribution, and so on.

But notice the next steps for Job in 1:21. He fell to the ground in worship! Oh, that I could respond to hardship in this way. He goes on to say that he came into the world with nothing and will leave with nothing. The Lord gave him what he had, and the Lord took it away. And even at that moment he proclaims, "Praise the name of the Lord" (Job 1:21b NLT).

In the case of Job, the circumstances did not happen as any direct result of what he did. However, in 2 Corinthians 6:3–10, we learn that Paul's choice to follow Jesus and His commandments directly led to his numerous hardships. But Paul also praised God! We can see the direct correlation. Paul tells us that our hearts ache, but we always have joy.

Life may hit us directly or indirectly, but our reaction to whatever comes our way is still the same. We should hold onto the joy and praise the name of the Lord. Much like we see in the lives of Job and Paul, the proper response will be beneficial to us personally, but also to both Christians and non-Christians watching our lives. For everyone, but especially Christians, we can anticipate that hardships and trials will be part of our lives. It is critical that we not only prepare for them, but that we have the proper response to them when they come.

– Mark

Kill Others with Kindness
Matthew 22:34–40

Immediately following my marriage to Mark in 1994, we moved to the East Coast, where, for the first time in my life, I wasn't going to school, performing, or working. I was twenty-four and knew that boredom would set in if I didn't figure out what to do with myself while Mark worked twelve-hour days! A month after moving in, a school in the area offered me a job as a K-12 music teacher, and I accepted.

Toward the end of the school year, the teachers and staff had a secret sister/brother event, where we drew someone's name and showered them with cards and/or gifts for a few months until the reveal at the end of the year.

God truly had a sense of humor when I drew the name of a coworker whom I had had disagreements with regarding her child's behavior in my classroom. Being a somewhat strong-headed twenty-four-year-old, I was tempted to withdraw from the event after seeing the name I picked. However, I knew in my soul that God was up to something good and I needed to put on my big girl pants and practice graciousness, especially to this person whom I had been frustrated with.

For the school year, I secretly helped this person, wrote funny cards, and made every attempt to kill her with kindness. In the meantime, my demeanor toward this individual changed, and my responses became softer and kinder. By the end of the year when our names were revealed, my attitude had completely been transformed. God did a work in me by helping me to put my petty frustrations aside and to honor someone whom I didn't feel like honoring. Radical kindness was the thing I needed to practice for God to do a greater work in the deeper part of my soul.

Through that experience, this coworker and I were able to resolve our differences and put them in the past. I saw God's faithfulness and healing lived out before me, and I am grateful for His patience with me.

—Tammy

Praise Him Always
Psalm 34:1–6

"I will praise the Lord at all times. I will constantly speak His praises. I will boast only in the Lord; let all who are helpless take heart. Come, let us tell of the Lord's greatness; let us exalt His name together" (Psalm 34:1–6 NLT).

When I was growing up, my parents were great encouragers to me. They told me often that they were proud of me, which meant a lot. In general, however, I was often praised by others because of the things I did, such as playing the piano or violin well or doing well in school. Although this meant a lot to me as well, there was a hole in me, desiring to be noticed for who I was as a person and not for what I accomplished. My character and integrity mattered so much more to me than the accomplishments I achieved. When it comes to praising God, I believe this same principle applies. I want to praise and acknowledge God, not just for what He does for me, but for all of who He is and all His attributes.

During a Zoom Bible study that I facilitated during COVID, I asked my group of twenty-nine to each list a characteristic of God, compiling a full list of His attributes and reasons why we praise Him. The following traits are what we came up with:

Who God Is: Forgiver, Father, Redeemer, Guide, Protector, Shelter, Hope, Safety, Rock, Tower, Stronghold, Slow to Anger, Compassionate, Sustainer, Way-Maker, Savior, Peace, Unconditional Love, Joy, Beautiful, Creator, Builder, Transformer, Healer, Strength, Our Song, Deliverer, The Alpha and Omega, Omnipotent, Always Present, Shepherd, and Faithful

There are many, many more attributes of God, but this list was a good start to being able to put words to our praise! Perhaps this list can inspire you to add some of your own words of praise, for the facets of His character and power are endless, giving honor and adoration to the Savior of our souls! Meditating on who God is and being able to verbally and specifically identify His lordship in our lives allows God to inhabit the very praises that we give. Let us praise Him always!

–Tammy

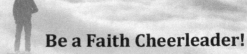

Be a Faith Cheerleader!

Lamentations 3:22–33; 1 Thessalonians 5:11;
Hebrews 3:12–15

I never was a cheerleader in high school. However, some of my friends have daughters who cheered and went to competitions around the country. I've always enjoyed sitting in the bleachers watching a game, hearing the cheers and marching band spur on the players from the sidelines! The game would lose a little "umph" without the roles of these encouragers.

Christian faith is a life journey that involves rough terrain, steep slopes, and dry days, while other days feel like we are drowning. At times like these, we need cheerleaders spurring us on to finish this race! I'm not talking pom-poms and acrobats (although that would be fun). I'm talking about being purposeful about encouraging one another in our faith, reminding others of God's faithfulness and presence. We all need a positive word saying "You can do this!" or "Keep holding on!" and then having someone to pray alongside us with encouraging faith.

> See to it, brothers and sisters, that none of you has a sinful, unbelieving heart that turns away from the living God. But encourage one another daily, as long as it is called "Today," so that none of you may be hardened by sin's deceitfulness. (Hebrews 3:12–13 NLT)

Faith cheerleaders help us to combat sin in our lives. Accountability and encouragement are biblical, and there is power in cheering our friends on to victory over areas of sin.

Lastly, we could all use a good cheerleader when it comes to being built up. As humans, we can be easily discouraged and give up too quickly when attempting to tackle a challenging situation or simply pursuing our faith journey. We don't always see ourselves through God's lenses, which is why 1 Thessalonians 5:11 encourages us to build each other up.

Today is a new day! One of the kindest things we can do for our fellow neighbors is to be a faith cheerleader, encouraging them right where they are in their faith, cheering them on to victory.

—Tammy

Week 6 Reflections

1. After reviewing the Scriptures for each day, name three to four passages that jumped out at you this week.
2. How can you practically apply these verses to your life today and the upcoming week?
3. What is your testimony? Are you prepared to share it with an acquaintance when the opportunity arises?
4. Name a situation going on right now that is affecting you (the 10 percent).
5. Write out two possible scenarios of outcomes to this situation based on your response (perhaps your human nature versus godly response).
6. Who is someone that is hard for you to love, much less like? How can you kill them with kindness this week?
7. Praise is affirming who God is, not necessarily what He has done. Who is God to you? Name ten attributes of God as your personal praise.
8. Are you a faith cheerleader?
9. What does being a faith cheerleader look like to you and the people around you?

"What's on Your Nose?"

1 Peter 3:16; Matthew 5:11

Many years ago, I worked at a place where we had an inside joke if a coworker were kind or offered to help our boss in any way, we would say they had a little "something brown on their nose!" We, of course were teasing, implying they had ulterior motives to be in her good graces. Although we joked and teased about the brownnosing, there was some small cultural truth in the subtle humor.

Going out of one's way to be kind is more the exception than the rule nowadays. In the busy world we live in, people often assume an ulterior motive in someone who is kind for no reason. I used to help a ninety-three-year-old lady after school named Florence. I knew life had been difficult for her, so I tried my best to be kind. I made cookies for her, sat with her, and listened to her life's stories. One day as we were chatting, her demeanor changed, and she accused me of wanting a piece of her will because I was being so kind to her. That came out of nowhere and certainly shocked me! I assured her that I had no such motive and apologized if my kindness came across insincere. Knowing her background as I did, I was not offended by this and certainly understood her reaction.

The sad reality is, in the world, people are known to be kind when it benefits themselves or if it doesn't cost them too much. For example, if we have extra time on our hands, we will offer our place in the grocery line to someone else. If we don't, we won't. If we receive a big bonus, we contemplate giving money to a missionary or someone in much need. If we don't, we don't.

Kindness is shown in simple ways. Taking the opportunity to write a note of kindness to a waitress, shovel the neighbor's driveway, make a meal for a sick friend, bring a plant to someone just because, text encouraging words to a teenager, or call some elderly friends are great places to start. I have found that being kind needs some creativity on my part. The opportunities are out there. I just need to be aware and act, regardless of appearing to have something brown on my nose!

—Tammy

Whom Do You Cling?

Deuteronomy 13:4; Matthew 10:39; 1 Timothy 1:19

A few years ago, I asked a group of college students where they believed God was. Some commented that they thought of Him far off in the clouds, seemingly beyond reach. Some replied that they knew in their minds that God was here in our midst, but they didn't really see or feel His presence. One student, however, responded that God's presence was so real to her that she relied on Him for every part of her being. She went on to explain that from having alcoholism and depression in the family, she had no choice but to cling to God.

I don't know about you, but I want to cling to my heavenly Father, no matter my circumstances. While having a strong family bond and wonderful friends, I can find myself complacent, making everything else seem closer to me than God Himself.

In Matthew 10:39, God describes the kind of commitment He desires from us. He doesn't just want us to cling to Him when life is falling apart. He wants us to cling to and fasten ourselves to His presence so that when we rise in the morning, He is the first thing on our minds. When we go about our days, His Spirit goes with us, impacting every word we say and everything we do. "Cling to your faith in Christ and keep your conscience clear. For some people have deliberately violated their consciences; as a result, their faith has been shipwrecked" (1 Timothy 1:9 NLT).

Has your faith been shipwrecked? Does God seem distant? To answer these questions, take a minute to quiet yourself, lean into Him, and listen to Him. For application, we are given some key action words in the following verse to help us, "***Serve*** *only the Lord your God and **fear** him alone.* ***Obey*** *his commands,* ***listen*** *to his voice, and* ***cling*** *to him*" (Deuteronomy 13:4 NLT).

Serve, fear, obey, listen, and cling! Ironically, clinging is freeing! He wants to be our God in every area of our lives. Let us make Him our God and cling to our faith in Christ Jesus!

—Tammy

Dr. Jekyll and Mr. Hyde
Luke 6:43–45

Robert Louis Stevenson inspirationally published his now-famous book, *Dr. Jekyll and Mr. Hyde*, in 1886. His inspiration for writing this classic came mostly from his curiosity of the good and evil of human nature, but also from a friend named Eugene Chantrelle, a French teacher convicted and executed for his wife's murder in 1878.

The story's plot begins when Dr. Jekyll, a scientist, is tormented by his bad impulses. Consequently, he creates a potion that separates his good self from his bad self, resulting in the monstrous Mr. Hyde. Even though they are the same person, the physical characteristics of them both are different from each other, symbolic to who they are. Jekyll has spent most of his life trying to be good and doing good things, so naturally his evil side isn't all that big. As a result, Hyde is smaller than Jekyll. Hyde is also younger because the evil part of Jekyll hasn't been worn out as much as his good self.

> No good tree bears bad fruit, nor does a bad tree bear good fruit. Each tree is recognized by its own fruit. People do not pick figs from thornbushes, or grapes from briers. A good man brings good things out of the good stored up in his heart, and an evil man brings evil things out of the evil stored up in his heart. For the mouth speaks what the heart is full of. (Luke 6:43–45 NLT)

These verses tell us about a good tree and a bad tree, reminding me of these two personality figures. I have learned the hard way that kindness in my own strength can wear me out if I am not kind through the Holy Spirit in me. My temptation to sin hits me hard when I am weak, and I can easily succumb to temptation if I'm not leaning on the Lord.

Unlike the mythical story of Dr. Jekyll and Mr. Hyde, good and evil cannot coexist in the same person. We are surrounded by good and evil, but when the Holy Spirit is in us, Satan has no home. Yes, we will make wrong choices and say and do things we shouldn't, but as we repent and turn from our sin, the Holy Spirit will nudge us forward to grow in our faith, not in our own strength, but through His power!

—Tammy

Son-Ripened Fruit
Galatians 5:22–23

My mom is an amazing pie maker. While I was growing up, she exposed my sister and me to many berry-picking excursions, yearly highlights for me because I anticipated the bountiful pies my mom would make in the weeks to come!

Years later when I had two boys my own, I carried on the tradition to go fruit-picking, including strawberries, blueberries, grapes, apples, and peaches. I remember picking peaches at an orchard in Mesa, Arizona, and the smell of peaches permeated through my senses, some of the sweetest peaches I had ever eaten in my life. Fruit that is ripened in the sun on the vine is very sweet and a direct parallel to how Scripture personifies the fruit of the Spirit.

> But the Holy Spirit produces this kind of fruit in our lives: love, joy, peace, patience, kindness, goodness, faithfulness, gentleness, and self-control. There is no law against these things! (Galatians 5:22–23 NLT)

Jesus is the vine on which our fruit grows. The fruit then ripens in the "Son" once we choose to follow Him. He will then produce the kind of fruit that is sweeter than anything we could muster up ourselves. That is an important concept because even without the Holy Spirit, it is possible for people to be kind, gentle, or patient. I know many people who don't have a relationship with Jesus who are very nice people.

But the kind of fruit that comes from being connected to the vine (Jesus) produces supernatural abilities to love the unlovable, to allow joy to coexist with suffering, and to experience peace that passes all understanding. Son-ripened fruit exhibits kindness that goes beyond our nature, stretching ourselves with goodness that reflects Jesus, not us.

Jesus softens my words and actions with gentleness and can help me control myself from doing things that are not pleasing to God. I anticipate sweet pies from the vine this week, from the Son-ripened fruit that only can come from the Spirit.

—Tammy

Eyes to See

1 John 3:16–18

I was in a store not too long ago when I assisted a legally blind woman and her seeing-eye dog. For those of us who do not have to rely on someone else's eyes or ears to get around, we can afford to be quite independent. But for this woman and others who are visually impaired, a seeing-eye dog must be a huge blessing.

Although I am not physically blind, I am fully aware that I can often be spiritually blind. Much like the relationship a blind woman has with her dog, I know I need the Holy Spirit to be my eyes to see the needs of others around me every single day. In the song, "Give Me Your Eyes," by Brandon Heath, the lyrics speak volumes about how we can be spiritually blinded to the needs of those who cross our paths each day. We can overlook prime opportunities to offer kind words, actions, or encouragement to someone that desperately needs it. There are physical needs out there in our own neighborhoods that are visible when we have the eyes of Christ. We can't afford to be spiritually blind when it comes to needing Jesus to open our eyes fully to see as He sees.

> This is how we know what love is: Jesus Christ laid down his life for us. And we ought to lay down our lives for our brothers and sisters. If anyone has material possessions and sees a brother or sister in need but has no pity on them, how can the love of God be in that person? Dear children, let us not love with words or speech but with actions and in truth. (1 John 3:16–18 NLT)

Seeing the needs and acting on the needs are two different things. Let's be honest. Our lifestyles can be so busy that, even though we see the needs, we ignore them or overlook them because we believe we don't have time. But we do have time! We oversee our own schedules. Some rearranging on our calendars may be in order, but we have an amazing opportunity to not only see the needs, but to act on them!

—Tammy

What Overflows?

James 1:21

Do you ever feel complacent when you are in a stable place in your life? Your marriage may be doing well, you're really enjoying your work, or maybe your relationships with friends and family are conflict-free. Truthfully, this is when I turn to God the least. The attitude of my heart says, "Nothing's wrong with me, God. I'll check back in once I'm struggling again!" Unfortunately, these are the times I need to be most cautious.

Sometimes I don't see what is brewing deep within until I am triggered, often blindsiding me. I forget that there are frustrations during these seasons in which I need God's wisdom and grace. Just recently, I discovered my boiling point at the grocery store when I could not find whipped cream! What should have been a five-minute trip to the store ended up taking twenty minutes looking for this can of sweetness. To add to my inconvenience, every slow person seemed to be in my way, topping my grocery visit off with self-checkout frustrations. I succumbed to my emotions and hit my boiling point.

On my drive home, I furiously made sure I was ahead of the cars next to me. "I'm not going to let you in!" was what I was stiffly saying to any car that tried to sneak in after I'd waited. It's a silly example, but I had been triggered. Whether it was stress from work earlier that day or the impatience I felt in the store, I chose to turn from God's holy mindset to my own worldly reactions.

In James 1:21 (ESV), it says, "Therefore, lay aside all filthiness and overflow of wickedness, and receive with meekness the implanted word, which is able to save your souls." My inclination to think only of myself was an overflow of wickedness that led to a bad attitude.

Implanting God's truth into my daily thoughts prevents these sins by calling me to confess my wickedness and laying it aside so that God's peace and love can overflow. There is no stress too small to surrender to God. I testify today that God can sanctify not only my negative attitude in the grocery store, but He is preparing me to have a sanctified heart in much harder times in the future.

—Hannah

Week 7 Reflections

1. After reviewing the Scriptures for each day, name three to four passages that jumped out at you this week.
2. How can you practically apply these verses to your life today and the upcoming week?
3. Name a time you were kind with an ulterior motive. Did you realize it at the time?
4. What does "clinging to the vine" practically look like for you in your daily life? Be specific of habits or schedule changes that need to be made.
5. We all have a good and bad side to us (Jekyll and Hyde). What are some fruits you have noticed in yourself that you know are not fruits of the Holy Spirit? What do you need to surrender to Him?
6. What are some sweet fruits God has developed in you that were not natural to your personality?
7. What prevents you, if anything, from having eyes to see? What is something you can stretch yourself to do the next time you see someone that is alone, sad, or stressed?
8. What "yuck" overflows when you are under pressure or stress?

Exercise and Discipline
1 Corinthians 9:23–25; Proverbs 3:1–4; Galatians 5:22

I'm not an athlete. I never wanted to be an athlete; nor was playing sports ever in my bag of gifts. On the contrary, I am a professional musician. But like an athlete who knows the benefits of keen discipline, I resonate with hard practice and utter instinct that is needed to be good.

Since I was five, I have become aware that the musical talent God gave to me is truly a gift from the Lord. With gratefulness, music has been part of my intuitive language, ingrained in me so I can communicate with notes even more than I can with spoken words.

However, there was a time in my life when I relied on my natural abilities alone, neglecting the hard work and discipline that was needed to win piano competitions and audition for violin chairs in the orchestra. I couldn't enter those things without strong technique, required memorization, and muscle memory that came from hours of practice, discipline, and time with the music itself.

Our spiritual lives are much this way. As God's children, some fruits of the spirit (love, joy, peace, patience, gentleness, kindness, goodness, faithfulness, and self-control) come easy to us, while other fruit is harder to produce unless we are disciplined to fertilize it, water it, and nurture it.

God wants us to grow. He wants us to exercise our faith muscles. If you've ever entered an exercise routine at the gym, it takes scheduling the time, dressing for the occasion, drinking water, and being present in the moment. This is all to begin the process to be healthy. Likewise, we need to schedule time in our day to make spiritual exercise a priority, spiritually "dressing" for the occasion, and letting the Holy Spirit water the dry seedlings in us.

Exercising is hard work, especially in the initial days of developing the healthy discipline so it becomes a habit. We cannot rely on our natural abilities, thinking these will be enough to get by with. No, God wants to grow all types of fruit in us so we can best love the world around us and glorify Him in the process!

—Tammy

Wait, This Is a Race?
Hebrews 12:1–13

Years ago in Cincinnati, five-year-old Scott said to me, "Mom, let's play a game and run around the house and touch these different things [certain plants, rocks, and bugs]." It was his idea of an obstacle course, and so I played along. When we were done, laughing and running, he screamed, "I won!" I told him that it wasn't fair because he never told me it was a race! I asked to do it again so I could put real effort in this time.

Since I didn't know it was a race, I didn't put my best foot forward the first time. I went through the motions of doing all the things Scott asked me to do, but I wasn't seeing it as a race.

> … let us strip off every weight that slows us down, especially the sin that so easily trips us up. And let us run with endurance the race God has set before us. We do this by keeping our eyes on Jesus, the champion who initiates and perfects our faith. (Hebrews 12:1–2 NLT)

The race Christ has set before us is not a race of speed, but of endurance. Notice how the author of Hebrews says that in order to run the race, we need to shed off anything that hinders us and is a potential to drag us down. If we are aware that this is a race that God has set before us, shouldn't that motivate us to run with everything we've got?

I don't know about you, but I do well with goals. Likewise, in our spiritual lives, God has given us goals and has set the bar high. We need to keep our eyes on Jesus, who perfects our faith. Yes, life is hard. Yes, life is unpredictable. Yes, we are going to have many struggles and pain. However, in this race of endurance, Jesus wants us to hold on to Him with everything we have, allowing Him to carry us when the race gets hard. He wants to run with us and to cheer us on with His glory and grace.

Once we accept Jesus as our personal Savior, we have entered the race that God has set before us. Don't let life creep up on you and drag you down. Keep running. Keep enduring. Shed off anything that trips you up, and you will be victorious in this race. And yes, this is a race!

—Tammy

Start Walking

Galatians 5:16; Ephesians 5:8; 1 John 2:6

My son Matt and I took a trip out to Zion National Park and Bryce Canyon after he had just completed his junior year of college. We decided to do this trip on a whim, as Mark and Scott were at that time in other states for other events. Of the many trails in Zion, one can opt to tackle one of the most strenuous hikes there called, Observation Point. On our first day there, Matt and I trekked this eight-mile, twenty-three hundred-feet-high hike. It was 105 degrees, challenging us even more because of the heat index. Step by step, we made it to the top where breathtaking views awaited us over the canyon below. Yet despite our physical success, the evidence of the feat of perseverance was our true reward!

I remember that day like it was yesterday. During the last few hours of the hike, there were many times I wanted to quit. I had to mentally tell myself to keep walking, breathing, and putting one step in front of the other. For a long time, the climb was unrewarding. It was dry, hot, rocky, and painful. But in the end, it was incredibly worth it. I learned a lot about myself and my ability to plow through, even when exhausted and full of self-doubt.

The correlation here with our spiritual walk is obvious. We all have our own faith journey. Some know Jesus at an early age, while some never make the commitment until adulthood. No matter how long you have been walking with the Lord, living your life through the Holy Spirit is a journey all on its own!

When the writer Paul wrote to the Galatian church, he said, "So I say, let the Holy Spirit guide your lives. Then you won't be doing what your sinful nature craves" (Galatians 5:16 NLT).

When we make the decision to follow Jesus, the walk can be strenuous, even painful to stay the course. But walking the road with the Holy Spirit is rewarding. We need to take one step at a time, putting one foot in front of the other, remembering this, "God is our refuge and strength, always ready to help in times of trouble" (Psalm 46:1 NLT).

—Tammy

Run from Evil

1 Peter 5:8; 2 Timothy 2:19–22

Two years ago, our family visited the Columbus Zoo and witnessed a Cheetah Run, an exhibit that shows how fast the cheetah can move when he is either hunting for food or running from a predator. As the fastest land animal, the cheetah has been known to run between sixty-eight to seventy-five miles per hour! This image is implanted in my mind when I read the following verse:

> Run from anything that stimulates youthful lusts. Instead, pursue righteous living, faithfulness, love, and peace. Enjoy the companionship of those who call on the Lord with pure hearts. (1 Timothy 2:22 NLT)

If we are going to run from evil, we need to be ready for action. Satan will attack us when we are most vulnerable. We need to remain alert with prepared hearts so we can have the ability to hear Satan's footsteps as he prowls around stealthily. By being prepared, we can run the other way and not allow him to trap us in his snare. Our running shoes need to be tied and ready. "Stay alert! Watch out for your great enemy, the devil. He prowls around like a roaring lion, looking for someone to devour" (1 Peter 5:8 NLT).

When I envision how I want to run from evil, the cheetah is what I think of, not hesitating and not jogging, but running at full speed in the other direction! This can be difficult for us because we are often resisting something that is fun. But God tells us to run because if we ponder and consider the temptations we're facing for too long, we may not get away in time.

Satan may be looking for someone to devour, but God has equipped us with the shoes we need to run from evil! Lean into that! Trust your spiritual legs, and God will set you straight on His path!

—Tammy

The Sword of the Spirit

Ephesians 6:10–18

Recently I was invited to a home where an impressive full-sized knight stood in the entryway. I remember the reaction I had and just stood there in awe of the huge piece of metal staring back down at me. I commented to the owners on the uniqueness of displaying a whole coat of armor as people enter and leave their home. They had bought that knight as a reminder of the spiritual battle their family faces every time any one of them walks out that door. I was awestruck, and the armor inspired me to look up Ephesians 6:10–18 again for my own review and application.

Paul writes to the Ephesian church about spiritual warfare, how we are not fighting against flesh and blood, but the forces of evil that invade this world (Ephesians 6:12). Paul uses a coat of armor to explain the spiritual weapons we need to be prepared with to face the unseen obstacles.

As you read Ephesians 6:10–18 today, I encourage you to make a visual of the symbolism Paul uses to describe the different pieces of armor that prepare us for battle. Pay careful attention to the sword of the spirit, the living Word of God.

> For the word of God is alive and powerful. It is sharper than the sharpest two-edged sword, cutting between soul and spirit, between joint and marrow. It exposes our innermost thoughts and desires. (Hebrews 4:12 NLT)

The Word of God separates the truth from the lie by sharply cutting to the quick. It causes someone to radically change by cutting off the old way. Personally, I need my sword! I need to live by the Word of God so it can cut through the deceit in my motives, the gossip on my tongue, and the idols in my life that slowly creep in.

In reading God's Word, we will be able to resist the enemy in the time of evil. Then after the battle is done, we will be standing firm (Ephesians 6:13). This is God's promise to us.

–Tammy

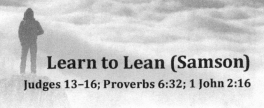

Learn to Lean (Samson)
Judges 13–16; Proverbs 6:32; 1 John 2:16

Do you ever read something in the Bible that just doesn't make sense to you at first? I know that I have. But I have also learned that if I have a response like that, it usually means I need to dig in and go deeper to find out more. So today, our reading is the story of Samson, a peculiar story, but one with a great message found in Judges 13–16.

Samson was born somewhere between the years of 1145 and 1100 BC and is one of four people in the Bible whose birth was preannounced by an angel. (Isaac, John the Baptist, and Jesus are the other three). Samson was a Nazarite, meaning he was "set apart" for God. This meant he was never to drink fruit or wine from the vine, go near and touch a dead person or animal, and was never to cut his hair. Scripture tells us that God gave Samson unrivaled strength through his hair (Judges 16:17), with the sole purpose of defeating the Philistines.

Samson was a faithful follower of God and a warrior who became the fifteenth judge of Israel. Despite having the Spirit of the Lord upon him, his sexual yearnings of the flesh controlled his life, ultimately causing him humiliation, defeat, disgrace, and eventually death. "For everything in the world—the lust of the flesh, the lust of the eyes, and the pride of life—comes not from the Father but from the world" (1 John 2:16 NLT).

Despite equipping us for what we need to follow God and His will, our gifts and personal sin can trip us up. Since He generously gives unique and special gifts and talents to use (like giving Samson strength), we can fall into the trap of leaning on those gifts instead of leaning on God. Like Samson, we can become too dependent on our own intelligence, strength, and talents. This self-dependence can readily lead to sin in our heart, giving in to the passions of the flesh rather than leaning on the Lord. Remember, God doesn't give us talents and gifts that will replace Him; rather He gives us those things to reflect Him and serve Him while we continue to lean on Him!

–Tammy

Week 8 Reflections

1. After reviewing the Scriptures for each day, name three to four passages that jumped out at you this week.
2. How can you practically apply these verses to your life today and the upcoming week?
3. Name a time in your life when you had to exercise discipline. Were you ever tempted to give up? Why or why not?
4. Where are you on your Christian journey? Are you staying put, walking, or running? Or perhaps you are walking backward.
5. What do you need to do to get in shape for the race? Even if you feel in shape today, we know that the enemy is prowling around. Where do you tend to fall weak?
6. Draw a picture in your notes of the knight and the spiritual armor so you can get a visual.
7. Take time to write a prayer asking God to give you the sword of the Spirit more than you ever have before.
8. Samson leaned on his own God-given strength. What strengths has God given you?
9. How are you tempted to lean on your strengths instead of God?

MONTH 3
To Whom Much is Given,
Much Is Required

A FAITH THAT STANDS
Produces Self-Control and Wisdom

To Whom Much Is Given

Luke 12:42–48

"When someone has been given much, much will be required in return; and when someone has been entrusted with much, even more will be required" (Luke 12:48 NLT).

God has given graciously to all of us. Yet so often we choose to compare our provisions, abilities, or opportunities with others, perhaps overlooking the gifts God has already given to us. We are reminded in Luke that God has an expectation for us to be faithful in the big and little things He so faithfully provides. This can pose a challenge for us if we don't put into perspective the gifts and talents He has given to us.

I've noticed that when God bestows gifts of leadership, giftedness, or intelligence upon a person, it is often difficult for that person to be faithful with the little things because he or she may feel equipped to have or do so much more. Frustration, discontentment, and pride can set in, potentially leading to a bad attitude. Luke understands these tensions, so he stresses the importance of being responsible, having the conscience toward right and wrong, the capacity for humility, and being faithful in all circumstances, big or small.

Are we faithful with little? Are we respectful and wise? Are we grateful for what we already have, putting forth the same amount of energy into the small opportunities as much as the big important ones?

Mark and I have moved around the country quite a bit. There have been moves where God has given me large opportunities that utilized my potential to the fullest and then other moves when the opportunities seemed smaller in importance to me. In those times, I found myself being pruned by God to teach me to serve purely out of love for the Lord with an attitude of gratefulness. I knew that if I weren't faithful with the little things, He couldn't trust me with the larger ones.

Are you faithful with little? Faithful with much? Are you grateful and content for what you already have, treating others with respect and keeping commitments and responsibilities in the day-to-day? Then celebrate all that God is doing in your life now and look forward to the open doors He has for you ahead!

–Tammy

Jealousy

Genesis 26:12–25; Proverbs 14:30; James 3:16

Before you read this today, please read the story in Genesis 26:12–26 first. You will enjoy this read!

We learn that there was a conflict over water rights and that jealousy was at the core of the problem. God had blessed Isaac with many riches and herds of animals. Out of jealousy of his wealth, the Philistines filled all of Isaac's water wells with dirt, the wells that his father, Abraham, had dug. Because of jealousy, Abimelech asked Isaac to move out of the area, for Isaac had become too powerful for Abimelech's liking. Nothing good comes from jealousy, which is why we need God's help.

Proverbs 14 tells us that jealousy is like cancer in our bones. It's not only painful, but it grows, spreads to other parts, and affects our strength and outlook on life. Jealousy is a response that often stems from discontentment, pride, and greed. It also comes from comparing ourselves to others, leaving us ungrateful, bitter, and questioning God. "For where envy and self-seeking exist, confusion and every evil thing are there" (James 3:16 NLT).

Ouch! When we covet or are self-seeking, we can't see straight! Jealousy clouds our vision to see clearly what God desires us to see. Evil hangs out in a spirit of envy, and God will reveal it to us individually. When I begin to feel jealous, I often get a pang in my stomach, sometimes even a heat that comes over me. When this happens, I have learned to get on my knees right then and there and confess my jealousy and ask God to help me. I start listing off to God all the things I am grateful for in my life and pray for the person I am feeling jealous of. It's hard, but I have found much relief in letting God help me.

My heart's desire is to be a person who can celebrate others with a high five without being intimidated or jealous. I long to be gracious and genuinely happy when others succeed. If you feel the pangs of jealousy begin, go to God immediately! Don't let it grow. God is pleased when we confess our sins and ask Him for His guidance. He loves us so much!

–Tammy

To Boast or Not to Boast?

Jeremiah 9:23–25

Growing up, I was taught never to brag or boast about anything, including talent, brains, opportunities, or possessions. My parents taught me that if I boasted in myself, I would be displaying pride, making myself look better than other people. This boasting could potentially cause others to feel "less than," which would not be pleasing to the Lord. "This is what the Lord says: 'Don't let the wise boast in their wisdom, or the powerful boast in their power, or the rich boast in their riches'" (Jeremiah 9:23 NLT).

Is it ever ok to boast? Yes! But not in ourselves. We are to boast in the Lord by giving credit to Him alone, praising Him for who He is!

> But those who wish to boast should boast in this alone: that they truly know me and understand that I am the Lord who demonstrates unfailing love and who brings justice and righteousness to the earth, and that I delight in these things. (Jeremiah 9:24 NLT)

Have you ever found yourself unprepared for an opportunity to give God the credit for what or how He has been working in your life? When we come to God asking for something to happen and then He comes through for us, there is such value in letting others know about it!

As you continue in your week in whatever you do or wherever you go, look for opportunities to boast in the Lord! Even right now, reflect on your provisions. If you have a roof over your head, a meal to eat, clothes to wear, health, or family, boast in the Lord for being your provider! Don't take those things for granted. When you are given a good job, great friends, certain abilities, or resources, boast in the Lord! Every good and perfect thing is from above. Let's recognize the times to boast in the Lord, not once, not twice, but as many times as you can!

—Tammy

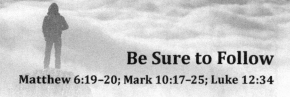

Be Sure to Follow

Matthew 6:19–20; Mark 10:17–25; Luke 12:34

As you read the parable of the rich man in Mark 10:17–25, there is a deep and challenging message that has the power to change you if you are brave enough to take the message to heart. The tendency in reading a parable such as this one is to rationalize what Jesus meant, to think that Jesus didn't really mean what He said. After all, he was talking to a rich man. (And I'm not rich. Am I?) Could it be that Jesus' expectations were too high? Unpractical? Too narrow? What does Jesus expect of me?

> "Teacher {Jesus}," the man replied, "I've obeyed all these commandments since I was young." Looking at the man, Jesus felt genuine love for him. "There is still one thing you haven't done," he told him. "Go and sell all your possessions and give the money to the poor, and you will have treasure in heaven. Then come, follow me." (Mark 10:20–21 NLT)

Jesus knew the heart of the rich man and so challenged him to see what the man was willing to give up in order to follow Jesus. The body language of the rich man said a lot as he lowered his head in sadness, unable to fathom his earthly treasures being gone. His life had been wrapped up in his world of possessions, servants, family, and power, even though his heart seemed good.

I have compassion for the man because as I reflect on my own life, there are certainly treasures (people, things, or activities) I have at one time or another, placed in higher importance than Jesus Himself. Although my intentions have been good, my heart has been undiscerningly divided. Luke tells us that where our treasure is our hearts will be.

The message? Be sure to follow. We can have all the good intentions in the world, but if our treasures here on earth crowd out the treasures of heaven, we are not putting Jesus in His rightful place as Lord of our lives. As we meditate on this parable, may we allow God to examine our hearts and identify anything or anyone that is keeping us from wholeheartedly following Jesus.

—Tammy

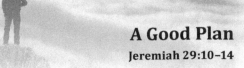

A Good Plan

Jeremiah 29:10–14

I enjoyed nearly all my classes in high school. I am not sure I fully understood their purpose for my future, but I knew success here would lead to a better college opportunity. Success in college would lead to a better job, and a better job would pay more. It's not a bad outline for a general plan, but clearly a lot of missing details.

My chemistry teacher, Dr. Schrader, had taught at the school for many years, and with his vast experience, he graciously saw some potential in me. He pushed me very hard in this class, and I felt good to check off the box of completing another math and science in the curriculum. Subsequently as I set up my classes for the following year, I found that advanced physics and advanced chemistry were offered during the very same hour. I would have to choose between them. After having chosen AP physics, Dr. Schrader approached me.

He asked why I did not sign up for AP chemistry. After my basic answer around having to choose one or the other, he generously recommended to me a special option during my study hall to take AP chemistry. I wasn't sure why I needed both, but I trusted Dr. Schrader.

It wasn't until later in college that I fully realized that he had seen my potential and had taken some of his normally free time to help prepare me for a future degree. He seemed to know what I was going to need, and he helped me move in that direction even before I knew it myself.

There are times in our lives when we will doubt or not even see the plan God has for us. I am thankful to many of my teachers who helped me with a plan regarding college and a career. I was fortunate to have some of the best! But even the best teachers are limited with their guidance and broad understanding.

I am far more grateful to know that I have a heavenly Father who knows me intricately. No matter what has happened so far or what circumstances I find myself in, He has a plan not to harm me but to prosper. That same heavenly Father also knows you fully and has a plan to prosper you. Seek Him and He will guide your plans.

–Mark

Seek It and Ask for It

2 Chronicles 1; Matthew 17:20; James 1

Have you ever started to pray, asking God to do something, yet you didn't believe He would do what you were asking from the moments your words began to form on your lips? I know I have. I am twenty-six years old, and although I have never once questioned God's ability to do anything, I confess that I have found myself doubting His intentions or desires before I even asked.

One of my favorite passages of Scripture is in 2 Chronicles 1, where God tells Solomon that He would give to Solomon whatever he asked for. Solomon's response blows me away. He asks God for wisdom so he can lead God's people appropriately and effectively. God granted him wisdom, but also gave him wealth, power, and much more than he could ever hope for.

Now, don't hear that you can just ask for wisdom and God will make you like Solomon. That's not the point. The point is that Solomon trusted God, and God went above and beyond. The cool thing about God is that He works with our faith, stretching us to strengthen and grow, giving us His desires as we ask Him and are obedient to Him. Solomon was walking in the way of the Lord, and God knew He could trust Solomon with what he asked for.

James 1:5–6 explains that we are **all** supposed to ask for wisdom from God. Then, when we do so, we are to not doubt … at all! Those who doubt should expect to receive nothing from the Lord! (James 1:7). Our relationship with Christ is not about what we can get out of it. We are called to worship Him and live our lives in the likeness of Christ. In seeking and serving the Lord, He will honor our obedience, sacrifice, and faith. He, in turn, is faithful and can be trusted as we seek Him with all our hearts.

What are you trusting God for right now? Do you believe in the power of God when you ask, or do you ask with a weight of doubt attached? God wants specific prayers, prayers that truly seek Him with unwavering trust. Jesus informed us that faith as small as a mustard seed can move mountains (Matthew 17:20). What is your faith moving?

–Scott

Week 9 Reflections

1. After reviewing the Scriptures for each day, name three to four passages that jumped out at you this week.
2. How can you practically apply these verses to your life today and the upcoming week?
3. Name a time when God gave you more than you had thought He would. What was your response?
4. If anything, what is an area in your life that you struggle with being jealous of someone else?
5. What does God say about jealousy and contentment?
6. Is it easy or difficult to boast in the Lord? What are some practical ways that you can boast in the Lord this week and tell others what He has done for you?
7. Do you believe God has a good plan for you? Why or why not? How can you discern what His plan is?
8. On a scale from one to ten, rate your faith strength. Do you believe that God is who He says He is and that you can trust Him without doubt?
9. What does God desire overall in your walk with Him today?

The First Step to Self-Control
2 Peter 3:1–11

I freely confess that I am a recovering shopaholic. After many years in my twenties and thirties of excessive shopping for clothes, shoes, and things for the house, one word finally sunk in, self-control!

On a deeper level than shopping, however, God began teaching me self-control as early as ninth grade. I remember vividly when my church youth group studied a series on self-control as it pertained to sexual purity and our tongues. As a ninth grader who was, overall, a moral Christ-follower, I was searching for understanding as to why God would ask me to abstain from sex until marriage and to avoid foul language. My strong personality needed practical reasons on the whys before I could commit.

> For this very reason, make every effort to add to your faith goodness; and to goodness, knowledge; and to knowledge, self-control; and to self-control, perseverance; and to perseverance, godliness; and to godliness, mutual affection; and to mutual affection, love. (2 Peter 5–7 NLT)

The attributes in this passage may seem impossible to achieve in our own strength. However, they are not impossible with the Holy Spirit, as He produces this fruit in us. The fruit of goodness leads to purity and moral excellence. Perseverance is a gift from God that gives us patience to practice discipline. Finally, godliness, and love for the Lord spur us on to pray for wisdom, strength, and discernment to make good decisions.

Once I began to dig into Scripture and accept that my new life in Christ was to reflect Him in all I do and say, I made the decision to grow in self-control. I made a promise with God to wait until marriage for sex. I then committed to clean up my language, including swearing and taking God's name in vain. Why? Because I made Jesus the Lord of my life and I was forever committed to Him.

My friends at school thought I turned prudish, but I didn't care. I knew that as a Christian, I had a responsibility to please God first, to be sanctified holy, and to strive for self-control through the Holy Spirit.

—Tammy

A Little Bit of Kindness
Proverbs 11:24–25

My husband and I have lived in apartments all four years we've been married because our financial burdens have prevented us to save up for a house. We drove my 2007 Chevrolet until we couldn't anymore. We tried to put money aside, but something always seemed to come up: snow tires, student loans, oh, and then … a baby.

Ok, enough of the excuses. If I'm being honest, we both really enjoy shopping! Before having our firstborn, we spent a lot of our days off together going to stores downtown. I mean, who isn't roped into sales or something that would fit just perfectly in the house?

After our first two years of marriage and a thousand dollars of unnecessary buying, we had to face the music about our spending. Our lifestyle desperately needed some changes. Proverbs 11:24–25 teaches us to give freely. Consequently, these verses revealed our problem of wanting more for ourselves while being stingy about giving to others. After swallowing that reality, we knew our spending habits needed to change. We wanted God to give us a spirit of kindness and generosity, even if it stung a little. Was it easy? No. But the muscle needed to be strengthened. We started small.

One thing I personally learned through this challenge that I want to pass along is this: don't do what we did and waste your time waiting to feel like giving. If you're finding it hard to be generous, ask God to change your attitude. Train yourself to think of others over yourself. Ask God what He wants you to give and how to give it! Let Him guide you. Next time you're at the store ready to buy an unnecessary item, pray about how that item could bless somebody else instead.

Flexing your generosity muscle can seem difficult when you struggle financially. My husband and I are in that stage of life right now! But even so, we have found ways to still give freely (pun intended). When we have asked God for ways and opportunities to give, He has shown us. He will show you too! A little bit of kindness goes a long way, and you will see what blessings God will put on your life!

–Carissa

Sexual Purity
Psalm 119:8–10; 1 Corinthians 6:15–20; Hebrews 13:4

"Marriage should be honored by all, and the marriage bed kept pure, for God will judge the adulterer and all the sexually immoral" (Hebrews 13:4 NLT).

When Mark and I were raising our boys, we talked to them regularly about sexual purity, especially between the ages of eight and eighteen. In our own lives, the desire for sexual purity has directly correlated to our desire to obey God, even if it hasn't always been popular or easy. We see purity as a gift that we give to the Lord as an offering, an inevitable result of self-control. Is sexual purity hard to achieve? Yes! But it is possible, and there is an abundance of peace and blessing from God when we stay pure.

Last year I spoke at a teen event about sexual purity. One of the students asked how we achieve sexual purity in today's day and age. I was thankful that I could personally testify that it could be done, but we read and focused on the following passage together:

> Don't you realize that your bodies are actually parts of Christ? Should a man take his body, which is part of Christ, and join it to a prostitute? Never! And don't you realize that if a man joins himself to a prostitute, he becomes one body with her? For the Scriptures say, "The two are united into one." But the person who is joined to the Lord is one spirit with him. Run from sexual sin! No other sin so clearly affects the body as this one does. For sexual immorality is a sin against your own body. Don't you realize that your body is the temple of the Holy Spirit, who lives in you and was given to you by God? You do not belong to yourself, for God bought you with a high price. So you must honor God with your body. (1 Corinthians 6:15–20 NLT)

I want to encourage you today that if you feel that sexual purity is impossible to attain, remember what it says in Psalm 119:9. Nothing is impossible when we remain in and meditate on God's Word.

—Tammy

Let's Talk about the Body!

1 Corinthians 6:19–20; Romans 12:1, 13:12–14; Colossians 3:4–6

"For the moment all discipline seems painful rather than pleasant, but later it yields the peaceful fruit of righteousness to those who have been trained by it" (Hebrews 12:11 NLT).

Our bodies are extremely complex. Last summer I was diagnosed with a rare blood disorder, essential thrombocythemia, where my bone marrow makes too many platelets. For years I had struggled with headaches, shortness of breath, and pressure in my head but thought I was just out of shape. Fortunately, through daily medication, I am able to keep the condition under control.

God desires for us to be diligent and care for our bodies. They are a temple of His Holy Spirit when we come into a relationship with Him. Paul instructs the Romans, "to offer your bodies as a living sacrifice, holy and pleasing to God—this is your true and proper worship" (Romans 12:1 NIV). For personal application and accountability of this verse, I broke down the parts of the body as a checklist for myself. I encourage you to do the same by allowing God to speak into each of these areas:

- **My Thoughts:** Am I taking my thoughts captive?
- **My Eyes:** Am I looking at shows, video games, or books that God would say are ok for me?
- **My Ears:** Am I listening to music or shows that are beneficial to my spiritual growth?
- **My Mouth (verbal):** Am I taking God's name in vain, swearing, slandering others, or using language not edifying to others?
- **My Mouth (consumption):** What am I putting into my mouth? Drugs, alcohol, chemical substances, smoking, or too much food?
- **My Heart:** Do impure motives, greed, lust, idolatry, unforgiveness, and selfishness dwell in my heart?
- **My Arms/Hands:** Am I serving others as God's hands and feet?
- **My Sexuality:** Do I accept the gender assigned to me at birth? Do I accept that God designed sex to be between one man and one woman in the context of marriage only?
- **My Legs/Feet:** Am I going to places that are pleasing to the Lord?

—Tammy

Weariness
Isaiah 40:28–41

Doing the right thing is usually the harder thing to do than to not. Let's be honest: our human nature can get pretty worn down from simply going against the worldly flow, the culture of our government, schools, workplaces, and institutions (sometimes even churches). The systems at play go head-on with biblical views, wearing down the believer by widely accepting ideas we know are not of God, in turn tempting us to grow immune to the evil lurking around us. I sometimes tell people that I feel like a salmon swimming upstream, going against the strong currents of my daily surroundings. I can become weary unless I hold on to the promises found in today's Scripture passage, one of my favorites!

As you read the following passage in Isaiah, I encourage you to highlight the characteristics of God that you see:

> Have you never heard? Have you never understood? The Lord is the everlasting God, the Creator of all the earth. He never grows weak or weary. No one can measure the depths of his understanding. He gives power to the weak and strength to the powerless. Even youths will become weak and tired, and young men will fall in exhaustion. But those who trust in the Lord will find new strength. They will soar high on wings like eagles. They will run and not grow weary. They will walk and not faint. (Isaiah 40:28–41 NLT)

We simply cannot fathom the magnitude of our God! His strength and power are like the vastness of the ocean and every crevice and creature that belong to it. We may become weary, but He promises to keep us going without fainting!

The Creator of all the earth who spoke everything into existence is in the middle of your trial. He knows where you are. He knows what you are facing. Lean into Him! Pour out your weariness on Him and stay the course. When you are tempted to give up and faint, remember those wings and legs that He promises. He is just waiting for you to ask!

—Tammy

Success and Generosity
Micah 6:8; Matthew 6:19–21; Mark 12:41–44

How do you measure success? By how much money you have or your level of happiness? The number of college degrees, how the kids turned out, or promotions over the years? Whatever you place importance on in your life is probably the very source from where your feelings of success come from. Subsequently, our feelings of personal success can directly affect our generosity if we are not careful.

Perhaps you don't feel successful because life has not turned out the way you'd hoped? The lack of success can lead to feelings of utter failure at times. Doubt and blame take their place in the heart, creating resentment that ultimately causes you to hold back from God. If this is you, take heart! There is encouragement in the Word of God.

In the story of the widow's offering found in Mark 12:41–44, the woman had nothing to her name except for a few cents, yet this widow gave everything she had out of her gratefulness to God. I'm sure she did not feel like a successful person. I'm sure she suffered more than even the story reveals. But she didn't hold back from God because of how she felt. Her love for the Lord was genuine and consistent, and she knew that this was not her final home.

> Don't store up treasures here on earth, where moths eat them and rust destroys them, and where thieves break in and steal. Store your treasures in heaven, where moths and rust cannot destroy, and thieves do not break in and steal. Wherever your treasure is, there the desires of your heart will also be. (Matthew 6:19–21 NLT)

These verses cause me to self-reflect because I don't want my generosity (or lack thereof) to God and others to be based on whether I feel personally successful or not. God's measurement of success is in the eternal things, not in the things here on earth. I can rest in the fact that He will always provide for me and give me joy, even throughout the unexpected turns in my life.

—Tammy

Week 10 Reflections

1. After reviewing the Scriptures for each day, name three to four passages that jumped out at you this week.
2. How can you practically apply these verses to your life today and the upcoming week?
3. What are your challenges with self-control on a small scale?
4. What are your challenges with self-control on a larger scale?
5. What are practical steps for you to take toward sexual purity (e.g., accountability, not putting yourself in vulnerable situations, etc.)?
6. What other areas of your body do you wrestle with purity and self-control?
7. When has doing the right thing become wearisome?
8. How do you measure your success?
9. How do your personal feelings of success weigh into your spirit of generosity?

Beware and Be Prepared!
1 Peter 5:6–10; 2 Peter 1:5–7, 12–13

"Stay alert! Watch out for your great enemy, the devil. He prowls around like a roaring lion, looking for someone to devour. Stand firm against him, and be strong in your faith" (1 Peter 5:8–9 NLT).

"Beware of Bears" signs are a common sighting along the trails of Glacier National Park. Tourists and hikers are encouraged to carry bear spray, along with a little bell to ring as they trek through the meandering trails. Bears are adorable to look at, but as the term "mama bear" derives from them, they are most protective of their cubs and will defend them until death. People need to be careful in their territory, especially during breeding season.

Although Peter is comparing Satan to a lion in chapter 5, not a bear, I think back to the bear warning signs and take heed to the meaning and application. Satan is prowling around like a lion, looking for his next meal, usually hidden from the target he is going after. Lions are patient and will wait for hours until they see their prey of choice. The best way to avoid both the lion and the bear is to stay away from the places where they are without proper protection and preparation.

As Christians, we need to be on the alert. We may look all around us and see life as it should be, trusting in our surroundings, only to be jolted by a pounce that will take us down. Satan is alive. He is not fictional. He will sneak up on us when we least expect it. But the good news? God gives us tools to prepare for the unexpected.

> In view of all this, make every effort to respond to God's promises. Supplement your faith with a generous provision of moral excellence, and moral excellence with knowledge, and knowledge with self-control, and self-control with patient endurance, and patient endurance with godliness, and godliness with brotherly affection, and brotherly affection with love for everyone. (2 Peter 1:5–7 NLT)

–Tammy

He Won't Compete

Malachi 2:1–2; Matthew 6:33–34

Malachi lived in the first part of the fifth-century BC and was the last of the twelve minor prophets. His book, bearing his own name, concludes the thirty-nine books of the Old Testament, preceding the birth of Jesus by about four hundred years. Malachi's name means "messenger," fitting for one whom the Lord used to share His message with the Israelite people. In Malachi 2, he warns the priests of their arrogance, disobedience, false teaching, and their defaming of the name of the Lord.

> For the lips of a priest ought to preserve knowledge, because he is the messenger of the Lord Almighty and people seek instruction from his mouth. But you have turned from the way and by your teaching have caused many to stumble; you have violated the covenant with Levi,' says the LORD Almighty. So, I have caused you to be despised and humiliated before all the people, because you have not followed my ways ... (Malachi 2:7–9 NLT)

God will not compete. In all His grace and mercy, His consequences for not following Him are harsh. These warnings are still in effect today in our society and culture. We have turned to other gods, defamed the name of the Lord, and watered down the message of salvation to allow us to feel comfortable. The narrow road has gotten wider and wider.

What competes with God in your life? Is it your time, work, family, or activities? There are so many things we can be doing that are all good things! But if we are "changing up the rules," so to speak, to adapt to our schedules and lifestyles, God will not tolerate that for long. He wants to be number one, the Lord of Lords and King of Kings. He wants you to trust Him, follow Him, and love Him with your whole heart, soul, and mind. "Seek the Kingdom of God above all else, and live righteously, and he will give you everything you need" (Matthew 6:33–34 NLT).

—Tammy

Make the First Move
Luke 17:1–10

"If another believer sins, rebuke that person; then if there is repentance, forgive. Even if that person wrongs you seven times a day and each time turns again and asks forgiveness, you must forgive" (Luke 17:3–4 NLT).

A professor asked the students in the class to explain their answers to the homework from the night before, specifically the process they used to get their answers. "Who wants to go first?" he asked, aware of the difficulty of the equations in question. Not one student raised his or her hand. Everyone looked around, waiting for someone else to go first.

While some of us may like to go first, I know that my initial tendency is to wait a few minutes until I first hear from others. After all, I don't want to look like a lab rat on a chopping block waiting for the ax to come down! Going first is risky, especially in the area of spiritual things and reconciling with someone else. It's a vulnerable and hard thing to do. We want to look right in others' eyes.

Reconciliation is complicated when both parties are digging their heels in, refusing to say "I'm sorry" first or making the initial move to talk things through. I compare the art of reconciling to a scab that has formed over a wound with an infection lurking beneath. Yes, it hurts when it is removed and is messy when the infection frees itself, but once it is healed, fresh starts can begin. In all reality, things will probably seem worse before they seem better.

Is there anyone you can think of that you need to reconcile with? Taking the initiative to do so can be uncomfortable. More importantly, it reveals where pride may be hiding in our heart. Do we want to be right more than we want to reconcile? Do we want to try to control the other person by sabotaging them and keeping them at bay? Maybe it's time to let down our guard and ask God to help us take the first steps toward reconciliation.

If I can offer any inspiration to you today, I encourage you to make the first move. Pursuing the high road and taking the initiative to go first is a pure act of humility before our brother or sister but, most importantly, before Jesus.

—Tammy

Sin in My Heart
Psalm 66:16–20

"Come and listen, all you who fear God, and I will tell you what he did for me. For I cried out to him for help, praising him as I spoke. If I had not confessed the sin in my heart, the Lord would not have listened. But God did listen! He paid attention to my prayer. Praise God, who did not ignore my prayer or withdraw his unfailing love from me" (Psalm 66:16–20 NLT).

Facial blemishes are annoying, especially during the teenage years. I've certainly had my share of imperfect skin to last me a lifetime. Yet, life is full of examples of nice things being polluted by the ugly, such as muddy footprints on the floor or weeds in the flower garden. But even more so, I remember going to a nice restaurant with Mark where I ordered one of my favorites on the menu. The excitement I felt when the broiled scallops came to our table quickly waned when I saw a long hair protruding from my fork, naturally only after it went into my mouth. Yuck!

Sin is that ugly thing in our lives that contaminates the good. It is like the facial blemish, the mud, the weeds, and the hair, tainting everything it touches. In Psalm 66, God specifically asks us to do a few things. First, He wants us to come and listen to Him. He wants us to fear Him, not in a bad way, but with a reverent fear, knowing that He knows every detail about us anyway.

God then wants us to praise Him as we petition Him for help. His divine will for us is that we confess our sin before Him. This is a crucial part of this passage because sin separates us from God! The sin in our heart contaminates us, yet His forgiveness wipes the slate clean. God loves us beyond belief. His love promotes discipline in us in hopes to make us more like Him. He promises to forever cast our sin as far as the east is from the west, and that is a long time.

Don't be afraid to confess. We are exposed anyway! God already knows the sin in our hearts, so once He reveals it to us, let us just be transparent with Him and confess what is deep within. He promises to give us a fresh start.

—Tammy

The Parable of the Rich Fool
Matthew 6; Luke 12:13–34

Years ago, Mark and I sat with a lawyer to make out our will. We wanted our estate to someday be divided evenly among the boys and their families, but also wanted to create a charity foundation that would reach others for Jesus long after we are gone. The process was somewhat painless, and we were able to put everything in writing so that later there will be no questions of our intentions.

But back in Bible times, things were not that clear-cut. When someone passed away, the hopes were that the family would be agreeable to divide up the assets accordingly to the expectations of the family. But this is not the case in Luke 12, when a person in the crowd asked Jesus to solve a dispute by instructing his brother to divide his father's estate with him. Jesus did not want to serve as an arbitrator because He was called to teach and reveal truth. So he responded to the man, "Beware! Guard against every kind of greed. Life is not measured by how much you own" (Luke 12:15 NLT).

Jesus proceeded to tell a parable about a rich fool who stored up wealth, building bigger and better barns to accommodate all his things. He chose material possessions over a relationship with God and giving to those in need. Jesus reiterates the importance of storing up treasure in heaven and not storing up wealth on earth, "Wherever your treasure is, there the desires of your heart will also be" (Matthew 6:21 NLT).

Based on Jesus' teaching, Mark and I have tried to be wise with our finances, saving for the future and being frugal when we can. However, Jesus warned us about being too comfortable like the rich fool, missing out on opportunities right in front of our eyes where we could store up treasures in heaven. This means that we need to be ready and willing to act on the needs around us as a way of life, adopting generosity and heavenly treasures as a regular way of thinking.

How is God speaking to you today about storing up treasures in heaven? What are you doing well at? What areas need some refocusing? May we learn from the lesson of the rich fool and embrace the words of Jesus so that we can be more like Him!

—Tammy

Want to Know a Secret?
Philippians 4:10–13

In 2009, our family went on a mission trip to the Dominican Republic to help build a church. One of my biggest takeaways from that trip was not in what I did there, but in what I learned from observing the native people living genuinely contented lives.

Life was very simple there. The homes of the villagers were constructed with cement walls, but often lacked floors and complete roofs. Open electrical wires were dangerously held together when they needed a light bulb, and they used the same dirty waterhole for bathing, laundry, and drinking. When they were hungry, they would grab a mango off the tree. The villagers diligently worked alongside the work team, talking with us and letting us hold their babies, who wore no diapers or clothes.

On Sunday we worshiped with them in a space no larger than a thousand square feet that had cement block walls, dirt floor, and no air conditioning in 110 degrees. Yet, the people there were dressed to the hilt, dancing and singing, lifting their hands to the Lord for the whole entire day. They took breaks to eat something midday, but went right back at it, reading the Word, singing, and giving God praise! Wow.

The people in that poor village in the Dominican knew what being content was all about. They acted as though nothing was missing. All they knew was that they were provided for with daily provisions. They were grateful to God, giving Him 100 percent of themselves on the Sabbath day. Were they comfortable in the extreme heat and humidity inside crowded cement block walls for hours? Probably not. Do you think they missed the comforts of what Americans count as necessities, such as coffee or snacks on a Sunday? No. They testified to God's holiness and power, and they gave Him glory and thanksgiving for all they had. This experience broke me and taught me an authentic lesson about true contentment.

So what is the secret to being content? Paul teaches us that gratefulness in living with plenty or in living in want is the key to contentment. He concludes Philippians 4 by instructing us that we can be content with whatever life throws our way because we can do all things through the One who generously gives us strength!

—Tammy

Week 11 Reflections

1. After reviewing the Scriptures for each day, name three to four passages that jumped out at you this week.
2. How can you practically apply these verses to your life today and the upcoming week?
3. Where have you seen Satan prowling around lately? Have you done anything to stop him in his tracks? If so, what?
4. What competes with God in your life?
5. What steps are you ready to make to ensure God is God and nothing else is standing in the way of that?
6. Sometimes God calls us to act first in reconciliation. Taking the high road is hard to do. How can you trust God with humility and go first in a certain situation?
7. Is there anything in your heart today that you need to confess? Please write that down. Take time to pray through that.
8. We all unintentionally store up treasures on earth if we are not careful. What treasures do you hold tightly? What eternal treasures are you storing up?
9. What is the secret to being content according to Paul?

Help! I Do What I Don't Want to Do!

Romans 7:14–25

One of my thrills is to play Chopin Études on the piano. The fiery Gb Étude is performed on the black keys at lightning speed. The Revolutionary Étude puts the left hand to the test with intense fast runs throughout. In order to practice both, the tempos must accelerate slowly, ensuring all fingerings are in place and comfortable in the hand. The process is tedious, but worth the effort. If I try to move the process along too fast, I will begin making the same mistakes over and over. Backtracking is painful, so I want to stay on task.

And so it is with life. We zip along at lightning speed, hoping we don't miss any beats along the way. Trouble is, if we aren't careful, we begin making mistakes that we don't want to make. Mistakes turn into sin, and before you know it, the sin nature within is taking over. Paul shows us the challenges of staying on task with God's will in our lives.

> We know that the law is spiritual; but I am unspiritual, sold as a slave to sin. I do not understand what I do. For what I want to do I do not do, but what I hate I do. And if I do what I do not want to do, I agree that the law is good. As it is, it is no longer I myself who do it, but it is sin living in me. (Romans 7:14–17 NLT)

We never should run ahead of God. If we do, we stunt the process of healthy spiritual growth, and we may put ourselves in situations we aren't ready to handle yet. Soon we may begin doing what we know is wrong, allowing sin to take hold. Consequently, we need to backtrack a little bit and revisit what God's principles are and what His Word says about running ahead of Him.

If you find yourself running ahead of God and beginning to mess up repeatedly, it is time to stop! Don't continue down this destructive path. Stop in your tracks and shout out to God, "Help! I do what I don't want to do!" And He will swoop down and come to your rescue.

–Tammy

Wisdom for Life

Proverbs 4:1–9, 9:9–11

I travelled with a Christian music group the summer before my senior year of high school, giving concerts all over the United States. We began in Colorado and drove on a bus through twenty-three states. As a group of about fifty students, we spent many hours on the bus together, making a family of sorts with peers from all parts of the country.

Each day after boarding the bus, we spent the first half hour in quiet time, whether it was reading our Bible or praying. We often would share with the person we were sitting with what we learned or read, mostly because we were sitting with that person for a few hours.

One hot summer day driving through Nebraska, the bus's air-conditioner decided to stop working. The humidity and heat were stifling, and so the driver dropped off the team at a park for lunch while the bus was taken in for service. One of the bass players and I struck up a conversation as he shared with me what God had been teaching Him during the morning quiet times on the bus. He explained to me how he had begun to read a proverb every day and that he was daily praying for wisdom in all the areas in his life. My peer pointed out that the book of James tells us to ask God for wisdom (James 1:5), therefore claiming God's promise by putting his faith into action!

I was so inspired with his goal that I decided to do the same thing for the rest of the summer. I was amazed at what God revealed to me and taught me during those quiet times on the bus each day! "Don't turn your back on wisdom, for she will protect you. Love her, and she will guard you. Getting wisdom is the wisest thing you can do!" (Proverbs 4:6–7 NLT).

Perhaps today you are needing direction in a relationship you are in or wisdom with disciplining your children. Maybe you are a student deciding what friends you should hang around. Whatever your situation, ask for God's wisdom, and He will give it to you. It is the wisest thing that you can do!

—Tammy

Embrace Wisdom
Proverbs 3:1–18

In Proverbs 3, King Solomon outlines all the many reasons we should seek out wisdom and embrace it. As you read the passage for today, see if you resonate with any of these reasons we should pray for wisdom:

1. You will live many years, and your life will be satisfying. (v. 2)
2. If you bind loyalty and kindness around your neck, you will find favor with God and people and will have a good reputation. (v. 3–4)
3. As you seek and trust Him, He will show you which way to go. (v. 5–6)
4. You will fear the Lord and turn from evil, therefore having healing for your body and strength for your bones. (v. 7–8)
5. Wisdom will speak to you to honor God with your first fruits, ensuring God's abundant provision for you. (v. 9–10)
6. Wisdom will allow you to accept the Lord's discipline and not be upset or reject it. (v. 11–12)
7. You will find joy and understanding, with the profits that wisdom brings. (v. 13–14)
8. The value of wisdom is more valuable than anything you could desire. (v. 15)
9. Wisdom will offer you long life and riches. (v. 16)
10. Wisdom will guide you down the right path and give you satisfaction. (v. 17)
11. Wisdom is a tree of life for all that embrace her; happy are those who hold her tightly. (v. 18)

When we pray and ask God for wisdom, we are asking Him for His insight and discernment in all of life's situations and relationships. Without embracing wisdom, we only have our own perspectives and intelligence to go on, which is nothing compared to what God wants to reveal to us through the Holy Spirit. He just wants us to ask for wisdom and then embrace it!

—Tammy

The Antidote of Wisdom
Matthew 6:33–34; James 3:13–15

The infection of pride often leads to the disease of jealousy. Jealousy consequently leads to discontentment and a bad attitude. This problematic condition we can so easily be affected with has the ability to contaminate the beautiful character that God wants to create in us. James 3:15 (NLT) teaches us that "jealousy and selfishness are not God's kind of wisdom. Such things are earthly, unspiritual, and demonic."

Whoa. That is a strong statement, but James writes it as God wanted it to be said, and he offers an antidote by seeking true wisdom from God.

I confess. I have dealt with this disease of jealousy. I remember a particular time in my life when I had jealousy toward someone in college. It seems insignificant now, but after I graduated, I moved to Cincinnati for my master's degree. This individual, however, went to Nashville (where I thought I wanted to be as a musician), and life's successes seemed to pour over her. Although I was genuinely happy for her, I occasionally had pangs of jealousy because God put me on a different path of life. My search for direction caused me to compare my path of life with hers, and I was plagued with thoughts of what could have been regarding my own music career. As I sought the Lord and His direction, He began to show Himself to me in a clear and tangible way, and in His wisdom, the jealousy faded and eventually went away.

I learned that being impatient for God's direction led to comparing my life to others. I also learned that to overcome jealousy, I needed to begin with gratefulness and surrender to God. In doing so, God altered my thinking to recognize that my life was on the path that God mercifully and graciously set me on. Through His generosity, I was given an amazing opportunity to accept a very specific calling that He had placed on my life, one I wouldn't have been able to identify without seeking His wisdom.

God has a unique calling for every single one of us. True wisdom through Christ means to, "Seek the Kingdom of God above all else, and live righteously …" (Matthew 6:33 NLT). He will then give you everything you need!

—Tammy

Fruits of God's Wisdom
James 3:16–18

Over the years, TV commercials have featured wise old owls to sell products varying from candy to insurance. Owls are symbols of wisdom, often depicted with glasses or a professor's cap to represent their profound astuteness! Expectedly, when I think of a person who appears to be educated and intelligent, owls like these come to mind. But the question here in today's Scripture reading is this: is wisdom an intelligence thing or a heart thing? Does wisdom imply smarts and brain power, sensitivity and insight of the heart, or both?

> For where jealousy and selfish ambition exist, there will be disorder
> and every vile practice. But the wisdom from above is first pure,
> then peaceable, gentle, open to reason, full of mercy and good fruits,
> impartial and sincere. And a harvest of righteousness is sown in
> peace by those who make peace. (James 3:16–18 NLT)

The wisdom James is talking about here is the wisdom that we get from God, not intelligence as far as IQ is concerned. I've known a lot of smart people that lack discernment and wisdom because they rely so much on their own brains. Biblical wisdom comes from the Holy Spirit giving us insight into His will, the ability to discern what is and what is not from God, and the ability to understand multiple facets of a situation. Godly wisdom also allows us to reason in order to solve a conflict and to be impartial in the process. I can't think of a relationship, job, or situation that does not require His divine guidance every day.

Yes, there are times when I feel self-sufficient, priding myself in being able to make decisions. Sadly, if navigating through a situation doesn't seem too difficult, I can easily forego asking God to give me His insight and rely on my own. I don't know about you, but as a leader and a mother, I need His discernment and ability to open my mind to reason that will subsequently lead to good decisions, real harmony and peace. When I do this, God fills me with His Spirit, where His fruits are on display!

—Tammy

Fabulous Future

Isaiah 43:1–3; Jeremiah 29:11–12

There are days when the demands of my job pile up or the problems seem to be getting the better of me. As I get older, there are times when this can lead me to think about the day I can retire and leave all these problems behind. Oh, if it were just that easy. I know that even if I were to retire, there would just be a new set of challenges to take their place.

Certainly the Israelites being exiled to Babylon was far worse than anything I have experienced in my life. But the clear message Jeremiah gave to the Israelites is the same message that God gives to each of us today. Regardless of our current circumstances, He has a plan for us that is not to harm us but rather to prosper us. Like most of us, I can desire for that plan to be here on earth and in fact for it to start today! I also can have a twisted sense of what that should be based on my own human desires. God sees things in such a greater way and with an eternity focus. I must remind myself when I am in these moments of difficulty that I am still in God's plan and to allow Him to grow me through these times.

As I reflected on the passage today from Isaiah, I found it interesting that the Lord was very clear that difficult times will happen in such a way as to expect these things. We will all have our own version of what these verses mean in our lives, but the same promise is there for each of us, the Lord will be there with us!

Sometimes these difficulties that come our way seem to be brought upon us by the people around us. These are some of the worst kinds of hurts as they feel so personal to us. But even in these moments, we can still be assured that the Lord is with us and has a plan for us. It is so healing and refreshing to be able to put our current pain and suffering to the side and allow ourselves to remember that the Lord has a plan for us. It does not mean that the pain goes away, but it does mean we can focus on knowing He is with us. I love knowing that He is preparing me for that fabulous future, and I want to be ready.

-Mark

Week 12 Reflections

1. After reviewing the Scriptures for each day, name three to four passages that jumped out at you this week.
2. How can you practically apply these verses to your life today and the upcoming week?
3. What things do you do in your life that you don't want to do, but your earthly flesh nags you about?
4. What are the reasons you personally need to ask for wisdom?
5. How can the lack of wisdom in your life lead to discontentment and potential jealousy of others?
6. What does God say about jealousy and contentment?
7. Is wisdom a head or heart thing? Explain.
8. Where do you see the fruits of God's wisdom in your life today?
9. People will hurt and disappoint you. How can God's wisdom penetrate your heart to handle those people with grace?
10. What does God desire overall in your walk with Him today?

MONTH 4
Transparency and Honesty Are Often Frowned Upon by Society

A FAITH THAT STANDS
Produces Boldness and
Unwavering Truth

Introduction to the Prophets
Nahum 1:1–15; Jeremiah 38

Throughout the Bible, God used prophets to speak on God's behalf, to communicate very specific messages or warnings to a group of people. Prophets are known to be extremely bold, not "tickling people's ears," but speaking truth in an authoritative way without hesitation. In reading the two Scripture passages for today, you will see the bold approaches of two prophets, Nahum and Jeremiah, as they deliver God's messages. God's authority is evident as they clearly state that God is the One who was telling them what to say. Likewise, when God calls us, we can stand boldly in what God says, even if it is unpopular.

In the Hebrew canon, the prophets are divided into two groups: the former prophets (Joshua, Judges, Samuel, and Kings) and the latter prophets (Isaiah, Jeremiah, and Ezekiel) and then the twelve minor prophets (Hosea, Joel, Amos, Obadiah, Jonah, Micah, Nahum, Habakkuk, Zephaniah, Haggai, Zechariah, and Malachi). The Bible names many prophets, but some of the most significant are:

1. Abraham, whom God himself calls a prophet (Genesis 20:7)
2. Moses, the greatest of the Old Testament prophets (Deuteronomy 34:10)
3. Samuel, anointed two kings of Israel on God's behalf (1 Samuel 3:19)
4. David, whose psalms were considered prophetic by the Jews (Acts 2:30)
5. Elijah and Elisha, who worked miracles and anointed (and denounced) national leaders on God's behalf (1 Kings 19:15–16)
6. Jeremiah, who warned Jerusalem's leaders that Nebuchadnezzar would take the city (Jeremiah 1:5)
7. Isaiah, who prophesied about the coming of Jesus, the Messiah. (Isaiah 7:1-17, 53:1-12)

Do some people have the gift of prophecy in the twenty-first century? Yes! Astutely aware to dishonesty and personal faults, someone with this spiritual gift is willing to suffer for truth. Regardless, God desires all Christ-followers to be bold and stand for what is right. Righteous boldness does not come easy, but as with the biblical prophets, He will tell us what to say.

—Tammy

The Devil Is in the Details

Deuteronomy 5:32–33

I'm not a baker, and to my mother's chagrin, I don't like to follow a recipe unless it needs very specific results. This innovative trait carries over into music, as I often find it stifling to play the notes on the page. As my improvising instincts take over, I quickly interpret the notes of the piece into a new arrangement as I go.

Contrary to my strong creative bent, I am a stickler for details when it comes to organization. My keen desire to plan large events, concerts, and services motivate me to have every detail planned, leaving room for the Holy Spirit to move.

> So, Moses told the people, "You must be careful to obey all the commands of the Lord your God, *following his instructions in every detail.* Stay on the path that the Lord your God has commanded you to follow." (Deuteronomy 5:32–33 NLT)

Moses' call to detail here is an exhortation that all of us should take to heart. God isn't looking for interpretive baking or musical improvising here. He is looking for detailed obedience. He goes on to say that God has *commanded* this! It's not open for interpretation, rationalization, or choice. We are to obey and stay on the path.

Staying on the path of truth is not widely accepted in modern society. Following Jesus will not make us popular. Oh, how the devil can get into the details with a few white lies. He is all about creating confusion, instilling pride, and capitalizing on our egos. He wants God's church to fail. I have witnessed the slippery slope, and my heart grieves in the rationalizing of small sins, of which there is no such thing. All sin is equal in God's eyes. We should use extreme caution if we venture off the path, for God has commanded us to obey all His commands, not just those up to our discretion.

Yes, the devil is in the details, but God is more into the details for the good of those who love Him. He desires to protect us, steer us, and guard our hearts in Christ Jesus. Our part is to obey and stay on the path.

—Tammy

The Call of Jeremiah
Jeremiah 1:1–19

Jeremiah is one of my favorite prophets in the Old Testament because while the Israelites sinned by turning to other gods, he spoke bold truth wrapped in a message of hope. Descending from a family of priests, Jeremiah was called to be a prophet at age seventeen. At age twenty-two, the Lord began giving messages to him with the purpose of revealing sin to the nation of Judah (southern kingdom of Israel), encouraging them to repent.

As you read Jeremiah 1:1–19, there are a few historical things to know in order to gain a broader understanding of the text. History tells us that five hundred years before the time of Jeremiah, King Solomon ruled over the Israelites. However, when his son, Rehoboam, became king, he messed things up, and Israel soon split, the northern kingdom of Israel and the southern kingdom of Judah, each with their own king. For centuries, both kingdoms were engulfed in sin and corruption, despite warnings from prophets sent by God. By 721 BC, the northern kingdom fell to the Assyrians, but the southern kingdom of Judah pulled itself together temporarily. Some wicked kings followed, reigning when Jeremiah came on the scene, until King Josiah, a good king, came to reign in 627 BC.

Why all the history? Jeremiah lived during a time of rebellion and contention. The challenges he encountered have influenced scholars to refer to him as the weeping prophet, yet also a prophet of hope. "For I know the plans I have for you, says the Lord, plans to prosper you and not to harm you; plans to give you hope and a future" (Jeremiah 29:11 NIV).

Jeremiah prophesied for forty years until Jerusalem was captured in 586 BC. He was appointed by God to proclaim truth in hopes that Israel would repent and turn back to God. He was later captured and stoned to death in 570 BC. I believe that God has called many Jeremiahs still today to be bold, speak truth, and give hope to those around us. We can't choose for others, but we can each be obedient to what God has called us to do!

—Tammy

Discernment and Training
Hebrews 5:11–14; Matthew 10:34; 1 John 4:1

"You have been believers so long now that you ought to be teaching others. Instead, you need someone to teach you again the basic things about God's word. You are like babies who need milk and cannot eat solid food" (Hebrews 5:12 NLT).

Yesterday, Mark and I watched a fifty-one-year-old golfer win the PGA golf major, the oldest anyone has ever won this tournament. When reporters interviewed him, he referenced the hard work and the changes he had to make with his training as he has gotten older. Skills that seemed to come easy when he was younger needed to be retrained and refreshed to continue into this next chapter of playing golf.

I can personally relate to this retraining in my spiritual life, needing to refresh and revisit lessons in God's Word. But unlike golf or other skills, I can make the mistake of likening it to riding a bike, thinking I will never forget how to lead a Spirit-filled life. The reality is, when I feel myself becoming stagnant or spiritually dull, I need to reignite the fire through Bible study, prayer, and accountability. If I am not growing, Paul says I am much like a baby on a baby bottle when I should be on solid food and training others. The more we are in God's Word and continue to learn and apply biblical teaching, the more we will have the insight and discernment of the Holy Spirit. Lapses of time and lack of use allow our faith to weaken if we are not regularly on top of it.

Being a Christ follower doesn't automatically produce discernment in the Spirit. I believe we are in the last days, when we especially need to spend time with God to discern what is true, pure, and authentic. There are many false teachers out in the world who make us feel good but lack truth.

> Dear friends, do not believe everyone who claims to speak by the Spirit. You must test them to see if the spirit they have comes from God. For there are many false prophets in the world. (1 John 4:1 NLT)

Let us be diligent in seeking after God through prayer and training so He instills His discernment in us.

—Tammy

Boast in the Lord
Proverbs 27:2; Jeremiah 9:23–24

As a boy growing up, I was very fortunate to be able to eat dinner with my parents most nights. We prayed before our meals every night, but we also had some other practices that happened during dinner such as sharing about our day and talking about the things we learned or accomplished. I enjoyed this part as I certainly liked to talk, but I also enjoyed sharing about learnings and successes of my day. Probably not too different from many young boys, but there was another especially wise practice we had at our dinner table.

Mom would make out little handmade cards with a simple Bible verse written out on each one. Clearly these were used for Bible memorization, a wonderful idea by itself. But as I grew older, I realized that I would often get a few of these little cards that I had seen before. At first, I assumed Mom just did not have enough to last without repeats until much later I realized a couple were repeated much more frequently next to my dinner plate. I do not remember others at the table getting repeats very often. One that was at the top of my list for repeats was, "Let another man praise thee, and not thine own mouth; a stranger and not thine own lips" (Proverbs 27:2 KJV).

As an adult, I look back with a thankful heart that my mom saw the areas that I needed growth in even as a young boy. She knew that this boasting, even at an early age, was part of an independent spirit that leads to pride and therefore is sin.

Jeremiah 9:23–24 takes the subject of boasting one step further. We are told again not to boast about our wisdom, strength, and riches, but rather if we are to boast, do so about our understanding that He is Lord. He delights in our praises of His love, justice, and righteousness.

When Jesus died on the cross for our sins, it included our pride. It was the ultimate demonstration of love, justice, and righteousness. Young or old, may we all remember that this is where our boasting should be so that others can hear about and be drawn to Him.

– Mark

Is Your God in a Box?
Isaiah 43:1–3; Mark 10:46–52

"Do not be afraid, for I have ransomed you. I have called you by name; you are mine. When you go through deep waters, I will be with you. When you go through rivers of difficulty, you will not drown. When you walk through the fire of oppression, you will not be burned up; the flames will not consume you. For I am the Lord, your God, the Holy One of Israel, your Savior" (Isaiah 43:1–3 NLT).

I believe we are living in the end times. As I sit here writing this, my heart is breaking for our Christian brothers and sisters around the world who are being persecuted and killed for their faith in Jesus. The fear of the unknown future in the world seems to have stunned the complacent church. Have we put God in a box, forgetting that we can come to God with expectation that He will act? I don't know about you, but I want to stand on the front line of prayer with expectation that God is working now and moving in our midst! He is not in a box, but sadly we put Him there.

In Mark 10, Jesus was walking through town. A blind beggar wearing the government-issued cloak of an official beggar stood on the side of the road. His name was Bartimaeus. As he stood there listening to the crowd around him, he learned that Jesus was coming his way. He began to shout, "Jesus, Son of David, have mercy on me!" (Mark 10:47b NLT). He threw off his beggar cloak and went to Jesus. There was no doubt in his voice or hesitation to go. He had already thrown the cloak off! He expected Jesus to do a miracle that day! He believed! He trusted!

I want to be a Christ-follower who expects God to move. For Him to do that, I need to take Him out of the box that I have put Him in and believe in the power of the most Holy God! I have seen Him move in the lives of my family. I have seen miracles of relationships restored and bodies and mental health healed. I have been a witness to God inhabiting the praises of His people!

What are you expecting God to do in your life? What promises are you standing on, believing on, and counting on? God is only as small as you make Him to be. God does not belong in a box! He is the Alpha and the Omega, so let's wait with expectation for Him today!

–Tammy

Week 13 Reflections

1. After reviewing the Scriptures for each day, name three to four passages that jumped out at you this week.
2. How can you practically apply these verses to your life today and the upcoming week?
3. Name the major and minor prophets in the Bible.
4. What are some characteristics of the biblical prophets? What about those who have the gift of prophecy today?
5. Where have you seen the devil getting into the details recently in your life? In those around you?
6. Describe Jeremiah. What can you learn from his boldness?
7. How is self-boasting a sin? How can you turn the boasting around, offering praise to God and encouragement to others in your life?
8. How have you put God in a box?
9. What do you expect God to do today in your life, family, workplace, school, and country? Be bold!

Bold Sharing
Matthew 5:11–13; Luke 12:34–36

"God blesses you when people mock you and persecute you and lie about you and say all sorts of evil things against you because you are my followers. Be happy about it! Be very glad! For a great reward awaits you in heaven ..." (Matthew 5:11–12 NLT).

Most people find it challenging to boldly share their faith. Why? If God is who He says He is and we have been transformed by His Holy Spirit, shouldn't this excite us and make us run to tell everyone of this saving grace? The answer is, "Yes, it should!" So what prevents us from doing just that?

1. We may be afraid of seeming unrelatable.
2. We may be afraid of offending someone.
3. We may not want to invade one's space, privacy, or time.
4. We may feel too much pressure if we are an introvert.
5. We may have not experienced the kind of suffering or persecution that Christians in other parts of the world have gone through, potentially resulting in us taking for granted this life-changing gift.
6. We may not be looking for opportunities.

Matthew 5:11–12 instructs us to be happy when we are made fun of or ridiculed for sharing our faith. Luke instructs us to, "Be dressed for service and keep your lamps burning ..." (Luke 12:35 NLT)

Be ready! Living the Christian life is not always easy. Once we have decided to follow Jesus, we become His ambassadors in a world that is not our own. I must ask myself every day if I am willing to lose my life, my reputation, or my standing for the name of Jesus.

Since I want so much to share my testimony, I try to find new ways to open doors to conversations. Loving others first and meeting their physical needs is often the way I start. I also strive to pray each morning for specific opportunities when I may need to free up my schedule to invest in people with services of love. I want to be bold in my sharing and rejoice when I am persecuted because Jesus gave His life for me!

—Tammy

I'm Not Ashamed of the Gospel

Romans 1:16–17

I love to read and watch mystery thrillers. For some reason, I don't get tired of the conventional plot of good versus evil, detectives seeking out the truth and bringing justice to the forefront. However, sometimes there are stories of people who have been wrongly accused of a crime and thrown into prison, sometimes for twenty to thirty years. During those hopeless and desperate years of living a never-ending nightmare, I can only begin to imagine what it would be like if a judge offered them a "get out of jail free" card, revealing new evidence to set them free! Could you imagine any better news, to go from utter misery and gloom to new life on the outside, free from the chains of bondage?

If you were that person, what would you do? Celebrate? Tell people? The greatest news of being set free after twenty-five years is not something I'd ever be embarrassed about!

In the spiritual realm, the gospel story has a parallel meaning. The gospel, which means "good news," is for everyone! Whether we are good people like the innocent prisoner or a mass murderer who took someone else's life, we are all sinners! We all deserve to be in chains because of our sin.

But the good news? Jesus came as a ransom for our sin, so that anyone who says "Jesus, I want you to be Lord of my life, I believe you died for me, and I am sorry for my sin" will be forgiven with the blood of Jesus shed for us on the cross. This gift of salvation is why we celebrate Easter! The result of His death and resurrection was a "get out of jail free" card with a fresh slate and our sin washed clean. This is the good news we all have the privilege of sharing! "For I am not ashamed of this Good News about Christ. It is the power of God at work, saving everyone who believes" (Romans 1:16 NLT).

We should never be ashamed to share the salvation that we have experienced. We were headed for spiritual death, and Jesus gave us eternal life through Him. And that, my friend, is something to be shared!

–Tammy

No Regrets

Acts 20:24

I had not seen or talked to him in over thirty-five years, and yet the news was startling and unsettling. Jon had passed away. Jon was my best friend growing up, and we roomed together our freshmen year in college. Some life choices did not bring Jon back to college our sophomore year, and so our close friendship quickly faded to the point that our lives did not again overlap. At times, I thought about Jon and wondered how his life turned out and if he had ever come to know the Lord.

Upon hearing of his death, not only was I hit with sadness, but I also wondered why I had not done more to share Jesus with Jon. I tried to live my life as a Christian around him and occasionally talked about spiritual things, but honestly, I don't ever remember sharing directly with him about needing Jesus as his personal savior. It was a miserable twenty-four hours as I thought about Jon and this possible miss on my part.

The next day I was hit by a clear thought in my head as I prayed. The Holy Spirit convicted me not to focus on the past with Jon, but rather focus on future opportunities to share Jesus with others by being fully prepared for these.

Just days later, someone who had worked with me indirectly twenty years earlier reached out to me. He was looking for help with finding a new job, but the conversation quickly led to our personal lives, catching up on what we missed. As a result, I found myself ready to be faith-minded, able to be more transparent with my faith.

In Matthew 28:16–20, Jesus gave the Great Commission telling us to go and make disciples of all people. Paul says in Acts, "But my life is worth nothing to me unless I use it for finishing the work assigned me by the Lord Jesus—the work of telling others the Good News about the wonderful grace of God" (Acts 20:24 NLT).

I want to be prepared to share my faith at all times and do my best so that in the end, I will have no regrets.

—Mark

Are Your Ears Itching?
John 14:6; 2 Timothy 4:1–5

"Jesus said, 'I am the way and the truth and the life. No one comes to the Father except through me'" (John 14:6 NIV).

Pastors today are on the front lines. With social media and live streaming, there are people who will watch four to five sermons on any given Sunday because they can! This is such a great resource. However, for a pastor who preaches, the pressure to be on and relevant is high.

Pastors have been called by God to speak truth about God's Word and how it applies to our lives. Yet truth is not always comfortable or accepted in today's culture. The human heart is universal and crosses the bridges of race, socioeconomic standing, and culture. When Jesus taught the many thousands of people, his mission was to address the condition of the human heart, nothing else. Jesus did not come to say what people may have wanted to hear.

> Preach the word of God. Be prepared, whether the time is favorable or not. Patiently correct, rebuke, and encourage your people with good teaching. For a time is coming when people will no longer listen to sound and wholesome teaching. They will follow their own desires and will look for teachers who will tell them whatever their itching ears want to hear. (2 Timothy 4:2–4 NLT)

> Jesus said to the people who believed in him, "You are truly my disciples if you remain faithful to my teachings. And you will know the truth, and the truth will set you free." (John 8:31–32 NLT)

There is no rationalizing when it comes to sin. When biblical truth is defended, our culture is offended. If we aren't careful, we can begin accepting terms like "brokenness" to replace sin, making it sound more like something we should embrace rather than something we should repent of. Yes, we are broken, but there is no middle ground. He forgives our sin, and we can live a life of victory over our sin! Got itchy ears? Run to Jesus.

—Tammy

Meditate on His Word
Joshua 1:7–9; Psalm 119

"Study this Book of Instruction continually. Meditate on it day and night so you will be sure to obey everything written in it. Only then will you prosper and succeed in all you do" (Joshua 1:8 NLT).

I was in a class yesterday in church. The teacher was gently challenging all of us to make Bible reading a priority in our lives, explaining a variety of resources from one-year Bible reading plans to Bible apps. A young person spoke up and asked this question, "If a person decides to follow Christ, shouldn't that person automatically have a hunger and thirst for God's Word?" Wow. That resonated with me, mostly because when I think back to times when I felt very dry in my faith, it was because I had grown complacent in reading the Word of God.

> Joyful are people of integrity, who follow the instructions of the Lord. Joyful are those who obey his laws and search for him with all their hearts. They do not compromise with evil, and they walk only in his paths. You have charged us to keep your commandments carefully. (Psalm 119:1–4 NLT)

When I become stale and find it difficult to find joy, this is exactly when I need to act and search for God with all my heart. I can't find something that I don't seek. I begin small by meditating on a verse, contemplating ways I can apply it to my day. As I grow from there, I look for Old and New Testament readings. Bible apps, reading plans, Bible studies, and online resources can aid in helping the most inexperienced Bible reader to the most experienced. The key is to not just read. We must think on it and apply it.

Are you feeling dry in your faith? Have you lost that fervor for opening His Word, reading it, meditating on it, and then acting on it? Come to the water! Take that first step today to seek the Lord with all your heart and listen to Him. Lean into His words. Meditate on His promises. He will never fail you.

–Tammy

Quick to Listen

Proverbs 18:13. 29:20; James 1:19

Personalities intrigue me. I have taken several temperament and personality tests, which are, in my opinion, very enlightening. The more I learn about what makes myself and other people tick, the more I can better understand the potential land mines in relationships as it relates to family, the workplace, and friends.

With my personality type, I am naturally not a good listener. I have worked on this for years and continue to do so, but my natural bent is to talk, not listen. I have always valued transparency and honesty, perhaps to a fault, and I love it when people are frank and honest with me. I have certainly been guilty of airing my own opinions!

God wants us to be wise and thoughtful with our words. Let's look at some passages of Scripture about thinking before we speak.

> Do you see a man who is hasty in his words? There is more hope for a fool than for him. (Proverbs 29:20 NLT)

> If one gives an answer before he hears, it is his folly and shame. (Proverbs 18:13 NLT)

> Know this, my beloved brothers: let every person be quick to hear, slow to speak, slow to anger. (James 1:19 NLT)

I wonder how many times in my life I have overlooked an opportunity to learn something because I have not been quick to listen. I desire to be a better listener. This includes not partially listening, pretending to listen, or airing my opinion first and then listening. I want to be a champion listener, for I do not want to be a fool, nor have folly and shame overcome me.

Yes, God wants us to speak up at the right times, take a stand for our beliefs, and speak for those who can't for themselves. But remember, God gave us two ears and one mouth for a reason. Let us bring joy to the Lord with how we use our tongues and how we are quick to listen!

–Tammy

Week 14 Reflections

1. After reviewing the Scriptures for each day, name three to four passages that jumped out at you this week.
2. How can you practically apply these verses to your life today and the upcoming week?
3. Out of the reasons listed in week 14 day 1, what are some of your reasons for not sharing your faith as much as you should?
4. Paul was not ashamed of the gospel in any way, shape, or form. Are you ever ashamed to share the gospel? Even if you don't want to use the word *ashamed*, what prevents you from being bold?
5. Who in your life right now needs to know Jesus? How can you be bold in your faith to those people?
6. People can rationalize the Bible and truth. How might you be rationalizing biblical truth to satisfy your lifestyle?
7. When it comes to God's Word, do you find yourself stale, stable, or growing? Explain.
8. What does the act of meditating on God's Word look like to you realistically in everyday life?
9. God desires for us to be quick to listen and slow to speak. How is God challenging you in this area?

Avoiding Conflict?

Romans 12:17–19; Ephesians 4:15, 25–27

We are instructed many times in Scripture to live in peace with one another, to not let the sun go down on our anger, and to reconcile with one another. Romans 12:18 (NLT) instructs us "to do all that you can to live at peace with everyone." Based on that, should we never disagree or have differing opinions? After all, how can we live at peace with so many varying perspectives and experiences of others? With peace being our long-term goal, let's look at what God says regarding conflict and His plan for how to resolve it.

There are two types of people with approaches to finding peace: a peacemaker and a peacekeeper. A peacemaker is willing to face and resolve turmoil in order to establish peace with others and themselves. With this approach, a person is honest and frank, coated in a spirit of love, and passionate about exposing sin, attitude, or behavior. This kind of honesty runs toward conflict with a long-term goal of having peace in a relationship or situation. Like a cut that has scabbed over and hasn't healed, the peacemaker may remove the scab to let the infection out so it heals properly and thoroughly, giving the wound complete healing.

A peacekeeper, on the other hand, desires to maintain peace by avoiding conflict. This approach places more value on the here and now by "letting sleeping dogs lie," not confronting things if they make themselves or others feel uncomfortable. This is a very common behavior, often displayed by those who truly desire peace, but find it very difficult to take the scab off and let it bleed a little. They are more comfortable with keeping the scab on long term, and unfortunately the infection is still there. This approach can create a false sense of harmony and lead to a repeat of behavior down the road.

Long-lasting peace is attained when we allow God to help us in a conflict by speaking truth in love, but also having the ability and humility to receive honest words from others. It is ok to be honest! We must face the conflict with respect and boldness and pray to God for the outcome He desires.

—Tammy

The Foothold of Pride
Proverbs 13:10, 13–14

A good leader knows his or her strengths and weaknesses and will strategically put people around him or her who will complement and fill in the gaps. On a team, this is very important. If everyone on a team is exactly alike, the team will stay stagnant and not challenge each other to move forward, stifling creative ideas for change and stunting needed growth that should take place for all members.

Proverbs 13 is excellent instruction for all people, young and old, to stay away from pride, as it will always lead to some form of conflict. My experience has been that when a leader or member of a team is unable to accept advice or a difference of opinion from others, the whole team suffers. The foothold of pride is a slippery slope that God desires to help us with. How do we get to the root of pride?

> "When he (Jesus) said to the crowd, 'If any of you wants to be my
> follower, you must give up your own way, take up your cross daily,
> and follow me'" (Luke 9:23 NLT).

Taking up our cross is a daily battle. Our way can easily consume us, often undetectable unless we allow God to search our hearts. Asking God to help us to be humble and to be able to take correction is a great first step. We all need advice and to remain teachable. When we make ourselves less, Jesus becomes more, and that is the goal we are striving for (John 3:30).

Pride in the midst of conflict hurts everyone involved. When we allow a foothold of pride to set in, our instinct is to defend ourselves, or rally people around us for our cause. With humility and forgiveness on both sides, many conflicts can result in victory by avoiding sinful reactions that lead to future consequences. As we seek God in this area, let us allow God to expose areas within where we need to give up our own way and follow Jesus, even if it hurts. He promises that we will see victory!

—Tammy

For Such a Time As This
The Book of Esther

The book of Esther is a unique book in the Bible where God's presence is woven through the whole text, yet His name is not mentioned one time. The author cleverly shows that God is always working things out for the good of those who love Him, and we can see this truth unfold throughout the happenings in this book.

There are four main characters: Mordecai and his niece Esther (both Jewish), King Xerxes, and the villain Haman. If you have never had the opportunity to read this book in its entirety, I encourage you to do so! The storyline is captivating, and you will be renewed in your faith of God's providence and faithfulness.

Esther was bold. She was also a Jew, yet her identity of her descent was kept secret from the king when she was chosen to be his queen. Esther was extremely beautiful, and because the king didn't know of her Jewish descent, God strategically placed her to free the Jewish people, her people. Meanwhile, Haman plotted to not only kill all the Jews, but Mordecai as well. When Mordecai heard this, he sent word to Esther, asking her to go to the king to have the decree to kill the Jews turned.

> Mordecai sent this reply to Esther: "Don't think for a moment that because you're in the palace you will escape when all other Jews are killed. If you keep quiet at a time like this, deliverance and relief for the Jews will arise from some other place, but you and your relatives will die. Who knows if perhaps you were made queen for just such a time as this?" (Esther 4:13–14 NLT)

You will have to read the whole story to know how it ends! The takeaway from this book is this: God has placed all of us strategically where we are for such a time as this. Whether or not we see it, God is always working and has called us according to His purposes.

Be bold! Esther had to be bold at risk of losing her own life! Today, remember that God is just. He is loving, He is the truth, and He has created you for such a time as this!

—Tammy

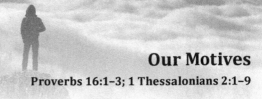

Our Motives

Proverbs 16:1–3; 1 Thessalonians 2:1–9

"We can make our own plans, but the Lord gives the right answer. People may be pure in their own eyes, but the Lord examines their motives. Commit your actions to the Lord, and your plans will succeed" (Proverbs 16:1–3 NLT).

As men, women, teens, and children, we daily make decisions by what motivates us in life. If we are motivated by people, we will invest our time in relationships and serving others. If we are motivated to be an engineer someday, we will strive for the education to do just that. If we endeavor to live a holy life that is pleasing to the Lord, we will pursue Him with diligence and commitment.

Motives say a lot about our personal character, priorities, integrity, and heart. Only God can see our hearts and the motives deep within us. Unfortunately, a consequence of being a human is that we are apt to judge another person's motive or evaluate someone else's heart, when we ourselves are just as human as the next person. Yes, God gives us discernment, but when we sit in the God chair, we are sitting in the wrong seat. Only God can determine what is in our hearts, and we can trust Him to act on what He knows! I can rest in the truth that God knows my motives, even if they are misunderstood by others.

In 1 Thessalonians 2:1–7, Paul, Silas, and Timothy recap their previous visit to Thessalonica because in their absence, people slandered and discredited them, assuming ill motives in them that could have potentially damaged the message of the gospel. With the sole purpose of defending the gospel message, Paul and the two other writers wanted to clear up false accusations, hence the reason for writing this letter. He didn't care about himself or need people's approval; however, he wanted to make straight the crooked path so they wouldn't have a reason to discredit the gospel.

God equipped Paul with unwavering boldness, wisdom, passion, and physical endurance to spread the gospel, but most importantly, his motives were pure, his faith didn't waver, and he was sold out to Jesus!

–Tammy

Communication Is Key
Galatians 6:9; Colossians 3:12–14

Communication on a heart level is so vital to any relationship. I have known many people through the years who never established that habit years ago. As I see their relational struggles from time to time, I can certainly relate. My motto used to be "peace at all costs." But as a seventy-seven-year-old mother, grandmother, and great-grandmother, I have learned that poor communication is an unhealthy behavior.

The lack of communication profoundly affects marriages, family relationships, and friendships. Poor communication models dysfunctional behavior to children and their children's children. Some of the people I love most neglected to seek conflict resolution with their relationships years ago because of fear, fear of an explosive or damaging reaction or fear of rejection. And the list goes on. How quickly we can predetermine others' behavior in assuming that they will never change. But "peace at all costs" is not God's way. He uses our communication with each other to help one another and be advocates for each other.

I want to encourage you today that if communicating is difficult, you are not alone. My husband and I were married for forty-seven years, and by the time we learned to communicate through the conflicts, we still had a lot of bad habits. I was fearful of his anger, so I thought that keeping my mouth shut was the answer. It wasn't. It made things worse. It not only affected both of us, but our girls as well.

As I sought answers for my problems, I grew closer and closer to God, digging deep into His Word beyond a surface level. I began to change. I studied the deeper meanings in a passage and discovered God's guidance and strength to speak truth in love, listen, and persevere.

Communicating through conflict will sometimes make you feel like things are getting worse instead of better. But let the infection out. Work through it, and you will see healing begin!

–Sharon

Feeling Powerless
Isaiah 40:28–31

"But those who trust in the Lord will find new strength. They will soar high on wings like eagles. They will run and not grow weary. They will walk and not faint" (Isaiah 40:31 NLT).

Feeling powerless is a horrible state to be in. I experienced this feeling just today on a very small scale. I had a nest of four killdeer eggs in my mulch, almost ready to hatch. Along came a group of crows and snatched all four eggs away. Even though I tried to protect them by working in the yard, I knew I couldn't be out there all day. Two hours later, all four eggs were gone.

There are many situations we will never be able to control in this life; thus we will all experience feelings of powerlessness at one time or another. The key is: who do we run to when these feelings set in? You may be going through a loveless marriage or taking care of a handicapped child or parent. You may be fighting no-win situations in school over moral differences and decisions or experiencing a natural disaster in your community. But where do you go, and whom do you turn?

> Have you never heard? Have you never understood? The Lord is the everlasting God, the Creator of all the earth. He never grows weak or weary. No one can measure the depths of his understanding. He gives power to the weak and strength to the powerless. (Isaiah 40:28–30 NLT)

God is here, ready to give you the strength and power you need to stand strong. He may give you the boldness you need to stand up for yourself and to speak truth in love to someone who needs to hear it. He may be calling you to seek help that He will provide for you and give you the ability to take a stand against evil in your child's school. No matter what it is, we are never powerless when we have the Lord. He is faithful and just, and when we trust Him, He promises that we will find new strength. We can rest in knowing that God is our strength and our shield, and he is the Rock we need to choose to stand on!

—Tammy

Week 15 Reflections

1. After reviewing the Scriptures for each day, name three to four passages that jumped out at you this week.

2. How can you practically apply these verses to your life today and the upcoming week?

3. Do you avoid conflict, or do you run to conflict or maybe somewhere in between?

4. How can God use conflict for good?

5. During conflict, pride can creep in when we least expect it to. How have you seen pride creep into conflicts you've had?

6. God created you to live in this day in age. Who, what, and where is God calling you to be bold like Esther?

7. Motives ignite our actions. How have your actions mirrored your motives lately (good or bad)?

8. Conflict can be solved by communication, but communicating can be intimidating and difficult. How can you better communicate when conflicts arise so that real peace can be made?

9. Bad relationships and situations around us can leave us feeling powerless. What does God ask us to do when we feel like that?

Jesus Is Truth
John 14:1–6; Hebrews 10

Have you ever doubted your faith? I know I have. In my early years of being a believer in Jesus, I was a skeptic to the core. I questioned parts of the Bible, and I wondered why there was such a narrow path to salvation. Wrestling with this brought me to a crisis point in my faith. I knew I loved the Lord, but I just couldn't wrap my head around the whys of certain biblical events, plaguing me with unbelief. Christians aren't supposed to question these things, are we? I had to be honest with God if I were going to grow in my walk with God.

This crisis in my faith caused me to search for answers. I did this by reading Scripture with friends, attending Bible study discussion groups, and crying out to God for wisdom and understanding. During this time, I was drawn to the whole chapter of Hebrews 10 and John 14. Please take the time to read these for yourself. There are some key points that I gleaned:

1. I needed faith to accept what I couldn't see or understand.
2. Jesus came as the final blood sacrifice, the sacrifice that takes away our sin.
3. When Jesus came, many Old Testament laws (polygamy, sacrificing animals for our sin, etc.) were done away with.
4. In the Old Testament, even though God was everywhere, God was experienced by people through the tabernacle and the Ark of the Covenant, where his spirit dwelt at that time. It was so powerful that you couldn't touch the ark, or one would die.
5. When Jesus came, however, he left the Holy Spirit with us, allowing every person to be the new temple of the Holy Spirit, having a personal relationship with Jesus.

If you are struggling with a little disbelief or have questions, I encourage you to delve into Scripture. The above points were things I personally wondered about, but for you, there might be totally different things. The main point is that there is one truth. Jesus said, "I am the way, the truth and the life!" (John 14:6 NLT). I celebrate today that Jesus is Truth, and I wouldn't doubt that anymore for anything.

—Tammy

Accountability—Honesty

Galatians 6:1–3

My colleagues and staff have traveled with me to many places, including spending time together overseas. It is very hard to spend nearly every waking hour of time together over the course of not only days but weeks without getting to know each other quite well. One of the best parts of these relationships are when we get close enough to truly see deeply into each others' souls, where we can trust that things we did or shared would be used in the best possible way. We have taken these relationships well beyond a normal employee-and-boss scenario. One of my colleagues knows that he has the tendency to allow things to become very personal and can therefore let difficult situations escalate to a point where he might react in a very emotional way. During our time together, I have been able to be there with him to help him through some of these situations. As we have gone through these together, it has been easier to see some of the signs of the upcoming situation and work to avoid the worst reactions. His giving me permission to step into his life at times when I see something coming has been a blessing to him but also to those working with us that would have been impacted by the reaction.

Our relationship has grown through this process to the point where we now meet on a regular, although random, basis to just get together and talk about work, family, and life. We use this time to check in on each other to build up our relationship and one another. As we have been open and vulnerable with each other, it has allowed for a much stronger process of accountability both in our work, but also in our personal relationships.

When considering Galatians 6:1–3, as we go to hold another believer accountable in some sin, we are to do it humbly and gently. I know in my work relationship, we have approached every meeting humbly and gently. This has been the cornerstone for our success as it has allowed us to be fully invested in the accountability process. While this accountability may have started in one direction, it has blossomed into a two-way process and one in which I know we both look forward to progressing.

-Mark

Knowing God and Being Known
1 Chronicles 28:1–10; Philippians 3:7–11

Ezra was an Old Testament prophet credited with writing 1 and 2 Chronicles in the fifth-century BC. In these historic books, he records a ceremony when King David assembled all the Jewish leaders in Jerusalem to pass on the crown of Israel to his son, Solomon. Never had a monarchy in Israel name a successor to the throne as one's own son until this time in Israel (1 Chronicles 28).

I'm sure David prepared Solomon to someday take the throne, but in this rite of passage ceremony, David stood up (as he was probably very old at this time) and had a fatherly exhortation for Solomon about how he could be a good king. There were three things David instructed Solomon to do:

1. He was to know God intimately with his whole heart, mind, and soul.
2. He was to worship and serve God with a loyal heart and a willing mind.
3. Whenever Solomon would look for God, he would be found by Him, but if he were to forsake God, the Lord would reject him forever.

There is nothing that is more important than knowing God, not just know of Him but to know Him intimately and be known by Him. For me, knowing God in such a way changes everything about the way I think, the way I hope, and the way I look at other people. It makes a difference in my work ethic, my daily disciplines, and my friendships. Knowing God allows me to have a relationship with Him, and I can ask Him for wisdom in parenting or my marriage. Knowing God gives me a reason to get up in the morning and purpose as I go throughout my day. At the end of my life, I want to be able to testify that I already know the God who I will be spending eternity with intimately. Nothing else matters.

> Yes, everything else is worthless when compared with the infinite value of knowing Christ Jesus my Lord. For his sake I have discarded everything else, counting it all as garbage, so that I could gain Christ and become one with him. (Philippians 3:8–9 NLT)

—Tammy

Tell Others

Psalm 107:1–9

"Give thanks to the Lord, for he is good! His faithful love endures forever. Has the Lord redeemed you? Then speak out! Tell others he has redeemed you from your enemies" (Psalm 107:1–2 NLT).

I was in college sophomore year driving our string quartet back to Belmont University from a Christmas party we had just played at. The rain was coming down in sheets, and my old and faithful Ford Tempo had bald tires. As I entered the highway, I saw an area up ahead with cones signaling one lane, but because visibility was limited and I was driving too fast, I swerved at the last minute. I proceeded to hydroplane, not only across the four-lane highway on our side, but across the median onto the other side of the ongoing highway traffic. Miraculously, we landed in a ditch, no one was hurt, and the car itself was only scratched. There is no other explanation other than a miracle to how we survived!

Following the incident, I couldn't help but tell my professors, my friends, my family, and even strangers how God had spared our lives on that stormy evening. I talked about that rainy evening with gratefulness, and I received a permanent notch in my faith belt to remind me what God had done for us that evening. God had mercy on me for driving too fast in a storm, and I will never ever forget it!

Psalm 107 requires us to open our mouths and tell others what God has done for us. If you have ever experienced the comfort and satisfaction God gives when you have feelings of loneliness, shame, or being lost, spread the word! Tell others of the faithfulness of God without hesitation. "Let them praise the Lord for his great love and for the wonderful things he has done for them. For he satisfies the thirsty and fills the hungry with good things" (Psalm 107:8–9 NLT).

When you explain to people what God has done in your life by transforming and redeeming you, your personal story and testimony stand on their own. No one can discount that or argue if it is true because it is your story! People need to know this amazing God.

—Tammy

Be Strong and Courageous
Joshua 1:1–9; Psalms 46:1

During my growing-up years and into my twenties, I loved the show *Little House on the Prairie,* inspired by the books of Laura Ingalls Wilder. The series portrayed the daily lives of pioneer families who had moved out West in the early 1800s. Hardships in life were commonplace. Diseases, extreme weather, lack of supplies, education, and medical care all instilled a sense of survival. They were dependent on God. As I reflect on the strength and courage it took to survive such an environment, I am inspired to live out my own faith with God at the helm.

In the first chapter in Joshua, we find out that Moses, who had passed away, was succeeded by Joshua to be the leader for the Israelites. God appoints him to lead the people across the Jordan River into the Promised Land. God's instructions to Joshua begin by commanding him to be strong and courageous, not wavering in his faith.

> "Be careful to obey all the instructions Moses gave you. Do not deviate from them, turning either to the right or to the left. Then you will be successful in everything you do. Study this Book of Instruction continually. Meditate on it day and night so you will be sure to obey everything written in it. Only then will you prosper and succeed in all you do." (Joshua 1:7–8 NLT)

In this passage, God gives a promise to the Israelites with a condition attached. If they obey God's Word, then they will prosper. Likewise, when we obey and live by God's Word, not deviating from His book of instruction, He will make our paths straight. Allowing God's Word to soak into our brains and hearts takes strength and courage to live a life of discipline.

There is a spiritual battle that rages all around us. One thing is for certain, "God is our refuge and strength, always ready to help in times of trouble" (Psalm 46:1 NLT).

We can't fight this battle on our own. As we obey His Word, meditating on it day and night, writing it on our hearts, He promises that we will prosper. Be strong and courageous!

–Tammy

Clothe Yourselves

Colossians 3:5–15

Clothes shopping is certainly a weakness of mine. Since I am inspired by color, my choices of outfits reflect colors that resemble my mood or feelings. As you can imagine, making my daily clothes selection can be a little challenging given that I may change my mind three to four times before the final choice!

You may or may not be able to relate to that small, somewhat silly, problem of figuring out what to wear, but everyone must get dressed when they go out. Some need more time than others to choose outfits and shoes in the morning. Yet somehow, we all seem to manage. We close the door behind us and go about our days. Scripture tells us that we should spiritually clothe ourselves as well.

> Since God chose you to be the holy people he loves, you must clothe yourselves with tenderhearted mercy, kindness, humility, gentleness, and patience. Make allowance for each other's faults and forgive anyone who offends you. Remember, the Lord forgave you, so you must forgive others. Above all, clothe yourselves with love, which binds us all together in perfect harmony. (Colossians 3:12–14 NLT)

I resonate with the metaphor of clothing, as the attributes in these verses are fruits we all need to wear as we follow Christ. When we clothe ourselves with these spiritual guidelines, we are covering our whole beings with these virtues. They encompass us and go with us wherever we go throughout the day. Our days could look very different when we take the time to pray and meditate on God's principles, being tenderhearted, merciful, kind, humble, gentle, and patient and demonstrating forgiveness and love to those we encounter.

As you think about and choose your outfits, shoes, or hairstyles this week, consider prioritizing the traits that the Holy Spirit wants to clothe you in each day as well. You will see the peace of God at work in you!

–Tammy

Week 16 Reflections

1. After reviewing the Scriptures for each day, name three to four passages that jumped out at you this week.
2. How can you practically apply these verses to your life today and the upcoming week?
3. Do you ever doubt your faith? If so, list your doubts here. (Be transparent.)
4. How can you resolve these areas of doubt? Make a list of steps you need to take to find answers for a stronger faith.
5. Do you have an accountability partner or group of people? How is accountability biblical?
6. How well do you know God? On a scale from one to ten, how much more do you want to know God?
7. Where have you seen God at work this week? Write them down and share those things with others!
8. How is God calling you today to be strong and courageous?
9. What fruits does God desire to clothe you in today?

MONTH 5

We Live, Create, Invest, and Build All of Which May Be Forgotten Someday

A FAITH THAT STANDS
Produces A Heart of
Surrender and Humility

Surrender

James 4:4–10

"Submit yourselves therefore to God. Resist the devil, and he will flee from you" (James 4:7 ESV).

Kingdom building is like a man building a house. He plans the blueprints, buys the land, hires the building team, and clears the property. The concrete trucks come, the foundation is laid, the walls go up, and the appliances, colors, flooring, paint, and windows are chosen. Every day he checks on the house, following up on all the details. The anticipation of the completed project is exciting, prompting him to continue eagerly to even do some things himself, putting his thumbprint on every part.

The day comes when the house is complete. The man gets ready to move in, but he is called to a new job across the country. His prized possession, now ready to inhabit, must be sold to someone else. All the blood, sweat, and tears turned out not to be for him to enjoy, but rather someone else.

Isn't building in the kingdom of God like that? We invest our money to serve others. We sacrifice our time and use our talents, all to accomplish what God has called us to. But then something happens, and He calls us to something else right at the end, and we don't get to enjoy the fruits of our labor. This very thing has happened to Mark and me several times over the years. As surrendered vessels for God to use, we have grown to understand that God often uses us to be builders, not maintainers, and humanly, this can be very difficult at times.

Surrender is hard, especially when it involves laying our talents, service, time, and finances at the feet of Jesus, knowing that we may personally never see the fruits.

I have learned to hold ministries I am serving in loosely, even if my passion drives me to fulfill the call that God has equipped me for. But I know that serving should never be about me. My ability to pass the baton to someone else after I put forth most of the work involves a selfless attitude on my part. Because of this, I need God's perspective. I am serving God, so when He calls me to something else, I need to be willing to let go.

—Tammy

It's Not About Me

Galatians 2:19–21

Occasionally I have some very weak moments when my emotional cup overflows. At those times, I find myself throwing up my feelings onto my husband, creating a tailspin of unfiltered responses. I am always amazed at how graciously he listens, but the listening often leads to some sort of comforting advice to help me diffuse emotionally. Sometimes I like this. Other times I don't.

I'll never forget years ago he said something that resonated with me and has always stuck with me. He said, "Tammy, not everything is about you. People aren't just sitting around thinking about you. They are thinking about their own stuff." Although embarrassed that he even needed to say that to a grown adult, his words spoke truth to me, and I recognized my unhealthy thought pattern at that time.

As followers of Christ, we can fall into a trap of placing our identity in the talents and gifts we use to serve God. When we serve others, our identity can be wrapped up in the actual serving instead of the God whom we are serving. Before you know it, we subconsciously find ourselves serving one another because we feel appreciated and noticed. Sometimes, however, someone will criticize us, hurt our feelings, or question the way we did something, throwing a big dart into our soul. Although we know that it's not about us, we have somehow made the situation about us. A root of pride has set in, and our defenses go up. "My old self has been crucified with Christ. It is no longer I who live, but Christ lives in me" (Galatians 2:20 NLT).

Oh, how I have needed to claim this verse repeatedly as I serve the Lord on this earth. I don't want my identity being wrapped up in the things I do. I want my identity to be in Christ alone. Period.

We all need to feel useful and affirmed. This is normal! But as we have been crucified with Christ, everything we do to serve God faithfully is to help build up the kingdom of God and those around us. It is never about us. It is all about God!

—Tammy

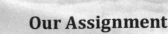

Our Assignment

1 Thessalonians 2:4–6; Luke 9:57–62; 1 Peter 2:9

For almost eight years, Mark and I felt called to assist, build, and lead a church as it experienced rapid growth. This assignment God had called us to was not an unfamiliar venture for us, as God had called us to similar positions throughout our married life. I speak for both of us that we have always enjoyed the challenges that come from investing, not only monetarily, but in people's lives. We love leading teams, having people in our homes, teaching classes, and serving in hands on ways. We also enjoy training and equipping others to grow deeper in their faith in service to the Lord.

Six years into our time there, however, Mark and I began to feel what ended up being a two-year tug of the Holy Spirit preparing our hearts for a new assignment. Truthfully, I didn't want a new assignment, as I had envisioned being there for many more years. We loved the people there! But that did not appear to be part of God's long-term plan.

I remembered Jesus' lesson in Luke when Jesus asked a man to come and follow Him, but the man said, "'Lord, let me first go and bury my father.' And Jesus said to him, 'Leave the dead to bury their own dead. But as for you, go and proclaim the kingdom of God'" (Luke 9:59–60 NIV).

Sounds a little insensitive, don't you think? But Jesus wasn't being insensitive. He just wanted the man to be sold out to Him. Similarly, Mark and I knew that Jesus was calling us to go elsewhere, even though we kept telling God, "We have so many friends here, and we love our jobs!"

1 Thessalonians 2 tells us that our purpose is to *please God*, not people. Looking back, we were probably too comfortable. God had a whole new assignment in mind. There is a cost to following Jesus. When we choose to follow, Jesus calls us to a very specific purpose, to please Him above all else by living a surrendered and holy life and by showing others His goodness (1 Peter 2:9).

Our lives are God's to use. We continue to invest as unto God alone, with both sets of hands open, and we are prepared and ready for our next assignment!

–Tammy

Hidden Gems

1 Corinthians 12:12–21

My wife and I have moved often because of my jobs. As part of these transitions, we have had the privilege of being a part of many wonderful churches. In most cases, Tammy has taken the role of worship director for our church. While she is personally gifted in music, she also has a unique talent for finding hidden gems.

Paul encourages each of us in 1 Corinthians 12:12–21 by defining our unique purposes using the analogy of the human body. Clearly, for the body to function at its peak, each part must do the role that it was intended to do. One part cannot say to the other, "I don't need you." As in the church body, there is no such thing as an unimportant part.

I notice with Tammy a very intentional aspect of her leadership in that she is always looking for signs of talents and spiritual gifting in the people she meets. She values everything they might have to offer to edify the body of Christ. Her astute awareness allows her to find diamonds in the rough, and the Holy Spirit uses that awareness to edify the body.

Sometimes, even when Tammy sees gifts in someone else, perhaps even gifts they do not see themselves, the person is still not ready to step forward. Tammy takes the next step to offer encouragement, but then takes the time to develop and train the person to use their gifts. I have seen it so often in our churches and even within our own family.

We so often look to choose our team from the obvious. In the example of Jesus, he chose his twelve disciples from a cast of characters that did not fit the mold with obvious qualifications. Rather he took those in whom he saw the potential in and developed, trained, and encouraged.

You might be a leader like Tammy, but you might be that hidden gem that someone will one day find. If you are a leader, I encourage you to look deep at those around you and see in them the potential that God sees. Pray for a way to encourage and lead them to use their gifts fully. If you are that hidden gem, pray that you would be ready when found and step up to be the part of the body that all the other parts so desperately need regardless of what part they play.

—Mark

That's My Territory

1 John 2:15–17

I grew up with dogs, but we now have a cat. If you've ever had one or the other, you will know how very different they are as pets! Despite their differences, they have one thing in common. They mark their territory, an instinctive act of survival.

Marking territory is innate when animals stake out a claim to a particular place or object, usually done by urine marking. Some of the reasons for this territorial behavior are to acquire food sources, protect nesting sites, or even to attract a mate.

Although humans do not go around marking territories with urine (or I certainly hope not), we have the same instincts for survival and to stake claims, physically and psychologically. During the Gold Rush in 1848, people would stake a mining claim, which allowed them to extract precious minerals within the boundaries of their claim. Later in 1862, the Homestead Act gave every person who asked for citizenship the right to claim government land. Having staked a claim, whether for gold or land, the territory was marked, and no one could claim rights to it.

We also do the same thing psychologically. We have staked our claims in certain friendships, jobs, ministries, coaching assignments, or anything we've created. Our human nature causes us to desire claim or control over those areas, which, if not committed to the Lord, can go against God's will.

> Do not love this world nor the things it offers you, for when you love the world, you do not have the love of the Father in you. For the world offers only a craving for physical pleasure, a craving for everything we see, and pride in our achievements and possessions. These are not from the Father, but are from this world … (1 John 2:15–17 NLT)

We do not have any claims in this world, for the world is fading away. Instead we have the divine privilege to put our stakes in the eternal things of God, to mark our territory in heaven, where He has all the claim!

—Tammy

For Yours Is the Kingdom

Matthew 6:13b; Exodus 15:18; Psalm 20:7–9, 146:10

On March 4, 1966, John Lennon said this to the *London Evening Standard*, "Christianity will go. It will vanish and shrink. I needn't argue with that. I'm right and I will be proved right. We're more popular than Jesus now; I don't know which will go first; Rock 'n' roll or Christianity."

As the lead singer, songwriter, and guitarist for the Beatles, John Lennon was "king of the world," or so he thought. With unrivaled record sales and popularity of his English band, The Beatles, he had made remarkable success for himself. Most people would have thought that he had it all, until that fateful evening on December 8, 1980, when he was shot and killed by a fan outside his New York apartment. He was forty years old.

As you read the Lord's Prayer today found in Matthew 6, you may note that the second half of verse 13 is not found in all Bible translations, "For Yours is the kingdom and the power and the glory forever" (Matthew 6:13b NKJV). Jesus closes his prayer with this phrase, clearly identifying that God's kingdom goes beyond anything we know here on earth.

People can easily be deceived that they can build their own kingdoms that result from their own successes. This is certainly a danger for the person who builds or creates anything such as a company, a church, a family, or even a football team. Self-importance can quickly grow within, implanting feelings of being indispensable or irreplaceable. The reality is that kingdoms will rise and fall, but God's kingdom stands forever.

> Some trust in chariots and some in horses, but we trust in the name of the Lord our God. They collapse and fall, but we rise and stand upright. O Lord, save the king! May he answer us when we call. (Psalm 20:7–9 ESV)

Sadly for John Lennon, he was not right about Christianity. People and music will come and go, along with kings and queens, presidents, pastors, athletes, and teachers. However, God and the Word of the Lord stand for eternity, and He shall reign forever and ever!

–Tammy

Week 17 Reflections

1. After reviewing the Scriptures for each day, name three to four passages that jumped out at you this week.
2. How can you practically apply these verses to your life today and the upcoming week?
3. Name something that God has asked you to surrender to Him. What do you think He would like you to surrender to Him?
4. We would like to think that the accomplishments we achieve and investments we have given to build have everything to do with us. But how might God desire us to prevent a feeling of territorialism, feeling ownership of a ministry, job, or person?
5. Are you aware that God has an assignment for you? What is your assignment now? If you don't know, ask Him!
6. Some day we will all pass away and pass the baton to someone else? How are you investing in the lives around you so that the work you have done continues without you?
7. Territorialism is a natural instinct, but God wants us to surrender that. How have you struggled with being territorial? How has this affected you and others?
8. God's kingdom is the only kingdom of worth. How are you investing in God's kingdom?
9. Sometimes we think we are investing in God's kingdom, but in essence, we are building our own empire. What caution signs do you see in areas of your life that could become that?

A Call to Holy Living
1 Peter 1:13–25

As a worship pastor, I have had the opportunity to write and direct several drama productions over the years. Many of the dramas focused on the reenactment of Scripture, particularly preceding Easter with the triumphal entry, Last Supper, and crucifixion. For the actors and actresses memorizing and living with the scripts for weeks, I have witnessed God's Word coming alive for them. In managing the finite details of each scene, I too have put myself in the setting. To imagine being a part of the crowd yelling to free Barabbas or to crucify Jesus (Matthew 27:16–26) or even denying Jesus three times as Peter did sends chills up my spine. The crucifixion scene has left me in tears, allowing me to remember my own sin that led Jesus to the place where He shed His blood for me.

1 Peter instructs us to live a holy life out of a response to loving Jesus, fully understanding the sacrifice he made as a ransom for us and our sin. According to 1 Peter 1:13–25, we are called to be obedient, exercise self-control, not slip back into worldly behavior, and have reverent fear of the Lord.

> For you know that God paid a ransom to save you from the empty
> life you inherited from your ancestors. It was the precious blood of
> Christ, the sinless, spotless Lamb of God. God chose him as your
> ransom long before the world began … (1 Peter 1:18–20 NLT)

Although we are not saved by our works, God still looks at the things we do. He will judge us based on our hearts and the fruit that pours out into works as a direct result of our love for Jesus. We are temporary residents in this world, and since we are a temple for the Holy Spirit to dwell, the Lord wants us to be holy because He is holy.

God is calling. He is calling you and me to live a holy life through His Son, Jesus. As the Holy Spirit fills us and opens our hearts to a new way, let us respond with gratitude for the greatest gift we ever could have imagined!

–Tammy

The Yawns of Life
1 Thessalonians 5:16–18

As a stay-at-home mom, sometimes every day looks the same. I wake up and do the same exact chores: get the baby, change her diaper, get a bottle, feed the dog, and let the dog out. If all goes well with those things, I'm free to get coffee, even though only a couple of sips will be hot before I get caught up in the whole cycle again: baby, laundry, dishes, and dog.

Do you ever drive to work and think there has to be more to life? Do you ever clean the kitchen after dinner and think, *I feel like I just did this*? Or maybe your days are jam-packed, always feeling like you're in a rush. Takeout menus become your friends because who has time to make dinner, let alone clean up afterward? Whatever you're doing, it seems like all your days collide together. As I ponder these things, I am aware of my need to snap out of this mundane mindset! God is working in the mundane, even though this season in my life seems like I'm not making a difference.

There are three actions I've gotten from 1 Thessalonians 5:16–18 to help with, what I call, the yawns of life.

1. **Pray often.** Pray before getting out of bed, pray in the shower, pray before meals, and pray before bed. Pray and don't stop. Even if you don't know what to say, pray anyway. Pray for your friends and family, pray for guidance, and pray for joy in the everyday duties.

2. **Count your blessings.** Even when you're feeling not so grateful, thank God anyway! Thank Him for the sense that you have, the job that you may dread going to every day, and the chair you're sitting in. Whatever you can think of, thank Him and do so often!

3. **Choose joy.** Every day we have choices. We choose to get upset when we get stuck behind a slow driver on the way to work. We choose offense when someone says something rude. Instead, flex that muscle and choose joy!

When you are tempted to feel like God is distant, embrace the yawns and gain a new perspective through the mundane!

-Karissa

Practice, Practice, Practice!

Leviticus 20:7–8

From the tender age of three, I was drawn to music, specifically the piano. We had inherited my great-grandmother's piano, who saved her vegetable and flower money from her garden for years to purchase the piano later in her life. She never got to fully enjoy it, as she fell, broke her hip, caught pneumonia, and passed away. The piano came into our home, and I was drawn to it like a bear to honey.

My mom was wonderful to allow me to exercise my creativity on the piano. Seeing my gift and not wanting to squelch it, she bought fun beginner piano books for me to learn from, teaching me what she knew herself. From that time on, no one ever had to ask me to practice. I was hooked, needing to express the music in my soul, stretching myself to new levels, and challenging my creativity through improvising and writing.

When I reached my junior year of high school, after being without a teacher for several years, Mr. Lombardo offered to teach me to get me ready for college auditions. He expected me to practice three hours every day but, more importantly, taught me the art of practicing. I later went on to receive two degrees in piano performance.

I tell you all of this because the term *practice* can sometimes create a sense of defeat before you even start. For me, practicing meant opportunity. When it comes to spiritual matters and living a holy life, God tells us in this verse, "So set yourselves apart to be holy, for I am the Lord your God. Keep all my decrees by putting them into *practice*, for I am the Lord who makes you holy" (Leviticus 20:7–8 NLT).

When we begin our faith walk with Jesus, the Holy Spirit in us directs us down a new and exciting path, setting us apart in every way. For many of us, that means we need to shed old habits, make different friends, or go to rehab to start a process. Faith is a journey, and we need to put God's principles into practice, meaning we must put in the effort. Practicing God's principles gives us opportunities to free ourselves of the sin that binds us, imparting a world of opportunity that only God can give.

—Tammy

Imitating Christ's Humility

Philippians 2:1–11

There is no greater example to me of what humility in Christ looks like than Philippians 2. The act of dying to self is a major step we all need to take in our sanctification process. Humility does not come easily in our natural human state. To compensate, we might try to force humility by putting ourselves down with negative self-talk. But is that what humility is?

The act of humility simply means to think of others as better than yourself, to care about their interests and to serve others when given an opportunity. It means to apologize without hesitation, to forgive with grace, and to serve without recognition by following His example. Humility allows us to be confident in who we are and the gifts that God has given to us without boasting in ourselves. Humility allows us to get our hands dirty and get out of our comfort zones when called to do so.

The Lord has been gracious to me over the years in teaching me how I can die to myself. Twenty years ago, some people we knew invited our young family over for a visit at Thanksgiving time. The couple lived in housing where gunshots, drugs, and homelessness were commonplace. I wasn't thrilled about going to see them because of the potential danger, and I told Mark I didn't want to stay longer than thirty minutes.

Unbeknownst to us, when we arrived, a small Thanksgiving meal had been prepared for us. The couple was overjoyed to see our family, and the table was set and ready! Shamefully, I realized how selfish I had been, thinking that they didn't deserve more than a half hour of my time. Yes, their living conditions were poor. Cockroaches had infested their apartment, and the facilities were not working adequately. Yet God gently taught me an important lesson that day. As explained in Philippians 2, Jesus made himself nothing, serving the poor, the unlovely, elevating those who were squashed by society. He loves every person equally. Who was I to think that I had any favoritism over anyone else?

The hearts of these people were pure gold, and God opened my eyes to see that. They are in heaven now, but from that day on, I have looked for new opportunities out of my comfort zone, remembering the example of Jesus, who laid down His life for the likes of me.

—Tammy

Perseverance

Hebrews 11:1–3; Revelation 21:4–5

Life is hard. Sometimes I just want to crawl into a hole and never come out for fear of something else being thrown at me. Just in the last several months, I have talked with people who are experiencing divorce, custody battles, wayward children, addiction, anxiety, health issues, or loss of employment. How do we handle life's heavy trials and curve balls without losing faith? How do we gracefully endure hardship without becoming bitter and depressed?

As Christ-followers, we know that God works all things out for the good of those who love Him (Romans 8:28). But in all honesty, there are times of wrestling with God, seeking answers to gain some form of understanding. Sometimes we might think, if we could understand what God was up to, we might endure our trials better by putting tangible outcomes to our faith. But where does that leave us when we can't make sense of our suffering?

As I read through the book of Job, I see a man who had lost everything important to him—his family, his livestock, and his health—yet left with a wife and friends who chastised or challenged God. Job openly wrestled with God, but ultimately recognized that his view of God was limited. Despite the pressure around him, he chose to persevere and stand on a rock of faith, trusting in His majestic Creator. Job came to a place of surrender in that he would never understand the reasons why. "Now faith is confidence in what we hope for and assurance about what we do not see ..." (Hebrews 11:1–3 NLT).

God loves you. Trust Him. Don't lose your faith because of what you can't see. He is righteous, faithful, merciful, and just. May you persevere by holding on to this hope in Revelation 21:4–5 (NLT), "He will wipe every tear from their eyes. There will be no more death or mourning or crying or pain, for the old order of things has passed away. He who was seated on the throne said, 'I am making everything new.'" And that is a promise!

—Tammy

Build Each Other Up
1 Thessalonians 5:11

David Willis said, "The world has enough critics, be rare, be an encourager." If you think about it, most times it is our natural reaction to find the negative in a situation or other people. It's easy for us to see all the ways we would do something differently or how something could have gone better. From our homes to our workplaces, churches, and relationships, it feels like the critics are often louder than the encouragers.

At the same time, have you ever been in a hard season or having a discouraging day and you receive a kind text or encouraging message from someone at just the right time? It is those moments when the love of God is being made tangible to us. What if we took seriously the instruction in the Bible to "encourage one another and build each other up" (1 Thessalonians 5:11 NIV)? What if we were the ones to seek out the positive, to see the good, to take note of others' gifts and abilities, and to not be shy in sharing it? In our homes, relationships, churches, and workplaces, we would be atmosphere changers. Through efforts to build up and not tear down, we would spur others on, encourage others to keep going, and strengthen those around us in ways we might not even realize.

Building others up is more than just being nice. It is a biblical command because God knew that in this earthly life we would need this from one another. More importantly, God would be made known through our love to the world. God sees more than we ever will. He knows personal heartache and struggles people are facing that we may never know. He doesn't ask us to know everything. He asks us to build each other up and not tear each other down.

Imagine if we started each day thinking about how we could encourage and build up those around us? The atmosphere would change, and the tangible love of God would be made known in ways we may not even realize. One of my favorite authors, Ann Voskamp, says it this way, "Only speak words that make souls stronger."

The world is already full of those who will tear us down. Let us be the rare ones and build each other up in the love of Christ!

—Shari

Week 18 Reflections

1. After reviewing the Scriptures for each day, name three to four passages that jumped out at you this week.
2. How can you practically apply these verses to your life today and the upcoming week?
3. What is the call for holy living look like according to 1 Peter 1:13–25?
4. Living a holy life is a choice we make when we trust God to transform our thinking and actions. How does God want to transform your thoughts and actions today?
5. The mundane tasks of life can seem fruitless. How does God want to give you joy and fruitfulness when life seems stagnant?
6. Practice takes discipline. The Christian life takes discipline. How can you begin or continue steady growth in this area?
7. God became a man who became obedient to death on a cross. What do you learn from Christ's example of humility?
8. Life is hard. How do you think God wants to help you persevere through your current situation(s)?
9. Who do you need to encourage in faith today?

A Time to Build
Ecclesiastes 3:1–8

"For everything there is a season, a time for every activity under heaven. A time to be born and a time to die. A time to plant and a time to harvest. A time to kill and a time to heal. A time to tear down and a time to build up. A time to cry and a time to laugh. A time to grieve and a time to dance. A time to scatter stones and a time to gather stones. A time to embrace and a time to turn away. A time to search and a time to quit searching. A time to keep and a time to throw away. A time to tear and a time to mend. A time to be quiet and a time to speak. A time to love and a time to hate. A time for war and a time for peace" (Ecclesiastes 3:1–8 NLT).

When Solomon became king, God told Solomon that he could ask God for anything and it would be given to him. Solomon chose to ask God for wisdom, and as a product of this God-given wisdom, King Solomon devoted himself to explore the meaning to life. We see his written thoughts in the book of Ecclesiastes, where Solomon refers to everything as meaningless as he wrestles with the mundane of life and our overall purpose under the sun.

Ecclesiastes is not a feel-good book of the Bible, for it highlights our humanity and daily struggles. However, God teaches us a very important lesson through this book, to build on our faith during every season we go through, including God in everything we do.

Although it is human to worry about the future or thrive to be rich, happy, or find purpose, we will find ourselves engulfed in an empty cycle of pursuits if we take God out of the equation. Much like summer, fall, winter, and spring, life takes us down meandering paths, unchartered waters, beautiful mountains, and scorching valleys.

God has a purpose for every season, and He is in them all. He desires for us to build on our faith through every high and every low, seeing His faithfulness at every turn. As you read today's passage in Ecclesiastes 3, take time to ask yourself how God wants to build your faith during the season you find yourself in today.

–Tammy

Our Foundation

Luke 6:46–49

My husband and I went through the process of building a house in 2017 in a new development that overlooks a pond and a horse farm, a place of sanctuary for me and a blessing from the Lord. We've had many homes because of all our moves, but this was the first time we picked everything out from the beginning.

In the initial stages of purchasing the lot, surveying the land, and drawing up the prints for the location of the house, the contractors began to dig. Not far into the digging, it became evident that, in order to support the house, concrete pylons were going to be necessary to build a firm foundation. If we didn't add the pylons, the house could slide down the hill in years to come. Twenty-seven loaded concrete trucks later, the pylons were laid, and the foundation was like Fort Knox. It was not going to move … anywhere!

Anything we build on needs a foundation. Our faith is one of those things. In the book of Luke, Luke recounts Jesus speaking to the disciples and a large crowd of people known as the Sermon on the Mount. People came from all over Judea and Jerusalem and along the seacoasts of Tyre and Sidon to hear Jesus. They also came to be healed from diseases and evil spirits. Jesus' message focused on the need for purity of the heart, embodying basic standards of godly righteousness. He closed with the following important teaching, instructing everyone to build a foundation of Christ-like love and obedience.

> I will show you what it's like when someone comes to me, listens to my teaching, and then follows it. It is like a person building a house who digs deep and lays the foundation on solid rock. When the floodwaters rise and break against that house, it stands firm because it is well built. But anyone who hears and doesn't obey is like a person who builds a house right on the ground, without a foundation. When the floods sweep down against that house, it will collapse into a heap of ruins. (Luke 6:46–49 NLT)

—Tammy

Mustard Seed Faith
Matthew 17:14–20

In third grade, I received a little card from Sunday school with the parable of the mustard seed on it, with an actual mustard seed glued to the card. The little seed was tiny. It could have been mistaken for a grain of sand or dirt if I didn't know otherwise.

In Matthew 17, Jesus uses a mustard seed to explain what faith in God is like. None of us are spiritual giants in our own strength, but having faith is the foundation to everything we believe in and live out in our daily lives. The mustard seed is the smallest of all seeds when planted in the ground but grows to be the largest of all plants, reaching heights of eight feet with several branches. Our faith is like this seed, whereas it begins small by acknowledging that there is a God and that He sent His Son Jesus to die for us. This is the start of our faith journey, but we don't stop there!

As we mature and grow, we will reach a point where God may transplant us, showing us a larger pot to grow in. Faith should never stay stagnant. It is meant to grow. If we find ourselves staying in the same pot for too long, we should probably take a hard look at what may be hindering us from further growth. Perhaps our language has gotten a little sketchy or we have developed some bad habits that haven't led to the best of choices. Sometimes we just need to be aware that we are taking some steps backward instead of forward and that we probably need a new pot. Perhaps we need a discipleship, a prayer partner, or a Bible study added to our weekly schedule. Whatever it looks like for you, remember, God wants your faith to grow and not stay stagnant.

I was transplanting an orchid this last week. It had given off many blooms this past winter, but now the leaves were wilting. When I looked at the roots, they had become a little rotten and embedded in the dirt. After some pruning the dead roots off, I transplanted it into a larger pot with new soil. It is now thriving in its new space with lots of new growth!

This week, ask yourself if your roots are starting to rot or get embedded into the same pot you've been in. God has much more for you on your faith journey, and He wants to renew your energy, thoughts, relationships, and lifestyle. He wants that mustard seed to grow!

—Tammy

Weighted Down
Hebrews 12:1–3

When our son Scott was two years old, we lived in Phoenix, Arizona. One of the luxuries we had at the time was a pool, something we utilized a lot living in the desert climate. One day when Mark was cleaning the pool, Scott followed Daddy outside, pretending he was cleaning the pool too. You can guess what happened. Mark heard a "plop" and turned around to see two-year-old Scott immersed in the deep end! As any parent would do, Mark jumped in fully clothed (jeans, shoes, and shirt) and retrieved his son, and all ended well.

I think of this image when I read Hebrews 12:1–3 (NIV), "let us throw off everything that hinders and the sin that so easily entangles. And let us run with perseverance the race marked out for us, fixing our eyes on Jesus, the pioneer and perfecter of faith." I don't know if you have ever jumped into water fully clothed, but when you get out, the weight of your clothes clings to you, making it difficult to move around or walk, much less run!

The term "fixing our eyes on Jesus" is key to this passage. Just like the wet clothes, we can get so weighted down by all the external weights of this world, like temptations, relationships, depression, and anxiety. Before we realize, we are fixed on those things instead of Jesus. We try to run, but the weight of what surrounds us is overwhelming.

How can we begin to change our focus when the walls of life grow higher and higher, crowding out Jesus, making Him seem unreachable? By shedding off everything that hinders us from running this race, things like sin, unbelief, impatience, selfishness, unforgiveness, immorality, and laziness, and the list goes on. God can't do His work to the fullest when we are carrying any of these things! We will lose our focus and potentially drown.

Jesus is the pioneer and perfecter of our faith! We either believe in Jesus Christ or we don't. We either allow the Holy Spirit to work in us and mold us, or we don't. There is no middle ground. The Holy Spirit can lift the weights if we let Him. He is faithful, and we can trust him. What is hindering you and weighing you down today?

—Tammy

Change in Focus

Hebrews 12:1–3

I love to watch and play sports. I am very competitive by nature, and sports has always been a great outlet for this characteristic in me. In many cases, that has worked out well for my teammates and coaches, especially those with a similar competitive nature. Generally, that has worked on a personal level too, but not always.

I have always loved to play golf, but the older I get, it has become my favorite sport to play. In my twenties and into my thirties, I played golf with the same approach I took with other sports I played. I wanted to win! It did not matter if my partners were better or worse as I even put pressure on myself to always shoot a particular score. Since I normally did not reach that score, I was often frustrated or disappointed at the end.

At some point on the golf course, I realized that I could change my focus from competing for a low number to actually enjoying the wonderful scenery, spending time with family and friends, and just relaxing in great weather. This change in focus has allowed me to find an entirely new and deeper love of golf.

In Hebrews 12, we are shown an even more important change of focus. First, we are told to strip everything off that slows us down, especially the sin that so easily trips us up. On the golf course, a bad shot can distract me from focusing on the next shot, let alone the beautiful scenery on some of these golf courses. The same is true of everything in our lives. We can put so much attention on the things weighing us down that we cannot see past them to the truly great things around us.

Hebrews gives us the ultimate approach with how to focus, by keeping our eyes on Jesus. When our focus is on anything else, we run the risk of growing weary and not finishing. We get distracted and worry about past mistakes. But if we focus on Jesus, we can see His example to endure all kinds of suffering and abuse because He had his focus on the joy that awaited him. So if you are weighted down by the things of this earth or even your golf game, consider that a change in focus on Jesus may be in order.

—Mark

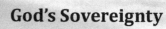

God's Sovereignty

1 Chronicles 29:11–12; Psalm 37:5;
Proverbs 19:21; Romans 8:28

Can we mess up God's plans for us? Since we have been given free choice, do we have the power to thwart God's ultimate purpose or intentions in our lives?

Fifteen years ago, I was afraid of messing up God's plan. Mark had received two amazing, out-of-state job offers simultaneously, one located out West and the other in the Midwest. Both would have required a move from Michigan, so with only one week to decide between the two, the whole family hopped on planes, making our pros and cons list of churches, schools, housing, weather, and jobs.

After weighing the two options, we were extremely confused. The pros and cons seemed about equal, and there was no clear answer. How were we to discern the Holy Spirit when both opportunities seemed equal? In situations like these, I must rely on the sovereignty of God. God is the God of the past, present, and the future, and nothing takes Him by surprise. In order to fully grasp that concept amid God giving humans free choice, we need to understand that nothing can stop the will of God. We cannot even begin to comprehend how God works out His will and plans despite us. Can we take a detour? Sure. Our sin can certainly delay or change the original course we were on. However, Romans 8:28 (NLT) says, "And we know that God causes everything to work together for the good of those who love God and are called according to his purpose for them."

When we were unsure of what to do in making the decision of where to move, we leaned into God's Word and poured ourselves into prayer. With these two biblical promises, we could rest in the Lord and trust in His sovereignty. "Commit everything you do to the Lord. Trust him, and he will help you" (Psalm 37:5 NLT). "You can make many plans, but the Lord's purpose will prevail" (Proverbs 19:21 NLT).

—Tammy

141

Week 19 Reflections

1. After reviewing the Scriptures for each day, name three to four passages that jumped out at you this week.
2. How can you practically apply these verses to your life today and the upcoming week?
3. There is a season to build. When is the last time you have been in that season (e.g., job growth, building a family, school, etc.)?
4. Building requires a foundation. What does your foundation consist of? What does God desire in your foundation?
5. Faith can be difficult, but how can the faith of a mustard seed benefit our walk with the Lord? Is your faith growing? Why or why not?
6. What weighs you down in life? What steals your joy?
7. What does it look like for you to fix your eyes on Jesus?
8. Life can be challenging if we are focused on the wrong things. Be specific on how focusing on Jesus can give you a different perspective.
9. We can take detours to God's plan, but God is sovereign. Explain.

The Word of God Is Alive!

Hebrews 4:12–14

The Institute of Museum and Library Services records that there are 35,144 museums in the United States, more than double the estimate of 17,500 from the 1990s. In the whole world, the number is over 95,000. Some of the most fascinating museums I have discovered across the world are *The Museum of Bad Art* in the United States, *The Dog Collar Museum* in England, *The British Lawnmower Museum* in England, and *The Cup of Noodles Museum* in Japan. If you've ever driven out West through the Dakotas, you will see the most unique museum I've ever been to, *The Spam Museum*, which was surprisingly awesome!

Most people find museums interesting because they represent history, preserving cultures of people by displaying collections of rare and valuable items, including ancient writings.

Speaking of ancient writings, let's recognize God's Word. The Bible was written by forty different authors, some known and others anonymous. From the beginning to the end, the Bible was written over a span of 1,500 years, the last books written in the first-century AD. This ancient text is the top-selling book in the world. Why? What sets it apart from being just another piece of work to observe in a museum?

> For the word of God is alive and powerful. It is sharper than the sharpest two-edged sword, cutting between soul and spirit, between joint and marrow. It exposes our innermost thoughts and desires. (Hebrews 4:12 NLT)

These ancient and sacred words are just that, ancient. But these words are still relevant today, transforming those who read it and take it to heart. God's Word convicts us, loves us, guides us, heals us, and strengthens us. It speaks to us, offering the path to salvation through Jesus Christ with His gift of redemption.

Unlike any item in a museum, meant only for display and educational purposes, the Bible interacts with us, transforming our hearts. For those who read it, His Word will come alive!

—Tammy

Bricks of Gold
Matthew 7:24–27

Did you know that the largest brick building in Europe took more than seven hundred years to complete? Yes, me neither. One day out of those seven hundred years seems so small, doesn't it? But each day was one to count toward an amazing architectural feat!

How cool to think that rearing children is very similar to constructing unique architectural creations. My husband and I just had our first daughter a year ago now. I stay home with her while my husband works full time. He and I decided this arrangement would work best for our family so I can witness all her firsts, but also be hands-on in teaching her our family values. That sounds nice as I write it out; however, the everyday chores get to be exhausting, and I soon miss adult interaction. Don't get me wrong! I'm extremely grateful for having the opportunity to stay home and raise our little one. It's just, sometimes I wonder how three loads of laundry in a week and taking a walk every day make a difference.

As I pray and talk to others about my feelings, I realize that every day I spend caring for our household is a day when I am laying a brick on the foundation of my child's character. Eventually the bricks will stand tall, leading her to a foundation that is built on the Rock of Jesus Christ.

> Everyone then who hears these words of mine and does them will be like a wise man who built his house on the rock. And the rain fell, and the floods came, and the winds blew and beat on that house, but it did not fall, because it had been founded on the rock. (Matthew 7:24–26 ESV)

Some days I don't feel like I lay any bricks at all, and that's ok. God and I are molding bricks of love, kindness, self-control, patience, integrity, commitment, humility, and so much more. These are more than clay and cement bricks; they are bricks of gold that will stand the test of time and last through eternity. And that, my friend, is priceless.

-Karissa

Let Him Plant and Grow
Colossians 2:6–8

Last spring, we planted five new trees. At the end of the summer, the larger of the five seemed like it might be dead. We had done everything by the instructions from the nursery, but the leaves were brown and falling off. This year, however, the same tree we thought was dead is full of life, full of new leaves, and we can tell it is now established enough where it is firmly planted and growing.

Each one of us is like a tree that God plants when we ask Him to be Lord of our life. He doesn't leave us hanging out to dry, but rather His Holy Spirit is alive in us. He spurs on to get deep into God's Word so we can grow and flourish, establishing our roots in Him. Life will throw all types of curve balls at us. People will disappoint us, and churches will sadly disillusion us, but God knows our confusion. He knows when our leaves get brown and start to fall off, which is why we must follow Him closely.

> And now, just as you accepted Christ Jesus as your Lord, you must continue to follow him. Let your roots grow down into him, and let your lives be built on him. Then your faith will grow strong in the truth you were taught, and you will overflow with thankfulness.
> (Colossians 2:6–7 NLT)

Paul wrote the book of Colossians in AD 60–61 while he was still in prison. He wrote this epistle because he had heard that Colossae was under attack from false teachers who were slandering the deity of Jesus. Paul addressed these issues head-on, correcting them that the nature of Jesus Christ as Creator and Redeemer was nonnegotiable. What had been planted was starting to wither and brown. In their dryness, people began listening to false teachers who were twisting the truth.

I often wonder what Paul would say to our churches of today. Are we planted in the truth, individually growing with deeply established roots? Or do we get sidetracked with watered-down truth and self-importance? I believe we are in the last days. God wants to plant and grow roots that stand strong.

–Tammy

Put Yourself in a Window

Psalm 80:3–7

Although Mark and I have a cat, we are not necessarily "cat" people. We love *our* cat! Nonetheless we know that most cats like to lay in a sunny spot, absorbing every bit of warmth that they possibly can. Our cat, Elsie, is all black, but she has turned a little brown from laying in the sun so much!

People also need and crave sunlight, as it is beneficial to our mental and physical health. Health benefits such as improving our sleep, reducing our stress, maintaining strong bones, strengthening our immune system, and fighting off depression, all come from the sun to help give us a longer life. In the Bible, understandably so, God is often paralleled with light. Jesus is the light of this world, and there are countless benefits to a relationship with Jesus.

> Again Jesus spoke to them, saying, "I am the light of the world. Whoever follows me will not walk in darkness, but will have the light of life." (John 8:12 NIV)

> The Lord is my light and my salvation; whom shall I fear? The Lord is the stronghold of my life; of whom shall I be afraid? (Psalm 27:1 NIV)

> But if we walk in the light, as he is in the light, we have fellowship with one another, and the blood of Jesus his Son cleanses us from all sin. (1 John 1:7 NIV)

> Turn us again to yourself, O God. Make your face shine down upon us. Only then will we be saved. (Psalm 80:3 NLT)

When you are not feeling your faith, not seeing God as your light in the darkness, you may need to put yourself in a spiritual window and bask in the light of Christ. Start by prayer and confession and begin your day with God's Word. May His face shine upon you, around you, and within you. He is the light!

—Tammy

WEEK 20

·········

Day 5

Get Yourself Watered!

Jeremiah 17:5–8

Landscaping is a strategic art. When working alongside our landscaper, I learned more than I ever thought I could about plants, flowers, trees, and their likes and dislikes in climate and habitat. In our backyard, we planted a grove of trees of a standard variety, doing our best to be mindful of the needs of each tree. Since river birch trees need lots of water and thrive in very moist areas, the edge of our pond at the bottom of our hill was the perfect place for these trees. They are thriving and seem to have everything they need!

On the other hand, the shepherd's tree, native to the Kalahari Desert (and not one of the trees in our yard) does not need to be planted in a moist area, but is just as green and just as big as the river birch. This hardy tree has the deepest documented roots of any tree, extending more than 230 feet deep into the ground. Why so deep? These unique desert trees grow deep roots to gather water that is far down under the surface of the earth, therefore sustaining every part of the tree, allowing it to thrive in the harshest of environments.

> But blessed are those who trust in the Lord and have made the Lord their hope and confidence. They are like trees planted along a riverbank, with roots that reach deep into the water. Such trees are not bothered by the heat or worried by long months of drought. Their leaves stay green, and they never stop producing fruit. (Jeremiah 17:5–8 NLT)

Jesus is our living water. In seasons of plenty, we are like the river birch trees, reaping the benefits of friends, a purposeful job, a joyful church family, and good health. We are regularly watered, and we can produce fruit generally with ease.

However, during seasons of drought, we are like the shepherd's tree. When the dry times come, we need deep roots to sustain us with living water that is commonly found during drought. When we get ourselves watered, God will grow the best fruit in us than any other time!

—Tammy

The Living Word

1 Peter 1:21–25; Romans 10:17

"For you have been born again, but not to a life that will quickly end. Your new life will last forever because it comes from the eternal, living word of God. As the Scriptures say, 'People are like grass; their beauty is like a flower in the field. The grass withers and the flower fades. But the word of the Lord remains forever'" (1 Peter 1:23–24 NLT).

How can we fully comprehend the word *forever*? We can't! Yet Peter writes about the Word of the Lord remaining *forever*! And not only that, but you who have been born again, who have chosen to follow Jesus and accept the gift of salvation, will have eternal life ... forever with God!

So what does this knowledge mean for believers in Christ, especially when forever is so hard to fathom? For me, it means that every choice I make needs to be an eternal choice, that every choice either leads me closer to God or further away from God. Since we have this living hope, there is no need to hold on to the things that don't matter. If we need to forgive someone, it is time to surrender that and do what we need to do. If we need to apologize to someone, now is the time to reconcile. We may need to make the choice to work fifty hours a week instead of seventy for the sake of our children. Maybe the choice is to be more intentional with our time, habits, and health.

Peter explains that our lives are temporary and our bodies as we know them will not be with us forever. Some of us are very thankful for that! But the things we are holding onto that are grieving the Holy Spirit need to be laid to rest and surrendered to the One and Only. God wants His Word, which is alive and active, to consume us in every way.

The art of surrendering is a learned one. The more we do it, the easier it becomes. Lean in to letting go and you will begin to see God working with your own eyes. The living Word has the power to transform us from the inside out. God is faithful. His Word stands forever, and we will see Him face-to-face someday.

–Tammy

Week 20 Reflections

1. After reviewing the Scriptures for each day, name three to four passages that jumped out at you this week.
2. How can you practically apply these verses to your life today and the upcoming week?
3. What is the evidence (or lack of evidence) of God's Word being alive and active in your life?
4. What are some of the bricks of gold that you are laying?
5. Describe an example(s) of watered-down truth that you have heard.
6. Faith needs more of the sun. In what practical areas do you need God to build or rebuild your faith?
7. If you were a tree, how would you describe your roots? Are they deep, shallow, dry, or other?
8. Have you been born again? What do others see as evidence of your new life in Christ?
9. What are you learning about total surrender to God?

MONTH 6

The Uncertainties in Our Lives Can
Cause Doubt and Discontentment

A FAITH THAT STANDS
Produces Trust and Patience

A Positive Outlook
Philippians 4:8

When I was a little girl, I am told that I rarely smiled. Like many families I know, we had our share of turmoil in the home, and my sensitivity to the turmoil gave me some baggage I needed to deal with later. As a musician, I feel very deeply, and I must work harder than most to see the glass half-full instead of half-empty.

As I sought to mature in my faith and process the hurts in my past, God brought me to a counselor in my early twenties, whom God used to help me shed the weight of much of the baggage I was carrying. When I shared my history with my counselor, she asked me, "So where was God in all of this? Do you think He abandoned you?"

To help me answer that, she asked me to recall times, places, and experiences that were positive, infused with God's spirit, and evidence of His faithfulness. Although I couldn't recognize them years earlier, I began to cry in recognition that God had never abandoned me. He was there in the middle of the storms, providing mentors, friends, provisions, and a mom who pursued her faith, ultimately finding Jesus in a personal way. As a result of her finding a relationship with Jesus, my sister Wendy and I, and eventually my dad, found Christ as well. God was there!

So when I read this Scripture passage in Philippians 4, God is not instructing us to focus on material things such as rainbows, chocolate, and diamonds. Rather He wants us to reflect on all of His goodness and His character. His faithfulness is something we recognize when we pay attention. Our negative thinking can be a stumbling block to focusing on what is true, noble, and praiseworthy.

To this day, I have to work at what it says to do in Philippians 4:8. With the Holy Spirit's help, I have chosen to fix my eyes on what is excellent and worthy of praise: His Word, His love, His faithfulness, His peace, His strength, His forgiveness, and His compassion. I meditate on the times when He has guided me, providing for me in every situation. Every opportunity I have is because of Him. Most important of all, I am a life that has been redeemed by the blood of the Lamb. There is nothing more positive than that!

—Tammy

Do Not Fret
Psalm 37:1–9

Do you ever wonder why we worry and fret over things that we have absolutely no control over? The Bible is very clear that in this world we will have trouble. There will be suffering and hardship, and there will be times when we don't see a way forward until we take our cares to the feet of Jesus. Let us see the power of God as we delve into Psalm 37.

> Don't worry about the wicked or envy those who do wrong. For like grass, they soon fade away. Like spring flowers, they soon wither. Trust in the Lord and do good. Then you will live safely in the land and prosper. Take delight in the Lord, and he will give you your heart's desires. Commit everything you do to the Lord. Trust him, and he will help you. He will make your innocence radiate like the dawn, and the justice of your cause will shine like the noonday sun. Be still in the presence of the Lord, and wait patiently for him to act. Don't worry about evil people who prosper or fret about their wicked schemes. (Psalm 37:1–7 NLT)

There are several promises here from God when we take the first step:

<u>First Step from Us: God's Promise to Us</u>

Stop worrying	The wicked will fade away
Trust in the Lord and do good	You will live safely and prosper
Take delight in the Lord	He will give you your heart's desires
Commit what you do to Him	He will be the justice of your cause
Be still and wait patiently	He will act on your behalf
Don't worry about evil people	He is taking care of them
Trust Him	You will possess the land

Though faith over worry may seem impossible at times, God promises to help us. Worrying is a sin and does not add a single moment to our day. We can trust God, and He delights in those who trust Him!

—Tammy

The Waiting Room
James 1:2–12

My son Matt was a senior in high school when he came home around 8:30 p.m. from a varsity basketball game with his friends. Mark and I were surprised they came home so early, and when they showed up laughing, we knew something was up. Matt proceeded to tell us that he had attempted a dunk with sweaty palms, causing him to over-rotate and fall to the floor. At first glance, he looked like he probably broke not one, but both of his wrists. The night was shot. Off to the emergency room we went!

We waited. We waited. And we waited. Finally, after almost two hours, Matt was taken back for x-rays. Sure enough, it was confirmed that his wrists were indeed broken. When I think back to that night, the thing I remember most was the waiting room. Although it seemed like a long time before we were taken back, Matt's friends, Matt, and I had the most wonderful conversations. I not only got to know them better, but some of the other patients waiting as well. The time was not wasted.

> Dear brothers and sisters, when troubles of any kind come your way, consider it an opportunity for great joy. For you know that when your faith is tested, your endurance has a chance to grow. So let it grow, for when your endurance is fully developed, you will be perfect and complete, needing nothing. (James 1:2 NLT)

Waiting patiently is a form of endurance. So often I am tempted to complain or worry when I am waiting for an answer to something. The longer I wait, the longer I think negative thoughts. But James instructs us to consider it pure joy when our faith is tested, for our endurance will have a chance to grow, and then it will eventually be complete.

I want to be a good waiter. I want to find joy in the waiting room, looking for opportunities around me that I may have missed before had I not been in this place. Waiting serves a purpose, and God does not waste time. We can trust Him completely. And when it is our turn, He will call us, and we will hear our name loud and clear!

–Tammy

God's Lemonade Stand
Psalm 30:22; Romans 8:28

"You turned my mourning into joyful dancing. You have taken away my clothes of mourning and clothed me with joy …" (Psalm 30:22 NLT).

You've heard the saying, "When life hands you lemons, make lemonade." In other words, when bad things happen to you, make the best of the bad situation.

We have all had challenges that have fallen into our laps, whether we expected them or not, or knew how long they'd last. Oftentimes we wonder how we got where we are in life. I have a friend that always envisioned herself married with a family. At age fifty-five, she has still yet to realize that dream. I've seen the news where senseless killings have taken place not very far from my own community. Still another acquaintance of mine passed away unexpectedly at thirty-four with three children and a loving husband. Talk about lemons! How can God do anything with those?

God is in the business of repairing shattered dreams that we have held onto. I used to wonder if God really heard my desires and cries of my heart because some of my dreams didn't come to pass. But God has done more than I imagined when I began to look through His lenses.

Asking the question why is our human instinct; however, God is in the business of doing the superhuman by taking our lemons to make the most refreshing and pleasing lemonade around! This way, He gets all the glory!

In moments of grief, confusion, and loneliness, God wants you to do this. Gather your bag of lemons. Label them one by one. Take them to the feet of Jesus at His lemonade stand and hand Him your lemons. Then sit on Jesus' lap. Sing with Him and wait. Let Him fill you with His strength and lean into Him until you fully know where you are, in His holy presence. He will restore you, refresh you, and make something beautiful out of your lemons. Trust Him! Jesus is the master lemonade maker! "And we know that in *all things* God works for the good of those who love him, who have been called according to his purpose" (Romans 8:28 NIV).

–Tammy

Godliness and Contentment

1 Timothy 6:6–10

Occasionally I'll catch an episode of a popular game show where contestants gamble by selecting hidden dollar amounts in boxes, hoping to end up with a high reward in the end. The gambling is addictive, and I've heard contestants say, "If I just get to a hundred thousand, I'll walk away." Sadly, when the $100,000 is achieved, they keep playing, only to lose the whole pot a few turns later.

We seem to want more, but when we get it, we aim higher for more still. What begin as little wants soon have the potential to become bigger wants. Seeds of discontentment can easily lead to sins such as greed, lust, pride, selfishness, and a critical spirit. Discontentment slowly robs our joy, keeping us on the endless search for something more. Ultimately, we become vulnerable to all sorts of temptations around us.

> Yet true godliness with contentment is itself great wealth. So, if we have enough food and clothing, let us be content. But people who long to be rich fall into temptation and are trapped by many foolish and harmful desires that plunge them into ruin and destruction. For the love of money is the root of all kinds of evil. And some people, craving money, have wandered from the true faith ... (1 Timothy 6:6–10 NLT)

King Solomon attained every bit of wealth, had over a thousand wives and concubines, and had all the wisdom in the world. But at the end of his life, God called him to write one more book called Ecclesiastes, in which Solomon explains in detail that he chased after wealth, women, and power, seeking the ultimate contentment. In the end, those things did not fulfill him. He said everything was meaningless under the sun because he had turned to pleasing himself rather than God.

Consequently, his discontentment led him further away from God. Likewise, if we are not alert, discontentment will consume our thoughts and monopolize our days, weeks, months, and possibly even years to come. Godliness with contentment is a treasure because we can rest, knowing that God is fully in control of every detail of our lives!

—Tammy

Joy in the Understanding
Nehemiah 8:1–12

I love learning about people of the Bible and the stories that go with them. Knowing the context behind the stories allows them to come alive and bring understanding to the reader. Today I'd like to explore the concept of understanding God's Word, for unless we understand the context of what we read, we might not know how to apply it. As you read Nehemiah 8:1–12, it's important to know who, when, where, and what is going on.

Nehemiah was a strong godly leader who was a high official in the Persian court at the capital city of Susa (modern Iran). As King Artaxerxes' cupbearer, Nehemiah was highly favored by the king. Therefore, when Nehemiah heard about the dismal situation in Judah, he asked the king for permission to go back to Jerusalem and rebuild the city and its walls. In Nehemiah's return in 445 BC, he was immediately appointed the provincial governor of Judah, surveying the damage and helping the people, protecting them from hostile neighbors.

Nehemiah 8 tells us that the people of Judah were hungering for a spiritual foundation. They called on Ezra, a priest and a scribe, to assemble with all the people and read the law of Moses (given by God). They asked for help in understanding the meaning of God's Word, and they stayed in full attention while Ezra spoke for the whole morning until noon.

The desire to understand is so valuable! We may read the Bible, perhaps the whole thing front to back, but if we do not understand it, how can we apply it? When I am mentoring high school girls, my desire is not to spoon-feed God's Word to them, rather to help them to seek it and crave to understand it. In Nehemiah 8, every person, old and young, yearned for a spiritual foundation found in God Himself. I'm sure they asked questions. Their motive for change in their lives caused them to take the time to seek it and understand it.

Whether you are a seasoned or a newer Christian or haven't yet figured out what you believe, pray that God gives you the desire to understand His Word. The more we understand God in His fullness, the more we will crave that personal relationship with Him!

–Tammy

Week 21 Reflections

1. After reviewing the Scriptures for each day, name three to four passages that jumped out at you this week.
2. How can you practically apply these verses to your life today and the upcoming week?
3. Do you tend to be a positive or negative thinker?
4. How does God want to infuse the Holy Spirit into your thinking?
5. When are you most tempted to worry? Be specific.
6. When have you been in a waiting room of sorts? What have you learned in the waiting room?
7. Label the lemons in your life. How does God want to make lemonade from your lemons?
8. Discontentment is a condition that can be habitual. When have you been most discontent in life? What is God teaching you about contentment?
9. What do you need to do in order to understand God's Word better?

The Art of Waiting
Lamentations 3:18–33

Nothing revs up my anxiety level like getting behind a pokey driver when I am running late for something important. In my youthful twenties, one might say I had occasional road rage. Having two small boys at the time certainly didn't help my habitual problem of being fashionably five minutes late. One day in the car with the boys, an incident happened when I was cut off by an inconsiderate driver, and I exhibited, let me just say, a poor example of how to act as an adult! My older son, Scott, asked me why I got so mad at the driver because I didn't even know him! I realized that my impatience and reactions were going to have a negative impact on my children if I didn't work on this.

I need more patience! If I get upset when a slow driver affects ten minutes of my day, what is my response when I am waiting for an hour, a day, a week, a month, a year, or a decade? As an American with a need for immediate answers and instant gratification, I am not disciplined as I should be to wait on God. Mercifully, it is through times of waiting that God teaches me valuable insights about Himself.

The book of Lamentations, probably written by the prophet Jeremiah, is a dark but beautiful book that reflects the pain of injustice and human loss. It's filled with crushing emotions: anger, desperation, fear, loneliness, and hopelessness. However, it reminds us that God's mercies are new every morning and that He is a faithful God who is trustworthy.

> I say to myself, "The Lord is my inheritance; therefore, I will *hope* in him!" The Lord is good to those who *depend* on him to those who *search* for him. So it is good to *wait* quietly for salvation from the Lord. And it is good for people to *submit* at an early age to the yoke of his discipline. (Lamentations 3:24–27 NLT)

Jeremiah calls us to five key action words: *hope, depend, search, wait,* and *submit.* Waiting is an art. It doesn't come easy. But as we come under God's authority, we can depend on Him and find peace in the waiting.

–Tammy

159

Losing a Loved One
John 14:1–4; Revelation 14:13b

One of my best friends died last night. I have such mixed emotions, joy that she is in heaven with her Lord and her beloved husband, who died two years ago, but true sadness knowing I will never be able to pick up the phone to talk with her again. Marian had a challenging life, plagued with many obstacles, debilitating diseases, and losses. For these reasons, I am glad she is not suffering anymore. But because I am human, I grieve. I already miss her so much. At times like these, God has given me Scripture to comfort me.

> Let not your hearts be troubled. Believe in God; believe also in me. In my Father's house are many rooms. If it were not so, would I have told you that I go to prepare a place for you? And if I go and prepare a place for you, I will come again and will take you to myself, that where I am you may be also. And you know the way to where I am going. (John 14:1–4 ESV)

> The Lord is my Shepherd; I shall not want. He makes me lie down in green pastures; He leads me beside the still waters; He restores my soul. Even though I walk through the valley of the shadow of death, I will fear no evil, for you are with me; your rod and your staff, they comfort me. You prepare a table before me in the presence of my enemies. You anoint my head with oil; my cup overflows. Surely goodness and mercy shall follow me all the days of my life, and I shall dwell in the house of the Lord forever. (Psalm 23 ESV)

God has an appointed time for each of us to die, although we do not know when that time is. The important thing is that we are ready to go when our time comes. I am comforted knowing that Marian is in heaven. I know that because she chose to follow Jesus as her personal Savior. I also know that I don't have to wonder where she is and I will see her again someday.

—Sharon

Joy Remembering Christ

Hebrews 10:33–35

Life can be tough. People can be mean. The author of Hebrews is aware of this, yet he gives a call to persevere during difficult times. As humans, we often have the tendency to shrink back from difficult circumstances and want to avoid the pain and pressure. But Hebrews is a great reminder to remember back to those first days when you learned about Christ. The early church was subject to ridicule, beatings, and even death. Yet with all of that suffering and loss, they accepted it with joy. This was something that those around them could not fully grasp.

We might experience some of this same suffering, or it might be in a different form. Tammy and I went through a difficult time when we felt called to leave a place of ministry of nearly eight years. After having poured ourselves into every aspect of this ministry, we felt the need to step away, which was heartbreaking but freeing all at the same time. After some initial tough days, I was able to remember my initial love for Christ and return to a place of joy.

One amazing aspect of this return to joy was through family and close friends reaching out to us. As we read in Hebrews 10:33, we will at times be the ones to go through pain and suffering, and at other times, it will be us helping those who are going through hardship. We focused our meetings together not on the situation itself but on the joy we have in knowing Christ.

In times of pain, my first reaction is not typically to find joy. However, I find that the Holy Spirit uses these times of difficulty to build up my patience, increase my endurance, and even add positive elements to my character. It is later in this process that I can return to a place of joy. As I go through tough times, I can get to that place of joy sooner based on past experiences.

We know that there are better things awaiting us that will last forever. In whatever suffering you might be going through right now, allow yourself to reflect on the early days when you first learned of Christ. In doing so, you will receive all that he has promised you, including joy!

-Mark

Worship in the Waiting
Luke 2:22–38

Luke tells us of a man named Simeon who was a very devout and godly man. The Holy Spirit was alive and well in Simeon, and God told him that before he died, he would see the Messiah with his own eyes.

At that time, the law of Moses required that if the firstborn were a son, he would be brought to the temple to be dedicated to the Lord with the proper sacrifices made, either two turtledoves or two pigeons. When Mary and Joseph had Jesus, they did as was required of them and took Jesus to Jerusalem to be dedicated. The Holy Spirit spoke to Simeon and led him to the temple. He talked with Mary and Joseph, held Jesus in his arms, and praised God, saying, "Sovereign Lord, now let your servant die in peace, as you have promised. I have seen your salvation, which you have prepared for all people. He is a light to reveal God to the nations, and he is the glory of your people Israel!" (Luke 2:29–32 NLT).

While this was going on, Anna, a prophet, was also at the temple. As a widow at the age of eighty-four, she never left the temple, staying there day and night, worshiping God with fasting and prayer. She came along just as Simeon was talking with Mary and Joseph, and she began praising God. She then told everyone about the child, praising God for His faithfulness!

Simeon and Anna, two elderly people who waited a lifetime for God to send His Messiah to redeem Israel and all people, waited patiently by trusting God, praying, fasting, and remaining in God's presence. They both worshiped God in their waiting, anticipating what He was going to do and believing it in their hearts before it ever happened.

When we are waiting on God's timing, His movement in our life, and His answers or provisions, it is easy to grumble or grow impatient. How can we better worship God in times of waiting? How can we personally grow in this area so we can wait on our knees in prayer, singing praises to Him, and not complain? When we put our trust in God, He knows it, and He helps us in the waiting. Let's worship Him and thank Him while we anticipate what He will do in the process!

—Tammy

Maturity in Action
1 John 2:13–15

"I have written to you who are mature in the faith because you know Christ, who existed from the beginning ..." (NLT 1 John 2:14).

Today was a good day! As my family and I walked over fifteen miles through Glacier National Park, climbing steep terrains with views I'd only seen in magazines or on TV, I was reminded once again of the beauty and splendor of our amazing God. We took in the landscapes, the lakes, the wildlife, and waterfalls, experiencing hiking on snow while dressed in shorts and T-shirts in eighty-five degrees! Yes, today was a good day.

But not too long ago, I found myself going through a season where each day brought pain and grief, a season I found difficult to find the joy amid all the negative. Times like these have indeed challenged my faith. Does God know what I'm going through? Does God hear me? But instead of digging my heels into resentment, bitterness, and anger, I have found that planting myself firmly at the feet of Jesus is the best thing I can do to mature my faith and draw me closer to God.

Have you ever found yourself in a wilderness at one time or another? Some of you may be going through that today. Maybe you received a discouraging health diagnosis, endured a miscarriage, or lost a loved one. Perhaps you just found out the news of an extramarital affair or have learned that you are going to lose your job. Yes, for many, today was a painful day. However, the more we know God, the more we experience God in ways we never have before.

God never changes. If the same God who adorned the earth with majestic mountains and glacier-fed lakes created me and knows me inside and out, He is certainly able to handle my bad days. Scripture promises that God is going to make beauty from ashes and turn my tears into joyful dancing (Psalm 30:11).

My faith cannot be dependent on my circumstances, but rather be rooted in Jesus Christ. It is here at the feet of Jesus where I have learned to trust Him and wait patiently for Him to do His work in me and around me. Being mature in my faith allows me to respond to God and others with consistency, despite how I feel or what I am experiencing.

–Tammy

Hope and Confidence
Micah 7:1–13; James 1:6

Lately I've been studying the prophets of the Old Testament, intrigued by their messages of boldness as chosen by God Himself. One of the twelve minor prophets, Micah, was a contemporary of the more famous prophet, Isaiah, and lived in a small town in southern Judah from 740 BC to 670 BC. Out of all the writers in the Old Testament, Micah is the most indignant, having grown up around the poor and seeing the constant injustice all around him. He spoke boldly and was not very popular because of his tenacity and strong words.

In Micah 7, we see a man who is spelling out for us what he sees and feels about the universal corruption, the discontent of finding little comfort or satisfaction in daily life, and bad things happening to good people. But after the first six verses, Micah changes his tone from complaining about injustice to complaining about himself, recognizing the badness in his own heart. He cries out, "As for me, I look to the Lord for help. I wait confidently for God to save me, and my God will certainly hear me" (Micah 7:7 NLT).

We can identify with Micah because we were all born into sin the moment we entered this world. But our minds get clouded by the bad in our culture, neglecting to attend to the sin in our own heart, our pride, impatience, or worry. Notice the confidence Micah has. He says he confidently waits on the Lord because God will certainly hear him. These words are unwavering. We too must trust that God will deliver us in due time from our greatest heartaches and afflictions.

> But when you ask him, be sure that your faith is in God alone. Do not waver, for a person with divided loyalty is as unsettled as a wave of the sea that is blown and tossed by the wind. (James 1:6 NLT)

I want to confidently wait on God to act. There is hope in the name of Jesus, and I am confident that He is always working in my life.

—Tammy

Week 22 Reflections

1. After reviewing the Scriptures for each day, name three to four passages that jumped out at you this week.
2. How can you practically apply these verses to your life today and the upcoming week?
3. Jeremiah calls us to five key action words to implement while we wait: hope, depend, search, wait, and submit. Which of these action words is the hardest for you?
4. Do you worry about death? Why or why not?
5. What might God be teaching you about enduring hardship with joy?
6. How can you better worship God in the waiting?
7. When is your faith tested the most?
8. Is your faith defined by your circumstances? Explain.
9. God is always working, even when we don't see it. How do you know that God is working in your life today?

I'm Listening ... I Think!
Proverbs 18:1–12

Have you ever attended a university lecture, eyes glued on the professor, your computer out and ready to take notes, only to come out of your trance an hour later, never retaining one word your professor said? I mean, you heard her with your ears, your eyes were fixed on her, and your fingers were busy typing, but nothing was understood or retained. You weren't actually listening to her, only hearing.

Listening is understanding. For those who listen, they are taking to heart what is being said in case there is a lesson to act on. Listening and understanding go hand in hand. Proverbs says many times that the fool lacks understanding. The fool also delights in airing his own opinions, lacks wisdom, is self-centered, and seeks his own interests before the interests of others. The fool's tongue invites a beating, and the fool is lazy and unproductive. "Fool" is an offensive word and a strong word that Solomon uses here to indicate the severe situation for a person who lacks judgment or sense, not listening to understand.

As you read today's Scripture passage from Proverbs, there is a lot to take in. Every verse has an instruction or wise counsel in it. When reading a passage like this, it is so important to take it apart, verse by verse, in order to find application in our own lives. Are we *understanding* the meaning? Is our heart *listening* to what it says and allowing God to check our spirit? When we take the time to understand, then we are truly listening. We allow the words to penetrate our souls and renew our thinking.

As a pianist and violinist, I have often memorized the music I'm learning while I am learning it. The slow repetition and attention to every detail allow for the notes, phrasing, fingering, and music to get ingrained into my mind and soul all at once. If I practice too fast, bad habits can set in because I've overlooked a finer detail that I should have paid more attention to. Likewise, dissecting Scripture to understand it welcomes God's Word to soak into our hearts and minds. We can then intentionally meditate on the application of what we read, which is key to refining us on the Christ-filled journey.

–Tammy

Stuck in Molasses
James 4:1–9

I have a recurring dream where I try to run, but my legs won't move. This feeling of paralysis thwarts my intentions to get where I am trying to go. I am stuck in molasses.

The dream parallels how I have felt with my relationship with God at times. In those moments, I'm trying to feel His presence, to move forward to something new, but with all my efforts, God still seems far away, and I feel stuck.

> So humble yourselves before God. Resist the devil, and he will flee from you. Come close to God, and God will come close to you. Wash your hands, you sinners; purify your hearts, for your loyalty is divided between God and the world. Let there be tears for what you have done. Let there be sorrow and deep grief. Let there be sadness instead of laughter, and gloom instead of joy. (James 4:7–8 NLT)

If our desire is to get out of the muck and draw close to God, He tells us how to do that in these verses. James tells us to purify our hearts by confessing our sin in humility. As we lament for our sin with tears, we will feel sorrow and grief. But He promises to raise us up and draw near to us as we take these steps toward Him!

Sin separates us from God. Sometimes, however, we feel stuck in our faith because the challenges and sin around us discourage us. We become numb and don't see a way forward. We need to get out of the molasses! We all have the unique opportunity to resist the devil and expect that God is always working in order to gain true joy.

As we humble ourselves before God today, let us resist the devil in our daily tasks and routines. May our efforts show that we are no longer divided in our loyalty to God and the world, and may we be diligent to repent with sadness over our personal sin. In turn, we will find ourselves in God's presence, never to be disputed. There will be no more barriers between God and us, and we will be examples of God's peace and hope.

—Tammy

Be Ready

1 Peter 3:14–16; Romans 1:16

We live in a time when there is a lot of pressure to be politically correct. Christian or not, we have been trained to guard our opinions to prevent offending anyone or appearing to be intolerant or judgmental. Pretty challenging, don't you think? We have grown so accustomed to keeping our views to ourselves that for many of us, we have lost the boldness that Jesus called Christians to as followers of Him. What do we say? What do we not say? What does God require of us as believers and followers?

I think the first question we should ask ourselves is this: where do we find our hope? 1 Peter 3:15-16 (NIV) answers, "But in your hearts revere Christ as Lord. Always be prepared to give an answer to everyone who asks you to give the reason for the hope that you have. But do this with gentleness and respect, keeping a clear conscience, so that those who speak maliciously against your good behavior in Christ may be ashamed of their slander."

If God is my hope, isn't He my neighbor's hope as well? No one can argue with my own story of what Christ has done for me. The hope I have in Jesus is directly related to the experiences I have had with God in my life. So why do I hesitate when it comes to sharing Christ with a neighbor or standing up for biblical principles at a meeting?

There is an important command in verse 15 (NIV), "But do this with gentleness and respect." *Gentleness* and *respect* are keys we need to explain to others the hope we have. We should never lord our beliefs over others, but rather boast about what God has done in our own lives. "For I am not ashamed of this Good News about Christ. It is the power of God at work, saving everyone who believes" (Romans 1:16 NLT).

Wow! Whether it is politically correct or not, I should never be ashamed to share my testimony. I need to be ready to share with gentleness and respect when the daily opportunities arise.

—Tammy

The Soft, Still Voice
1 Kings 19:9–18

Often Tammy will ask me how I can remain calm or even happy during a difficult situation. First, I must say that I have been blessed with a natural tendency to see things in a positive way. I also had amazing examples in both my parents as they modeled joy to me in their words and their actions. But even for me, there are times or circumstances that arise when I am vulnerable to letting discouragement take over. Ironically, these times of downheartedness often come immediately following great victories or accomplishments.

In 1 Kings, there is a wonderful story about the prophet Elijah. For me, it culminates in chapter 18 where he takes on the 450 false prophets of Baal by challenging them to a remarkable showdown. He puts his faith in the one true God, trusting Him to act with fire in a situation where there is no way for victory unless He is who He says He is! And oh, how God shows up. He comes through loud and clear, leaving no doubt that He is God!

After a victory like that and seeing how powerful God is, how could one ever become fearful or sad? But after hearing of this great victory, Jezebel, King Ahab's wife who worshiped other gods, sent word that she would have Elijah killed. Rather than put his faith again in the Lord, he fled and hid.

Mercifully the Lord does not let the story end there. He pursued Elijah, as He does each of us today. The Lord told Elijah to wait for Him, which he did. As a windstorm passed by, the Lord was not there. Then an earthquake shook the ground, but the Lord was not there. Eventually a fire broke out, but the Lord was not there either. Finally in the calm and stillness, Elijah recognized a gentle whisper. It was the Lord.

The story of Elijah is first a reminder to me that the times of difficulty or loneliness can come quickly after I am on the mountaintop enjoying great success and happiness. Yet the biggest reminder for me is that I need to faithfully listen and look to the Lord in all circumstances. Often it will be when I calm myself before Him and allow Him to speak in His soft, still voice.

—Mark

Gratefulness
1 Thessalonians 5:17–18

It was a long day of working a double at the restaurant when I came home to the best surprise I've ever had. I walked through the door to spot two beautiful green eyes peeking at me from behind the coffee table. I immediately dropped to my knees and started bawling happy tears. My husband of only two months drove an hour to pick up the little black cat we soon named Pippin.

Fast-forward three years. We've since added to our family a black lab mix, Finn, and our first child, River Noelle. I am very grateful for all that God has blessed us with over the past few years. Even through our challenges, I have always made sure to thank God for my little family, for they bring me so much joy.

Although it is always appropriate to be grateful to God for the good things we enjoy, we show even more faith to thank Him during our times of sorrow. I'm preaching to myself here because recently my sweet kitty, Pippin, went missing. Cats are curious creatures, but they usually wander back home after a few days of adventure. We prayed for his return and put out his food so he could smell his way back home. We called all the area humane societies and posted him online and on flyers around our area. We did everything we could think of.

Now we wait and pray. It would be so easy to meditate on our loss. God is perfectly capable of bringing Pippin back to us, if that is His plan. But if it's not, I need to grow my faith bone a little more and choose to thank God for the time I did have with Pippin and let go. That isn't easy though! How do I choose gratefulness when I'm in pain? "Pray without ceasing, give thanks in all circumstances; for this is the will of God in Christ Jesus for you" (1 Thessalonians 5:17–18 ESV).

Gratefulness is not always our first response when pain and loss afflict us. Yet as we pray to God continually, He instills a grateful heart in us.

–Karissa

A Lesson from the Conservatory

Psalm 1:1–3, 119:97–99

After graduating from Belmont University in Nashville, I went on to Cincinnati Conservatory for my master's degree in piano performance. One of the classes I had to take was piano literature, primarily a listening class designed to familiarize every pianist with the broad repertoire of piano literature. I remember spending hours preparing for the exams, getting to know piano concertos, sonatas, études, nocturnes, and preludes in such a way that I knew their form, their keys, and the motifs throughout. Some of these pieces had multiple movements, meaning altogether lengthy, some being up to fifty minutes.

The exams consisted of the professor dropping the needle of the record player (remember those?) at any point on the record. We then had to identify the composer, the piece (and which movement), the key, and the structure. Sound overwhelming?

My system to memorizing music is basic but effective. I will listen to the music while I am falling asleep so it will absorb into my brain. I will listen again in the morning while I get ready and then set aside time during the day to listen again. Listening must be a priority for memorizing. David uses the same principle to meditate on God's Word.

> Oh, how I love your law! I meditate on it all day long. Your commands are always with me and make me wiser than my enemies. I have more insight than all my teachers, for I meditate on your statutes. (Psalm 119:97–99 NIV)

To know God's Word is to know God more, allowing Him to bear fruit in us with His wisdom and insight for life. We are so fortunate in this day and age for the countless ways to learn and meditate on God's Word. We can listen to it in the car, on our phones, and on our computers and can read it from apps with correlating studies. We have Scripture at our fingertips twenty-four hours a day. We can listen, memorize, and apply His Word, but most importantly, we need to take the time to memorize. When we do, we have learned a valuable lesson from the conservatory!

–Tammy

Week 23 Reflections

1. After reviewing the Scriptures for each day, name three to four passages that jumped out at you this week.
2. How can you practically apply these verses to your life today and the upcoming week?
3. Scripture can be read but easily forgotten if we are not listening. What habits can you put into place that will help you listen and apply God's Word?
4. When is the last time you felt stuck on your faith journey? How does God want to free you and help you resist the devil?
5. On a scale from one to ten, how ready do you feel to share your faith with someone else?
6. God doesn't always speak loudly. When have you been able to discern God speaking to you? If you haven't been able to, what can you do to prepare yourself for listening to His voice?
7. Gratefulness is not always our first response, especially during trials. What are you grateful for today? Be thorough.
8. What are you learning about right now in your faith? How are you applying it?
9. Put a plan in place for memorizing and meditating on God's Word.

I Stand in Awe
Matthew 5:8

In Bill Moyers's book, *A World of Ideas II* (Main Street Books, 1990), Jacob Needleman remembers,

> I was an observer at the launch of Apollo 17 in 1975. It was a night launch, and there were hundreds of cynical reporters all over the lawn … The countdown came, and then the launch. The first thing you see is this extraordinary orange light … then comes this thing slowly rising up in total silence, because it takes a few seconds for the sound to come across … the sound goes through you. You can practically hear jaws dropping. The sense of wonder fills the whole place, as this "thing" goes up and up … until total silence. It's gone. People just get up quietly, helping each other up … These were suddenly moral people because the sense of wonder, the experience of wonder, had made them moral.

Imagine being present at Apollo 17's monumental launch. Now imagine what Christ-followers will experience when we see God! But how and when will we see Him? "Blessed are the pure in heart for they will see God!" (Matthew 5:8 NIV).

Seeing Jesus face-to-face will be nothing short of sublime. The promise in this verse is that if we have a pure heart, we will see Him. So then, how do we go about attaining a pure heart?

The word *pure* means to be free from inappropriate, inferior, and contaminating matter. Once we have a relationship with Jesus, the Holy Spirit in us will purify our hearts, instilling in us desires to be more like Him. Only through Him can we have a heart that is uncontaminated by the desires and pleasures of this world. We will have eyes to see and ears to hear, and our lives will be forever standing in awe in His presence.

—Tammy

Create in Me a Clean Heart
Psalm 51:1–12; 1 John 1:8–10; 2 Samuel 11–12

One of the things I used to get in trouble for in my growing-up years was being mouthy in situations when I should have kept my mouth shut. At times I could be disrespectful, opinionated, and strong-willed, and as a child, getting my mouth washed out with a bar of soap was a regular occurrence. Consequently my parents sent me to my room until I was ready to apologize. Sadly, I was often there for quite a while because I felt justified in what I said and how I said it and even blamed others for my outburst! Oh, life would have been so much easier for me had I been able to admit I was wrong and take ownership of my own behavior.

As you read Psalm 51 today, you will also want to read 2 Samuel 11–12, for the context of this psalm correlates directly with the events coinciding. David writes this psalm of confession after he sinned against God by committing adultery with Bathsheba followed by a snowball of sin. David was the king. He could generally do whatever he wanted without a whole lot of accountability (other than God and some advisors). But in this psalm, he clearly communicates lament over his sin and confesses with every inch of his soul to God, asking Him for His mercy and forgiveness. Moreover, David asks God, "Create in me a clean heart, O God. Renew a loyal spirit within me" (Psalm 51:10 NLT). David's desire is to change from the inside out, and he recognizes that only God can do that through the power of the Holy Spirit.

Confession and lament over our sin is inevitable if we want to continue growing on the Christian journey. No one arrives, no matter how biblically educated we are, how much we serve God, or how many hours we spend doing ministry.

> If we claim we have no sin, we are only fooling ourselves and not living in the truth. But if we confess our sins to him, he is faithful and just to forgive us our sins and to cleanse us from all wickedness. If we claim we have not sinned, we are calling God a liar and showing that his word has no place in our hearts. (1 John 1:8–10 NLT)

–Tammy

Get Out of the Fishbowl

Mark 1:16–20

I've owned many fish over the years: goldfish, beta fish, algae eaters, guppies, and angelfish. The list goes on. Some of them thrived in a small fishbowl, but for the larger fish, a larger fish tank was necessary. Once the fish were placed in their respective tanks, they were able to live out their days protected from predators and with the same-finned friends.

People are like fish. We are placed in our communities, growing comfortable with our familiar finned friends, and neglect to venture outside the bowl very often. Why? Because we feel safe and content in our bowl. Jesus wants us to get outside our fishbowl and cast our nets wider.

With this concept in mind, let's look at Mark 1:16–20 when Jesus called His first disciples. Simon and his brother Andrew were fishing in the Sea of Galilee. They were fishermen by trade, and as Jesus saw them on his walk along the shoreline, he called out to them, "Come, follow me, and I will show you how to fish for people" (Mark 1:17 NLT).

Jesus connected right away with Simon and Andrew through their livelihood of fishing. With a very simple to understand, yet sacrificial, call to action, Jesus asked them to come and follow Him. He asked them to drop everything, and they did. They left their daily job, their comfort zone, and their means of survival, and by faith, they chose to follow Jesus.

"Come follow me," (NLT Mark 1:17) Jesus says to us today. This means we may need to drop what we're doing, get a little uncomfortable, and venture outside our tank. Following Jesus may very well mean that we need to be willing to leave our fishbowl of family, friends, and community, if that is what Christ calls us to do.

Today, pray and ask God what getting out of the fishbowl means for you. Begin praying for those fish that are just outside your bowl. Pray also for God to give you joy in venturing out. As you follow in obedience, God will be glorified, as you will be a fisher of people as well!

–Tammy

Peer Pressure

2 Chronicles 20:1–19

You've probably heard the expression, "Jumping Jehoshaphat!" It sounds a little funny today, but it emerged in the nineteenth century during a movement to replace swear words and other offensive sayings with more unoffensive ones. The name Jehoshaphat directly derives from the biblical King Jehoshaphat who came to reign c. 873–849 BC at age thirty-five. He was a good king, and he removed many foreign baals (gods) from Israel. When you read this passage in 2 Chronicles, try to put yourself in that setting. Armies from the Moabites, Ammonites, and Meunites were declaring war on Jehoshaphat. Then the Bible says,

> Jehoshaphat was terrified by this news and begged the Lord for guidance. He also ordered everyone in Judah to begin fasting. So, people from all the towns of Judah came to Jerusalem to seek the Lord's help … As all the men of Judah stood before the Lord with their little ones, wives, and children, the Spirit of the Lord came upon one of the men standing … He said, "Listen, all you people of Judah and Jerusalem! Listen, King Jehoshaphat! This is what the Lord says: Do not be afraid! Don't be discouraged by this mighty army, for the battle is not yours, but God's … But you will not even need to fight. Take your positions; then stand still and watch the Lord's victory. He is with you." (2 Chronicles 20:1–19 NLT)

Do you ever begin to panic when outside pressures come upon you? Adults and children alike face peer pressure and can get easily persuaded to do things they wouldn't normally do without the pressure.

In Jehoshaphat's panic, the very first thing he did was beg the Lord for guidance. He then ordered everyone to pray and fast. The result? The Spirit of the Lord came upon them, and they stood still to watch the Lord work! May we all follow this example when pressures rise around us. May we seek God immediately, pray and fast, and allow Him to fight the battles that wage and press in on us. He will be victorious when we seek Him first!

—Tammy

Serenity in the Fire
Daniel 3

Think about the word *serenity* for a moment. I imagine that some of you had a very similar thought to mine, sitting on a soft, comfortable couch with that person you are closest to. You probably have a soft blanket thrown over you and, of course, a warm glow coming from the fireplace. The troubles of this world are probably far away from your mind.

My wife and I often enjoy time sitting by the fire, and serenity would describe that feeling. The story in Daniel 3, however, has the same elements of close friends and a warm fire, but a far different scenario going on. When I read this passage, I normally do not think of serenity!

The Jews were in captivity in Babylon during the reign of King Nebuchadnezzar. The king had a gold statue built that stood ninety feet tall. He decreed that at the sound of musical instruments, everyone should bow and worship King Nebuchadnezzar's gold statue. Failure to do so would mean being thrown into a blazing furnace. Knowing this worship of the gold statue would be a violation of God's commandments, this created a point of decision for the Jews. Three of those Jews we read about are Shadrach, Meshach, and Abednego. They refused to bow down.

Upon hearing of their refusal to bow down, the king summons them to his side and gives one last chance to bow before being thrown into the fire. Their reply was, "If we are thrown into the blazing furnace, the God whom we serve is able to save us … But even if he doesn't, we want to make it clear to you, Your Majesty, that we will never serve your gods or worship the gold statue you have set up" (Daniel 3:17–18 NLT). They knew with confidence their God could deliver them from something as impossible as the blazing furnace, and yet they also knew that even if He did not deliver them, they would not bow to another.

When I sit in front of the fire of serenity, things are either going well in my life, or I am taking a moment to put bad thoughts aside. The three men in Daniel have the utmost serenity in a situation that is direr than anything most of us have or likely will experience in our lives. Let us seek Him first and find this level of serenity in the fire.

—Mark

Loneliness in Widowhood
Ecclesiastes 4:12–13; Matthew 28:20

Loneliness in widowhood is very real. The void is painful, no matter how good or bad a marriage was. It is never easy when a loved one dies, but without God, the reality can be devastating.

My husband of almost forty-seven years passed away of colon cancer. We had a unique relationship, unlike any other. When Dale died, I felt like part of me had died too. I was numb for a while, but in time (and that's different for every person), I experienced a closeness with God that is indescribable.

> And one standing alone can be attacked and defeated, but two can stand back-to-back and conquer; three is even better, for a triple braided cord is not easily broken. (Ecclesiastes 4:12 NLT)

Even though Dale has gone on to be with the Lord and I now live alone, I know that I am never alone because God was the third part of the cord. But what about the marriage that had a lot of pain, maybe lacking the third strand, perhaps even yours? Loneliness may be an all-too-familiar feeling that you have lived with for years already. God wants to reach down and draw you close to Him. His presence is like nothing you have ever known, and He wants to be your comfort and your hope. He is here.

Being alone has its challenges, but the feelings of loneliness can be felt even amongst a crowded room. God can help us from being lonely. If you are lonely, I want to encourage you to seek God. Yes, there are times when I feel isolated, wishing I had someone to come home to. But I can catch myself by asking, "Am I keeping my eyes on Jesus and taking steps toward Him?" Am I balancing my alone times by being with friends and loved ones? God gives us new beginnings in widowhood.

I am comforted by this verse, "And be sure of this: I am with you always, even to the end of the age" (Matthew 28:20b NLT). When I feel lonely, I turn to God's Word and sing songs of praise to Him. His promises sustain me, and He always lifts me up!

—Sharon

Week 24 Reflections

1. After reviewing the Scriptures for each day, name three to four passages that jumped out at you this week.
2. How can you practically apply these verses to your life today and the upcoming week?
3. When have you experienced awe? How did you respond?
4. The content in our heart will at some point come out of our mouths. When has your mouth revealed to you what was truly in your heart?
5. Describe your fishbowl. On a scale from one to ten, what is your comfort level with your fish?
6. How can you get out of the fishbowl and reach out to people outside your circle?
7. We all face peer pressure in our lives. What does God say is the way to combat peer pressure in 2 Chronicles 20:1-19?
8. What is the big lesson from the story of Shadrach, Meshach, and Abednego?
9. What does God's Word tell us when we feel utterly alone? How is loneliness and being alone different?

MONTH 7

A Life of Good Deeds May Never Be Recognized by Anyone

A FAITH THAT STANDS
Affirms Our Purpose Through Christ

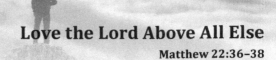

Love the Lord Above All Else

Matthew 22:36–38

When my husband and I were first married, we took a marriage class on love languages through our church. The five include words of encouragement, quality time, acts of service, gift-giving, and affection. Only being married two years, we were struggling with communicating love to each other and seeing eye to eye on important issues. At one point, we even discussed having our marriage dissolved, which was not in our belief system, because the issues we were having seemed impossible to tackle. As we learned more about the ways we communicated love to each other, the more we realized that we had opposite love languages!

From that point on, the awareness of how to love each other better and more completely and effectively saved our marriage. Today we have been married for twenty-seven years and can tell you that hard work, humility on both our parts, and the intervention of the Holy Spirit have helped us to be the best of friends, which we are still today!

Like marriage, when it comes to God, do we know how to love Him above all else? Are we cognizant of what pleases Him and what best gives Him honor and praise? And if we do know, are we acting on what we know with discipline and hard work?

If we are going to love God, we must first know *who* He is. He is our El Shaddai (Lord God Almighty), Jehovah Rapha (The Lord My Shepherd), Jehovah Rapha (The Lord That Heals), Jehovah Tsidkenu (The Lord Our Righteousness), Jehovah Jireh (The Lord Will Provide), and Jehovah Shalom (The Lord Is Peace). There are several more names for God in Scripture, but these are just some of His qualities! We praise Him because of these attributes and many more.

Knowing *who* God is allows us to connect with Him and draw close to Him. There is no greater privilege than to know and love our Creator. Loving God above all else requires us to first see Him for who He is. He then teaches us to love our neighbor in the same way, living our lives faithfully and completely surrendering to Him.

May we strive to know God so intimately that we are able to love the Lord above all else.

–Tammy

Love Others Like He Does

Matthew 22:39; John 13:34–35

It was late on Christmas Eve, and our family was eager to see both sets of grandparents over the Christmas holidays. We had a long trip ahead of us, so we decided to get a head start that evening to be able to arrive earlier the next day on Christmas. We packed the car with our suitcases, loading the presents we had for everyone, including the handmade gifts Scott and Matt had made in their woodworking classes. A few months prior, we had bought Scott a new trumpet, which he also packed in order to play for the grandparents. Yes, there was much excitement for this visit.

Late on that cold and snowy evening, we pulled into the hotel parking lot. We were roughly halfway on our trip, and we were very happy to get tucked into our warm and cozy beds. Just thirty minutes into our sleep, the telephone in the room woke us. It was the front desk asking us to come down to the lobby, as there was an issue with our car. When Tammy and I got there, we saw two police officers who informed us that our car had been broken into and that everything was stolen. After taping cardboard over the broken windows, we returned to our room, unable to sleep, wondering how we could go on tomorrow.

The hotel night manager gave me a name of a guy he recommended to help with repairs. I called him on Christmas morning, and he arranged to meet me at his shop. We managed to use plastic and tape to get us on the road to family, where we later got proper fixes completed. Who gives up their Christmas morning to help a stranger? We talked about Christmas as we worked together to patch up the windows and realized that we were both Christians. He was fully exemplifying the two passages for today and taking them to their fullest in many ways.

The repairman's example to our family demonstrated that everyone he meets is his neighbor. Jesus tells us in John that our love for each other will prove to the world that we are His followers. Showing this love to our neighbors won't always be easy for us. But if we follow Jesus' commandment, what an impact we might have on our neighbors in their daily lives on earth and quite possibly in eternity.

– Mark

Just Say No

Titus 2

"For the grace of God has appeared that offers salvation to all people. It teaches us to say 'No' to ungodliness and worldly passions, and to live self-controlled, upright and godly lives in this present age" (Titus 2:12 NIV).

In 1982, then-First Lady Nancy Reagan launched an anti-drug campaign famously known as "Just Say No." Mrs. Reagan poured out every effort into this campaign, speaking in schools, writing and producing newspaper articles and editorials, and seeking support from the movie theaters to support her cause in her public announcements.

Since that time, some people have criticized this slogan, saying it was out of touch with reality and that it was too simple-minded for teens to accept, consequently turning it into a pop-culture joke in years to come.

But was this slogan really out of touch? Biblically, Paul gives us the same instructions, "to just say 'No' to ungodliness and worldly passions" (Titus 2:12 NIV). If you think about it, every decision we make is a yes or a no. There is no gray area when it comes to following God. We can't pick and choose what we follow and what we don't, for God calls us to live self-controlled, upright, and godly lives. Godliness and worldly passions cannot coexist.

There will always be criticism from those who don't understand God and His Word. We can't expect them to understand, as we did not understand before we knew God either. If we are going to do good in this world and set a godly example for others, less is more. "No" is a straightforward answer to the temptations that come our way, luring us into potential sin areas. The more we use it, the easier it gets.

Nancy Reagan's slogan about saying no to drugs may not have been very popular; however, saying "no" to the world is not popular. We might as well accept that when we choose to follow Jesus. How do we represent Jesus in our actions and set a godly example to those around us? By acting in a simple way, to just say "no" to the temptations in life and follow His leading.

—Tammy

Accountability in Conflict
1 Peter 3:8–12; Galatians 2:11–16; Philippians 4:2–3

Relationships are messy. Whether we like it or not, people will disappoint us, betray us, and do and say things that hurt us. Conflict is very difficult unless we are intentional about making amends with those individuals who have hurt us. I have learned over the years that I desperately need godly, objective people in my life to hold me accountable to nudge me toward unity and peace when I am faced with opposition or personal misunderstandings.

One biblical example we see of accountability is in Philippians 4:2–3. Two women, Euodia and Syntyche, had an unnamed conflict that they could not resolve. Paul challenged them in these verses to settle their disagreement so they could put the conflict behind them for the sake of the kingdom. I love the boldness of Paul to speak truth in love and provide an outside voice to a situation that wasn't getting resolved.

Another example of accountability is in Galatians 2:11–16 when Paul writes to the Galatian church, telling them about the time he had to confront Peter face-to-face. Paul explains that Peter had been taught by Jesus that faith in God and love for others outweighed legalistic laws that had for so many years governed the Jewish people. Yet Peter succumbed to the swaying a few of James' friends to not eat with the Gentiles after finding out they were not circumcised (Jewish law). Peter knew this was wrong and hypocritical, but in his humanity, he was afraid of criticism by James' friends. This unintentionally influenced Barnabas to the same hypocrisy, and Paul was bold in reminding them of their offense to God.

The Christian life was never intended to be lived alone. We need each other! We were never meant to live a holy life without the Holy Spirit or godly influences connected with us. And as always, the holy Word of God is our best accountability ever as we continue to run this race until our final reward in heaven (1 Peter 3:8–9).

—Tammy

The Power of the Example
Proverbs 22:6; Matthew 5:16; Titus 2:7–8a

I am seventy-seven years old. The older I get, I find myself wondering, *What will people remember about me when I'm gone from this earth? Did I make an impact in this world? Did I do things that really mattered?* "In the same way, let your light shine before others, so that they may see your good works and glorify your Father, who is in heaven" (Matthew 5:16 NIV).

In everything I do, I ultimately want to bring honor and glory to God. I asked my daughter what she remembered about me in setting an example for her while she was growing up. She first made a joke and said, "I remember you didn't like to fold socks!" But then she seriously replied, "I remember you sitting at the dining room table every morning, reading your Bible." I had no idea she was watching me. I was just doing what I did without giving it much thought. "Show yourself in all respects to be a model of good works, and in your teaching show integrity, dignity, and sound speech that cannot be condemned ..." (Titus 2:7–8 NIV).

Truly, our example speaks louder than words and is more powerful than we could ever imagine. God is watching. Family is watching. Everyday people are observing our habits, our reactions, our language, and mostly our love for others. Indeed we do teach by example. Now, both my daughters are mature Christians, serving the Lord in many mighty ways. I encourage you today that the example you set will leave a legacy for generations to come.

"Direct your children onto the right path, and when they are older, they will not leave it" (Proverbs 2:6 NLT).

—Sharon

Suffering Never Wasted

Genesis 50:20

Mark and I recently took a trip out to Missoula, Montana, to see our son Scott, who is assisting in growing and pastoring a church plant. We had never been to that part of the country before and were in awe of the exquisite beauty of the five mountain ranges that surround the city.

While we ventured on some sightseeing, we learned about forest fires on those mountains, viewing one of the mountain ranges that had been hit by fire two years ago. Forest fires can destroy everything in their paths and take a long time to heal. However, the fires are also doing something good that couldn't be done without them. They refresh the soil, spur on new growth of seeds, and cleanse the area of disease and destructive insects.

What nature destroys, God uses to create something new and good. Similarly, what Satan means for bad in our lives, God turns the devastation into something new and amazing. Today I encourage you to read the story about Joseph in Genesis 50. Joseph was horribly mistreated by his jealous brothers, but as you look at the end of the story, you will see how God's plan unfolded. God used Joseph's imprisonment, lies against him, and eventually his royal position to mold Joseph into the godly, influential leader that he was. When Joseph's father Jacob passed away, Joseph's brothers were concerned that Joseph would turn on them for revenge.

> But Joseph replied, "Don't be afraid of me. Am I God, that I can punish you? You intended to harm me, but God intended it all for good ..." (Genesis 50:19–20 NLT)

Joseph's mercy represented God's mercy. I'm sure there were still scars from the damage that was done to Joseph in being sold into slavery by his brothers. However, God used every bit of Joseph's suffering to fit into a divine plan that God laid out. No one can understand God's ways, but if we are faithful through our hardships and count it all joy, God will not waste one minute of it. He loves us so much. Hold on to Jesus and put your trust in Him. Our suffering is never wasted!

Week 25 Reflections

1. After reviewing the Scriptures for each day, name three to four passages that jumped out at you this week.
2. How can you practically apply these verses to your life today and the upcoming week?
3. Who is God to you, and how do you show Him that you love Him?
4. What neighbors has God put in your path this week? Were you able to show them God's love? If so, how?
5. Who or what do you need to say no to? Pray about this. Ask a friend or family member if they see something in your life that you don't see.
6. People are watching you: how you respond, how you follow Jesus or not, and how you love people. What do you think people are noticing in you?
7. Name a time when something of yours was destroyed but God used it for the good.
8. What does God want you to remember the next time you go through a loss?
9. When it comes to leaving a legacy, what is the most important thing(s) to you?

The God Who Sees

Genesis 16:1–13; Deuteronomy 31:8; Matthew 25:21

1990 was the year when the movie *Ghost* came out. The main character had been killed, leaving his ghost behind to track down who had murdered him. Since he was invisible, he had the unique opportunity to do things without anyone seeing him at all. Perhaps being invisible for a day might be fun. But being invisible would probably be a very lonely existence.

In the story of Sarai, Abraham, and Hagar in Genesis 16, Sarai is unable to conceive a child. Consequently, she sends her husband, Abraham, to lay with her servant, Hagar, in order to have a baby. Hagar conceives and has a son but looks on Sarai with contempt. Sarai then treats Hagar terribly and eventually causes Hagar to run away. God sends Hagar back to Sarai, but before that, He listens to Hagar and draws close to her.

Hagar exclaims, "You are the God who sees me!" (Genesis 16:13 NLT). She must have felt alone and invisible. This had not been her idea to lay with Sarai's husband; nor did she find it too exciting to have his child. On top of that, Sarai mistreated her, and Hagar had no defender. In her greatest time of loneliness and grief, God saw her and drew close to her!

As human beings, we thrive on being known by other people. We yearn to have purpose and a place to belong. We don't enjoy feeling invisible, and we long to be seen. But God sees us! He sees the way we live our life. He sees the sacrifices we make and the people we love. He sees our acts of service and our words of kindness. God sees. He knows. "Do not be afraid or discouraged, for the Lord will personally go ahead of you. He will be with you; he will neither fail you nor abandon you" (Deuteronomy 31:8 NLT).

Someday we will pass on and people will celebrate our lives. The music will play, eulogies will be read, and a message will be given. But we won't hear any of it. Recognition won't matter. Appreciation won't matter. All that will matter is that God saw every breath we took and heard every cry. He is the God who sees you now and your God forevermore.

–Tammy

Health Is Fleeting
Psalm 73:25–26

At age eighteen, I met Mary, my wife-to-be. We quickly fell in love, soon became engaged, and married in about two years. It was during this second year of dating that I realized Mary had a hearing loss. She was born with 90 percent hearing loss in one ear and 30 percent loss in the other. How could I have not noticed? Mary was skilled at placing herself in the best position to hear others. She also taught herself to do some lip-reading.

In our first year of marriage, I had an aunt and uncle (a pastor) who would write us to let us know they were praying for Mary to have a healing from God. One of those letters contained information that would change our lives forever. They told us of a healing evangelist who was going to be in a town close to us and encouraged us to attend one of the services. We made the trip and attended.

The first half of the service was a message of salvation, and at the close of this service, we gave our hearts and lives to Jesus. The combination of peace and joy we received was amazing.

The second half of the service was a message of God's healing power. At the close of this service when the call to come forward for physical healing was given, Mary looked at me and said, "I believe I have already received the reason I'm here today." For the next nearly sixty years, Mary's life showed me that she had been correct.

Mary experienced many other health problems such as migraine headaches, osteoporosis, tumors that affected both hearing and vision, facial paralysis, and Parkinson's disease. Yet, through all these health issues, I saw Mary live by these words, "I desire you more than anything on earth. My health may fail, and my spirit may grow weak, but God remains the strength of my heart; he is mine forever" (Psalm 73:25–26 NLT).

Even though Mary's body seemed weak, the peace and joy of the Lord that Mary received the day she accepted Jesus as her Lord and Savior remained strong to the moment she left us, to the beginning of the promised life with perfect health forever. Health may be fleeting, but our souls live on for eternity when we know Jesus as our Savior.

—Dean

Hope in Despair

Job 3:20–26, 42:12–17

Nothing can affect the soul like utter despair. Extreme loss and grief can inflict the kind of pain that can paralyze even the most energetic, strong, and positive of people. I have walked alongside friends who have gone through a time like this. I have also experienced my own personal losses. Yet the accounts of loss that Job went through seem incomparable.

Although we know little of the timing of when Job lived, most scholars believe the book is the most ancient in the Bible and that Job was probably a contemporary of Abraham, Lot, and Isaac, putting his life around 2200 BC between the flood and Moses.

Clues that indicate this timing are that his wealth was measured in livestock rather than gold and that he personally offered sacrifices for his family (instead of a priest). Job also gave an inheritance to not only his sons, but also to his daughters. This indicates that he lived before the law of Moses.

The book of Job begins with an introduction to Job's character. He is described as a godly and blessed man with many children, lots of land, livestock, and wealth. The Lord's praise of Job prompts a fallen angel called Satan to suggest that Job served God simply because God blessed and protected him. Therefore, Satan asked God for permission to torment Job to convince him to turn his back on God.

God said ok to this if Job himself were spared, so Satan killed all of Job's children, livestock, and servants and inflicted Job with horrible sores all over his body. But Scripture also tells us, despite his wife wanting Job to "curse God and die" (Job 2:9 NLT), Job praised God, saying, "I came naked from my mother's womb, and I will be naked when I leave. The Lord gave me what I had, and the Lord has taken it away. Praise the name of the Lord!'" (Job 1:21 NLT).

Job's faith was strong, and he never sinned in his anger. Because of this, the Lord blessed him abundantly. Job became wealthier than before his inflictions and was given ten more children and numerous animals. I want to be like Job. If I lose what is valuable to me, I want to close my eyes, praise Him, and trust Him to bring hope through my despair.

—Tammy

Life is But a Breath
Psalm 39:1–7

Sometimes I feel small. Ok, if I'm honest, I feel extremely insignificant when I consider the whole world. I don't feel depressed, but rather minuscule in consideration of all that God has made. Have you ever flown in an airplane looking down at a massive city in lights and considered all the life that is represented in just a few square miles? So many people! Just one little me.

Feeling insignificant and small is not necessarily a bad thing if we use those feelings to embrace the pathway to understanding God's power and authority. Making ourselves less so that He can become more only deepens our understanding of the miracle of a unique purpose God has given every person. Even the animals, every plant and weed, every grain of sand, and every star that is millions of miles away have a purpose through God. Yes, we may feel small, but God's grand purpose involves you and me. He knows you better than anyone on this earth because He formed you from scratch, inside and out, and in His image!

> Lord, remind me how brief my time on earth will be. Remind me that my days are numbered—how fleeting my life is. You have made my life no longer than the width of my hand. My entire lifetime is just a moment to you; at best, each of us is but a breath … (Psalm 39:4–5 NLT)

So what do we do with this? Does our life not matter because it is only like a breath to God? No! Our lives matter. He created us to love Him and to love others as Jesus loves others. He wants to be actively and intricately involved in our decision-making, our goals, our relationships, and our work. We can't get hung up on our insignificance that comes from recognizing our mortality. We might give our life away in service for the Lord, only to be forgotten tomorrow. But the legacy of love we leave will leave its imprint on the generations to come, leading others to know the same Jesus we do. That alone will stand forever!

–Tammy

Dead Bones Walking

1 Corinthians 15:35–58; Ephesians 5:15–17

Years ago, a missionary came to our church to speak. The part of his message that caught my attention was how naturally and freely he shared his personal testimony with others. "Dead bones walking" is the phrase he used when referring to his transformed life through Jesus. His astute awareness of the victory he experienced through Christ gave him an eternal perspective that challenged me to reevaluate my own life. In terms of the eternal, I needed to take to heart daily that following Jesus was much more than saying a prayer to accept Him, going to church and serving. Jesus had called me to share my testimony with others.

1 Corinthians 15:35–58 reminds us that the sin in our lives equals death. I compare this to having a loved one who has passed away whom I am grieving the loss. If that person were to suddenly rise and walk, even though they were dead, I would know that I had just witnessed the most amazing and glorious miracle. Likewise, Paul is writing here that the sin in our lives is death. Period. When we repent of our sin and decide to live for Jesus, we are like the dead person coming to life again, and this is news we need to share!

> {Jesus said}, If any of you wants to be my follower, you must give up your own way, take up your cross daily, and follow me. If you try to hang on to your life, you will lose it. But if you give up your life for my sake, you will save it. (Luke 9:23–24 NLT)

The question for all of us today is this: If we decide to follow Jesus, daily taking up our cross to follow Him, does this knowledge sink in so deeply in our soul that we are "making the most of every opportunity, because the days are evil" (Ephesians 5:15 NLT)?

Or do we live as though this is our final home, looking for comfort, safety, wealth, and acceptance from others? Jesus told us that we will suffer and endure hardships for following Him. Remember, if sin is death, people are dying all around us. The time is now to be a living testimony, a witness that we too are "dead bones walking."

—Tammy

The Missing Puzzle Piece

Luke 15:1–32

During COVID, when many of us were quarantining for several months, jigsaw puzzles were my go-to. The bigger the better, and I spent hours putting one thousand- to three thousand-piece puzzles together. I didn't do these alone. After all, I had a helper! For those of you who have a cat, you will understand that my little puzzle helper in furry form loves to play with the pieces, occasionally knocking them onto the floor. This poses a problem for me toward the end of the puzzle when I realize that one or two pieces are missing. Every piece is important. 1,999 pieces may be in, but the picture is not complete until I have all pieces accounted for.

Jesus taught a parable very similar to this. If a shepherd has a hundred sheep and one goes astray, the shepherd doesn't just forget about the one because he has ninety-nine left. No! He goes and looks for that lost sheep because every sheep is valuable to him. They complete his flock.

A good shepherd is protective of his sheep and will sacrifice his own safety for the life of one of his own. He is trustworthy and knows what endangers the flock or what can make them ill. Jesus is that good shepherd. Perhaps you've backslidden and fallen into a bad time in your life. Did you know that Jesus is trying to pull you back? He is taking his staff to hook you back to him. He has not forgotten you, even if you have temporarily forgotten about Him!

Jesus wants you to come home. The time is now. He is not ashamed of you or shocked by your sin. In fact, Scripture tells us, "Tax collectors and other notorious sinners often came to listen to Jesus teach. This made the Pharisees and teachers of religious law complain that he was associating with such sinful people—even eating with them!" (Luke 15:1–2 NLT).

Jesus spent lots of time with sinful people because He loved them too much to let them stay in their own sin. The same goes for you and me. He loves us way too much to let us walk away from Him and not come back. If you feel that nudge that you have wandered off, stop in your tracks. Don't look back. Close your eyes, picture Jesus' face, and start walking to Him. After all, He's running after you!

—Tammy

Week 26 Reflections

1. After reviewing the Scriptures for each day, name three to four passages that jumped out at you this week.
2. How can you practically apply these verses to your life today and the upcoming week?
3. Name a time when you have felt invisible. Have you ever wished you were invisible? Why or why not?
4. Other than physical healing, what are all the ways we can count on God to heal us?
5. What can we learn from Job and his response to God through his suffering?
6. We may feel insignificant at times, but God has given us divine significance. What do you believe your significance and purpose is? Be specific.
7. Are you an example of "dead bones walking" through Jesus? What does that mean to you?
8. There is an urgency to follow Jesus because life is unpredictable. What, if anything, is holding you back?
9. When it comes to spiritual discussions, do you find them stressful? That could be an indicator that your soul is searching. Don't be afraid. Write your thoughts out and pray.

Focus on the Unseen
2 Corinthians 4:17–18

My heart breaks every time I see news about someone being murdered in the community around me. The breakdown of the family and morals in society has left me questioning whether little old me can do anything to help. While homelessness and mental illnesses wreak havoc on those we know and love, the problems seem too large for any one person to tackle, except through prayer.

Every Thursday morning, I pray with a friend who talks and prays through some of these issues with me. We agree that the systemic and heart issues are so overwhelming that all we can do is lay them at the Lord's feet and ask Him to show us our part in making things better. If we are not careful, we can be swept away with grief and discouragement. The spiritual battle is raging around us, and we need to have faith that God is working despite all that we see.

Paul writes a letter to the Corinthians to encourage them to live out their faith in Jesus, explaining how he has personally endured such sufferings. This is what he says to them,

> For our present troubles are small and won't last very long. Yet they produce for us a glory that vastly outweighs them and will last forever! So we don't look at the troubles we can see now; rather, we fix our gaze on things that cannot be seen. For the things we see now will soon be gone, but the things we cannot see will last forever. (2 Corinthians 4:17–18 NLT)

We will never be able to solve the universal problems that plague our world. However, as we faithfully trust that God is always working and moving in our midst, we can do our part by interceding in prayer for others. We can focus on heavenly things rather than the evils of this world. We can love people one at a time and pray for people every day. No, we can't see the spiritual battle with our own two eyes, but it is raging all around us. Let us not be fearful Christians. Let us willingly focus our eyes to see the power of an almighty God.

—Tammy

Weary in Doing Good
Galatians 6:9–10

Being a construction worker, I had many times when I was tired and weary. This weariness was generally physical tiredness, but at times it was emotional exhaustion. In Galatians 6, Paul encourages us not to get tired of doing what is good. He also tells us that at just the right time, we will reap a harvest of blessing if we don't give up.

I am ninety-two years old. But years ago, my wife, Mary, and I, along with our three kids, were asked to help start up a Sunday afternoon church in a tiny town thirty minutes away. This church had no pastor and was struggling to remain open. The church met in a very old building with three single wires hanging down from the ceiling with single light bulbs. It had no running water, so the outhouse was just beyond the building. After three months, the pastor who invited our family to come informed us that he would no longer be able to help, now asking us to take the lead. We had seen some growth to thirty people, and this was our first blessing that led us to say yes to the pastor and to the Holy Spirit.

Two years later, the congregation had doubled again to sixty. They were given land outside of town, and the desire to build a new church was started. After much prayer and meeting some goals we had established, we began what would be a nineteen-month building project. This was all done during evenings and Saturdays while still being a full-time bricklayer and a lay pastor on Sundays and beyond. I was certainly given an opportunity to grow weary, even in doing good.

Despite the full schedule and physical labor, we witnessed many amazing things happen during the building project. Not just people from our church, but some of my construction friends as well volunteered to help build this new church. We had materials donated or given at deep discounts. Most importantly, however, we were seeing people give their hearts to the Lord, which encouraged us greatly.

During this period of our lives when Mary and I should have been the weariest people around, God provided a harvest of blessing at just the right time so we would not give up. We are forever grateful.

—Dean

Not by Works
Ephesians 2:7–9

I knew an individual years ago whose family went through a myriad of back-to-back tragedies. People from all over the community reached out to help. Sadly, whenever others would try to help, whether with financial provision, groceries, or simple care, the family was not able to accept the charity. They felt guilty, feeling the need to earn what was given, and did not want to be in debt to other people. However, they eventually came around and graciously received help even though it was not easy for them.

I have been there, finding it uncomfortable to be on the receiving end of a gift, especially when it is something far beyond what I would expect from someone. In times like those, I begin to question myself whether I expressed my thanks sufficiently or entertain ideas of what I should give to that person in return. Human nature urges us to not get something for nothing, which explains why earning our way makes us feel better in receiving from others.

Subsequently, because of our nature, the gift of salvation is hard to grasp and receive sometimes. Receiving such an unfathomable gift for free can seem incomprehensible. It is much easier for people to believe that they can do good works to help pay for salvation, earning their way into a love that was divinely given by our Creator than to accept this gift with no strings attached. This love is personal, and God gives it to all who accept it for free.

> God saved you by his grace when you believed. And you can't take credit for this; it is a gift from God. Salvation is not a reward for the good things we have done, so none of us can boast about it. (Ephesians 2:8–9 NLT)

God delights in our good works. Good works are fruits that come from allowing the Holy Spirit to be alive and well in us. Works are a direct result of the choice we make to accept His gift of salvation. They do not pay for this gift, but beautifully edify what has already been given to us!

—Tammy

Spiritual Gifts
1 Corinthians 12:1–11; Galatians 5:22

I am fascinated by God's creativity and generosity in how He bestows spiritual gifts to every Christ-follower. By giving us gifts of the Spirit, God allows us to be a part of His grand story by loving and edifying the body of Christ.

In 1 Corinthians 12:1–3, Paul makes it very clear that the Holy Spirit gives gifts only to those who say that Jesus is Lord and refuse to bow down to mute idols. There are several gifts that God gives to people, but all in the same Spirit and serving the same Lord. Now, one thing to understand is that spiritual gifts are not the same thing as the fruits of the Spirit. Fruits of the Spirit come from having the Holy Spirit dwell in us. They are listed as "love, joy, peace, patience, gentleness, kindness, goodness, faithfulness, and self-control" (Galatians 5:22–23 NLT). These fruits are nurtured in every single Christ-follower, while God additionally and uniquely gives out spiritual gifts to His children.

Some of the spiritual gifts are listed in 1 Corinthians 12: wisdom, knowledge, faith, healing, miracles, prophecy, discernment, tongues, and interpreting tongues. Other gifts are noted throughout the Bible, such as teaching, encouragement, helping, pastor/shepherd, leadership, hospitality, and more.

Spiritual gifts are designed to reflect Jesus and to be used to build one another up. They are never to be abused by developing pride in us or taking advantage of others. For example, one of my spiritual gifts is leadership, but that doesn't mean I have to lead everything and everyone all the time. Being a good leader means being a good follower and serving others as well. Additionally, the gift of helps is not as natural for me. However, this does not exempt me from helping in certain situations just because the gift of helps isn't "my gift." God wants to strengthen this area in me by helping and serving others.

If you'd like to learn what your spiritual gifts are, I encourage you to go online and take a spiritual gifts test. Then pray that God will show you how, when, and where you can best use your gifts to glorify Him and edify the body as a whole! Be encouraged!

–Tammy

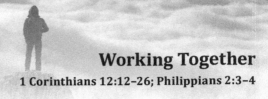

Working Together

1 Corinthians 12:12–26; Philippians 2:3–4

Our bodies are complicated. Have you ever had vertigo and the whole room spun around you? I have experienced this several times, mostly in my adult years. In the times I've suffered from this, I have not been able to walk, eat, see, or do anything that required movement. I have been, in essence, paralyzed.

You may know where this is going, especially after reading today's Scripture passage in 1 Corinthians 12. Christians make up the body of Christ. We are to function together in unity, understanding that this is the greatest need if the body is going to be a healthy body. We can't be a hand who wishes they were a brain or be jealous of a foot because it gets to walk. Jesus stresses the importance of unity among believers because when Christians work together for the same purpose, God is glorified, and people will come to Christ. If one part of the body goes astray or isn't well for one reason or another, the result is that it hurts the body as a whole.

Somewhere between AD 53 and 57, Paul visited Corinth and stayed there for about eighteen months. As he went on to continue spreading the good news of Jesus to other cities, he heard of the disunity in the Corinthian church. The leaders had caused division in the church by claiming that some spiritual gifts were superior to others, creating a hierarchy of sorts in the body of Christ. Paul proceeded to write a letter to the church of Corinth (the book of Corinthians) to address this issue. He explained that there is no hierarchy or favoritism in the Christian body. We are to work together with mutual respect, humility, and reverence for God.

I have seen firsthand in modern-day churches the importance placed on those with gifts on stage versus those with gifts behind the scenes. How can we model the body of Christ better in our churches? By heeding the words of Paul,

> Don't be selfish; don't try to impress others. Be humble, thinking of others as better than yourselves. Don't look out only for your own interests, but take an interest in others, too. (Philippians 2:3–4 NLT)

–Tammy

Action Plan

James 2:14–20

Think about a time when you set a goal. Most of the time when I set a goal, it is with faith that I can achieve that result. Goals wonderfully keep me pointed toward a true north. If you are like me though, you probably can think of some goals you achieved and some you missed on. Those I missed were mostly due to not having an action plan. I might be excited about achieving the goal and envisioning success. However, without an action plan, those goals are at great risk.

At work, I take this even further. I set up action plans with timing for key steps to be completed. Then I will assign people and a budget as necessary, establishing metrics to track with reviews along the way to measure progress. I want to see the actions that allow me to know that the goal is possible. If someone on my team tells me they have a goal, but they have no action plan, I will question them about how they expect to see their goal to completion.

I love the book of James for its practical nature. In chapter two, he tells us of a debate going on about faith and deeds. James asks what good is it if someone claims to have faith but has no deeds. James gets right to the point as he states that faith by itself, if not accompanied by action, is dead. That point should be a wake-up call to each one of us.

But James also does not leave us with deeds alone at the expense of faith. Rather he reminds us of some key examples where Abraham and Rahab, both in very different situations, put actions to their faith. In doing so, their faith and actions were working together. In the case of Abraham, James states that his faith was made **complete** by what he **did**. The word *complete* says to me that God finished what He started in Abraham, meaning that God will do the same for you and me.

In my work example, goals and actions are both great and necessary to achieve complete success. But one without the other clearly has something missing. James is clear that both faith and deeds are wonderful, but one without the other leaves us incomplete. Let's take action as the Holy Spirit leads us so our faith can be made complete.

Week 27 Reflections

1. After reviewing the Scriptures for each day, name three to four passages that jumped out at you this week.
2. How can you practically apply these verses to your life today and the upcoming week?
3. What did Paul mean by focusing on the unseen rather than what is seen?
4. We can become weary in doing good. How does God promise to help when this happens to us?
5. Have you ever felt that you needed to earn your way to heaven?
6. What does God say about our works in regard to our salvation?
7. Have you taken a spiritual gifts test? I encourage you to go online and take the test. What are your gifts?
8. The body of Christ is designed to work together in unity. What is your part in the body?
9. Faith and actions work hand in hand. How is the Holy Spirit calling you to act on your faith?

Unity in the Body
Ephesians 4:1–16

Unity carries with it a high calling. Jesus placed utmost importance on forgiveness, patience, and humility, all leading to unity in the church. Relationships can be sticky, but as Christ-followers, the love we have for each other is a testimony of God's love.

> I (Paul) beg you to live a life worthy of your calling, for you have been called by God ... Always be humble and gentle. Be patient with each other, making allowance for each other's faults because of your love. (Ephesians 4:1–2 NLT)

Why do you think Paul begs? If we are Christians, shouldn't we automatically desire to live a life worthy of our calling? But Paul saw dissension taking hold in the church of Ephesus, and he felt strongly about addressing it with these instructions. The biggest challenge I have seen in the church is making allowance for people's faults. There seems to be an expectation that when a person begins to follow Jesus, faults will begin to diminish. But let's clarify something: faults are not necessarily sins. Yes, sin should start to diminish, but faults include our personality quirks, our baggage we carry from our upbringing, and a lack of gifting in certain areas. We all have faults.

Years ago, I knew an amazing pastor with deep integrity and heart for God who lacked business sense. He is now in heaven with the Lord, but at one time in his career, he was deeply hurt by a church who treated him terribly for unknowingly mishandling finances. This was a fault, not a sin, and certainly not a reason to be treated poorly.

Similarly, I am a musician with an artistic temperament. I am a leader and passionate about what I do. However, that same passion leads to deep emotions and boldness at times. Yet I have suffered the hurt of unforgiveness and misunderstanding from others because of those traits.

As we move forward in our faith walk, let's not have to be begged to make allowance for others' faults. Instead, let us make every effort to live in the Spirit with peace, patience, and humility.

—Tammy

Not in Our Strength
Matthew 11:28–30

We just finished watching the Tokyo Olympics. Every couple of years when the Olympics are on, we become familiar with athletes who have trained for much of their lives. I am sure that they sometimes experience weariness, potentially even having thoughts of quitting a race or the sport altogether. The Tokyo Olympics was especially tough on the long-distance runners as the heat and humidity was a burden they could not have normally trained for. We saw many world-class athletes drop out of the races as they could not continue under these conditions.

Beyond the physical struggles we can face at times, we will also face burdens that will tear at our souls. This pressure on our souls can come from burdens placed on us by other people in our life or even burdens we place on ourselves.

In the New Testament, we read about the Pharisees who continually added rules to the Ten Commandments given to Moses. Eventually they added over six hundred man-made rules that placed great pressure and stress on the people. We can imagine the difficulty for the people to remember all these rules, much less to be able to follow them every day. Where would they find relief to these burdens? Where can we find relief from our burdens today?

"Jesus said, 'Come to me, all of you who are weary and carry heavy burdens, and I will give you rest'" (Matthew 11:28 NLT). This sounds great until we next read that we are to take his yoke upon us. At this point, we are reminded that following Jesus is not easy and will have challenges and hardships. But unlike the no-win obstacles of man-made legalism, Jesus offers something so much better, His promise to teach us.

Because He is humble and has a gentle heart, if we are willing to come under His authority, He offers for us to learn from Him. What an amazing thought to know our Creator is willing to teach us how to navigate the challenges of our lives. He has been through it all before and knows exactly what we can handle and how we should approach each step in our lives. We will have the strength to persevere because He is always with us.

—Mark

Our Identity and Purpose
Psalm 39:4–5; Jeremiah 17:5–8; Galatians 5:22–26

I am what some may consider to be a morbid thinker by nature. I sometimes ponder what people might say about me at my funeral. Will they be things based on what I did or characteristics of who I was as a person? Highlighting my performances or my integrity? All I know is this: I have one life to live, and I want to make the most of it.

When I was young, I engrossed myself in music, primarily the piano, and would play for hours a day after school. I performed well as a musician. I knew that God had given me these gifts, and as I grew older, I found my identity and worth in these abilities. Often people openly recognized my talents, praising me for my abilities, allowing me over time to see my worth solely in the talents that I possessed.

I hit a crisis point in my twenties when I was not chosen for a position that I felt I deserved. The reasons don't matter now, but this rejection hurt me far greater than it ever should have. The evidence from my stomped-on identity came out in light depression, anger, and jealousy of others. It was then I realized that my identity and purpose were in my gifts and talents rather than in who I was in Christ Jesus.

Through working with a counselor, I relearned what my purpose and identity through Christ looked like, something I didn't fully realize thoroughly until even later into my thirties. This is what I learned:

1. God made me to stand alone as me, not to be compared with anyone else.
2. I am not what I do.
3. When I become less, He becomes more.
4. Accomplishments are temporary, but serving God and others is an eternal legacy.

As we read through Psalm 39:4–5 and Jeremiah 17:5—8, we are reminded that our time here on earth is short. But if we find our purpose and identity in Jesus Christ, planting ourselves in Him, then our roots will grow deep, and we will not fear when the world goes against us. We will stand firm in our identity that reflects the love of Jesus in all we do and speak. This is our purpose, and this is our legacy after we are gone!

—Tammy

"Repurposing" Paul

Acts 9:1–31

One of my favorite stories in the New Testament is the conversion of Saul to Paul. It pulls at my heartstrings because Paul did a 180-degree change when Jesus got a hold of him. That gives me hope that God can transform me and use my weaknesses to serve as strengths when God gets ahold of me!

Saul was a pharisee. Because of that, he persecuted Christ-followers and murdered and imprisoned those who believed Jesus was the Son of God. Saul was extremely passionate about his role, and he was well-known for his brutality and severe harshness. Quite frankly, Saul was the last person anyone would have expected to believe in Jesus and especially to fight for the opposite cause.

Then, years after Jesus' death and resurrection, something miraculous happened! Saul, later known as Paul, was walking on the road to Damascus when he saw a very bright light and heard a booming voice. It was Jesus. Although Saul was blinded and could not see Him, he heard Him, as did his fellow friends. Upon hearing Jesus, Saul was led by his friends to Damascus where he fasted and prayed for three days. As Ananias was instructed by God, he entered the house where Saul was and placed his hands over Saul's eyes. The scales fell off and the Holy Spirit came upon him. Saul believed In Jesus and was immediately baptized.

Paul spent the rest of his life using the same passion and fervor to build the church instead of going against it, leading people to follow Jesus. Paul trained missionaries such as Timothy and Titus and traveled ten thousand miles by foot to over twenty-seven cities in Greece, Turkey, and Syria. Paul established at least fourteen churches, and the church continues today, recognizing the same transformative power of Jesus as back in Bible times.

God repurposed Paul by redirecting his passion to spread the gospel instead of fighting against it. Likewise, when God changes our hearts, He will do some amazing things in us and through us.

Paul left a legacy. He was later imprisoned, beaten, tortured, and murdered for the sake of Christ. Even as he lay in prison, writing letters to the churches he had planted, he had absolutely no idea that his God-breathed words would someday be a part of the Bible, impacting hundreds of generations to come.

—Tammy

Faith like Enoch

Genesis 5:21–24; Matthew 25:21; Hebrews 11:5–6; Romans 3:23–24

"It was by faith that Enoch was taken up to heaven without dying—'he disappeared, because God took him.' For before he was taken up, he was known as a person who pleased God" (Hebrews 11:5 NLT).

If I could go to heaven like Enoch, that's the way I'd want to go, no pain and no disease to suffer with until I take my last breath. But more than the desire to die a painless death, I want to be known as a person like Enoch, one who pleased God with his faith. I envision the purest kind of faith, one that seeks God with sincerity and diligence, never wavering or compromising. I want God to look me in the eyes and say, "Well done, my good and faithful servant" (Matthew 25:21 NLT). I want to please Him with my whole life, passing that faith on to my children, their children, and their children's children.

Does having a faith like Enoch seem impossible to achieve? I admit, for me, it most definitely does. But God knows we are not perfect.

> For everyone has sinned; we all fall short of God's glorious standard. Yet God, in his grace, freely makes us right in his sight. He did this through Christ Jesus when he freed us from the penalty for our sins. (Romans 3:23–24 NLT)

> As we live in God, our love grows more perfect. So we will not be afraid on the day of judgment, but we can face him with confidence because we live like Jesus here in this world. (1 John 4:17 NLT)

As we live in the Lord, our faith grows. Like Enoch, we can trust God when we can't see the next step for our job. We can trust God when we are waiting for the right spouse. We can trust God when we have a temptation we can't seem to shake. We can trust God when we have a wayward child that has turned his back on the Lord. We can trust God with a diagnosis that has devastated us. We can trust God when our finances have plummeted. We can trust Him! We can have a faith like Enoch!

—Tammy

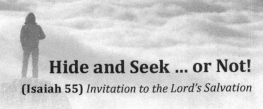

Hide and Seek ... or Not!

(Isaiah 55) *Invitation to the Lord's Salvation*

A favorite pastime is a good game of hide-and-seek. Over my life, I've seen a wide variety of people play this game: children, teens, and even grown men and women. We love to search for what is lost, and it gives us great pleasure to finally find what we have been looking for!

I remember an Easter twenty years ago when I took Scott (three and a half) and Matt (two) to an Easter egg hunt. Because of their young ages, the eggs were not really hidden; rather they were laid out in the grass right below their noses. Humorously, my older son, Scott, thought this was way too easy and thus proceeded to search behind, under, and around other objects with hope in finding mysterious Easter eggs. To his disappointment, no eggs were found in the harder places he had looked. As a result, he ended up with two eggs.

Have you ever tried to search for God as if He were hiding somewhere you couldn't see, playing some sort of game with you? I mean, come on, it can't be that easy! But there is a comforting message in Isaiah 55 with an invitation for each one of us to come to God. With this invitation, however, there is also some urgency, "Seek the Lord while you can find him. Call on him now while he is near" (Isaiah 55:6 NLT).

Why would Isaiah say this? If God is not playing games with us or if He is that accessible, why does he say *while* you can find Him? Is God going away? Is He hiding? Is He only available sometimes but not others? The truth is that God wants all people to seek Him, to repent from their sin, to run toward Him, and to commit their lives to Him. However, many will continue to put this commitment off to a later day, maybe after having a little fun or if illness strikes.

But what happens when death knocks at our door sooner than we anticipate? When this happens, there will be no more tomorrows or next years. Our time will be up, and we will no longer be able to seek the Lord and find Him. Please meditate on the words in Isaiah 55. Let them sink in deep. God is calling us to seek Him, know Him, love Him, and live for Him. He is not hiding. But someday the door will be closed.

—Tammy

Week 28 Reflections

1. After reviewing the Scriptures for each day, name three to four passages that jumped out at you this week.
2. How can you practically apply these verses to your life today and the upcoming week?
3. Why did Jesus stress the importance of attaining unity in the body of Christ? Have you ever witnessed disunity in the church? How has this hurt the church?
4. Jesus wants us to come to Him and lean on Him for strength. Where do you need Him to give you strength?
5. God has given everyone strengths that usually parallel weaknesses. Like Paul, what are some of your weaknesses that God has used for strengths?
6. Why was Enoch taken up to heaven? What can we learn from Enoch?
7. Name a time when you experienced God hiding or not showing Himself to you in a way you could recognize Him?
8. What is God teaching you about genuine faith and actions?
9. What element of faith are you wrestling with?

Imitating God

Ephesians 5:1–20

When our son Scott was around two, he loved to imitate animal noises from a book of unique animals, pressing the buttons that correlated their pictures with their sounds. If I were in the grocery store or out and about, I could distract him by asking him what a hyena or baboon says and he would mimic the sound of the animal, entertaining those in the store who were listening!

As he grew, his imitating sounds turned into imitating actions of Dad, such as mowing the lawn, shoveling snow, reading the paper, or watching sports. He would imitate me vacuuming, making crafts, and playing the piano. But more importantly, Scott would memorize Scripture by repeating what we said, putting us to shame with what he knew just by repeating back what he heard.

As parents, we have one of the biggest responsibilities to train up our children in the way they should go. We are to be imitators of God, reflecting God's love, faithfulness, goodness, and purity to our children and others around us. When I had children, my mom told me that my example would speak louder than words. She was right! Mark and I were not perfect parents and had to apologize many times to our sons for not having the right response, attitude, or behavior that God wanted us to have. Hypocrisy is damaging, and we wanted to be transparent with the daily struggles that came along with humble hearts and confession.

Ephesians 5 gets specific on what behaviors God detests, like sexual immorality, impurity, greed, bad language, idolatry, and drunkenness. But God also detests pride, selfishness, hate, impatience, and laziness. If we are lazy, chances are, our kids will be lazy. If we have poor language, likely our children will use bad language.

Jesus Christ was God in the flesh and taught by example how God desires us to live our lives as a reflection of His love. Jesus also left his Holy Spirit to dwell in us when he ascended into heaven, allowing us to be aware of how to be imitators of Christ. May His Spirit dwell in us richly today so that when our children, peers, or coworkers see us, they will see God because we are striving to imitate Him.

—Tammy

Can You Ask Someone Else?

Exodus 3, 4:10–17; Isaiah 6:8

"When the Lord saw Moses coming to take a closer look, God called to him from the middle of the bush, 'Moses! Moses!' 'Here I am!' Moses replied" (Exodus 3:4 NLT).

Have you ever felt unqualified for something that someone else asked you to do, but later realized that they asked because they saw something in you that you did not see? That happened to me when I was twenty-five years old. We had just moved to Ohio from Arizona when our pastor approached me about being a worship leader for the summer months. I had never done anything like that before; nor did I feel qualified. My degrees were in piano performance and violin, so I felt out of my element. I asked him if there were someone better qualified, but he told me that he saw potential in me and hoped I would give it a try.

Months passed in this new role, and I realized God was calling me into worship ministry. The way God called me reminds me of the story of Moses that we are reading today in Exodus 3 and 4. Moses was slow of speech and felt unqualified when God asked him to go and speak to the Israelites. Although he made himself available to God, he probably felt like God was making a poor choice, hence why he asked God if there were someone else he could send. But God knew Moses' heart and gave Moses the gifts he needed to do what God had called him to do.

And so it is with our lives. As we walk in this journey of faith, we need to keep our eyes and ears open, to be sure that we are sensitive to the Holy Spirit and His calling on our lives. God sometimes calls those who least expect it because He knows our hearts more than we do. With both hands open, ears in tune, may we be able to say "Here I am!" when God calls. He promises to equip us for whatever it is He has called us to do. He won't ask someone else!

—Tammy

Seasons of Life

**Genesis 8:22; Jeremiah 17; Proverbs
6:7–8; Song of Solomon 2:11–12**

Years ago, I wrote a song about the tree we read about in Jeremiah 17. No season in life lasts forever, but God's sustaining faithfulness through every season is my testimony.

SEASONS OF LIFE
Words and Music by Tammy Thurman, 1999

This tree standing by a stream, its arms stretched toward the sky
Has felt the warmth and radiance of the sun,
Yet has also known the drought it can bring.
This tree then begins to change, the colors turning to gold
The high winds blow, and the leaves begin to fall
But the roots of the tree have prepared for it all.
Through the seasons of life, I will hold the hand of God.
There will I find the love that keeps me strong
In Summer I feel His warm touch,
In Autumn, He guides me
In Winter, He restores my soul
In Springtime, He gives me joy, yes, He gives me joy!
Now standing alone and bare, its age reveals its strength
This tree holds on through the chill and icy storms
Obtaining its food from the soil
But then the cold passes and flowers start to bloom
The birds all sing, and the leaves begin to grow
Because the roots this tree have prepared for it all!

What season do you find yourself in right now? God allows us the privilege to go through every season so we can see more fully who He is. He is the God of our sorrows and the God of the happy times. He helps us grow and helps us end well. God is sovereign through them all.

—Tammy

The Team Approach
Hebrews 10:23–25

"Let us think of ways to motivate one another to acts of love and good works. And let us not neglect our meeting together, as some people do, but encourage one another, especially now that the day of his return is drawing near" (Hebrews 10:23–25 NLT).

Last week, we and our grown children went to Glacier National Park in northwest Montana. Twice while we were there, we experienced whitewater rafting. If you have never rafted before, one of the key instructions for the team is to be in sync with the two lead rowers, paddling in the same rhythm. That seemed normal common sense to me. However, what I was not prepared for was learning how to get into the raft if you fall in the water. I remember thinking, *This is no big deal. How hard could that be?*

Well, it was harder than I thought! One by one, we dove in for a swim. Then each had to climb back into the raft. My whole family was able to do it with no issues, except for me! Setting my embarrassment aside, I had no choice but to accept help from my family members.

And so it is with the body of Christ. We are a team. We have a responsibility to work together, sometimes by encouraging one another to press on or other times by physically helping to carry the heavy weight of someone else's burden. There are moments when we are spiritually able to get into the raft by ourselves, but when those times come, we are even more able to help someone else. The author of Hebrews instructs us to "think of ways to motivate one another to acts of love and good works" (Hebrews 10:24 NLT). This does not always come easy for us, to think of ways to encourage and motivate, but God is asking for us to be intentional about doing this.

The verses go on to tell us not to neglect meeting together. Since COVID swept across our world, many people who used to attend church stopped going completely. The church needs to stick together. Let us be encouraged that a revival is happening and God is doing a new thing. This especially gives us reason to meet as the church and spur others on in the body of Christ as God intended. The time is now, and the urgency is great. Let us take the team approach as we work together.

—Tammy

Samuel: Here Am I, Send Me!

1 Samuel 3:1–21

I love surprises! Unexpected interruptions in my day are often welcome because they cater to my creativity. Mark, on the other hand, is a planner to the letter, and there isn't much going off the beaten path with him. This difference in us is magnified when we plan vacations together. I vividly remember years ago when I explained to him my desire for some spontaneity in our vacation planning. I wanted to play things by ear with some element of unpredictability.

Well, he pulled off the surprise of the century! One summer day after work, Mark instructed the family to pack our bags to leave the next morning to a destination unknown! The excitement filled the house as Scott, Matt, and I anticipated the road trip ahead. Mark drove us out west through Minnesota, Wyoming, and South Dakota, stopping at sites along the way. To this day, that adventure was the most fun and exciting vacation we have ever taken as a family!

Similarly, as we read the story about God calling Samuel, Samuel did not have all the plans from God laid out in front of him to be able to decide if he would answer God's call or not. Instead, he just trusted God and believed that God would reveal His plans along the way. Because of that simple faith, Samuel was able to say, "Speak, for your servant is listening" (1 Samuel 3:10 NIV). God was pleased with Samuel, knowing that his trust was pure and unobstructed, making himself available to God for whatever lay ahead.

Sometimes we can be so planned out that we not only miss God's call, but we overlook the small opportunities along the way to do a simple act of kindness for someone else. Sometimes we even turn down opportunities because we don't have all the details to satisfy our planning nature. When God calls us, we may not have all the plans. We may only know the first step. However, following God is a faith-walk … period. The bottom line is: are we able to trust God and boldly respond to Him with faith and say, "Speak, for your servant is listening" (1 Samuel 3:10 NIV)? We never need to doubt or be afraid of God's surprises. He just wants us to respond with trust and open ears. You will be pleasantly surprised!

—Tammy

True Religion
James 1:27

When I was a baby, my parents had me dedicated to the Lord, committing to raise me in the faith alongside the help of our church congregation. Years later I was eleven, and my dad had been killed suddenly, stunning our entire family, friends, and church. Even though we no longer attended the church I was dedicated to, the pastor was one of the first to show up the next day when our friends and church family came by to mourn with us. I remember playing games with them and even laughing that day, just one day after my dad passed away!

As the months and years passed, families in our church continued to come alongside our family. One family invited me to join the worship team and brought me to Christian conferences with them. It was at these conferences that I entered a personal relationship with Jesus! Someone else from church invited me over weekly to cook with other young women. Other families took me on camping trips and day trips to the beach.

Years later, the same pastor, James Schuppe, published a book called *Choices: From Deception to Blessing: The Letter from James* (Shenandoah Press, 2020). Before my mom mailed it to me, she had him sign it. He wrote, "To Hannah, this is to let you know that your dedication to the Lord, which I performed 22.5 years ago, HAS NOT EXPIRED!"

I reflected on how big of an impact the intentionality of our church had on my faith and me. They displayed their commitment to help my parents raise me in the faith by coming alongside me in the hardest years of my life. They lived out the verse in James, "Religion that is pure and undefiled before God the Father is this: to visit orphans and widows in their affliction, and to keep oneself unstained from the world" (James 1:27 NIV).

People like those in my church growing up were a part of the continuation of my faith, so that twenty-three years later, I am still dedicated to the Lord. They showed that the church was not just a building to gather in each week, but a group of imperfect people that love God and then show that love to the people around them every day of the week.

—Hannah

Week 29 Reflections

1. After reviewing the Scriptures for each day, name three to four passages that jumped out at you this week.
2. How can you practically apply these verses to your life today and the upcoming week?
3. List as many attributes of God that you can.
4. When we are taught to be imitators of God, what does that practically look like for you in your daily walk? Be specific.
5. Has God ever asked you to do something you did not feel equipped to do or did not want to do initially?
6. What season do you find yourself in right now? Describe the season.
7. What is God teaching you through this season?
8. God's church needs to work together. What does that look like for the church in your area? How can you help toward unity?
9. Opportunities to serve the orphan, widow, and single mother are all around us. Are you ready to say "Here I am, God. Send me"? What does that look like to you?

MONTH 8
Sometimes We Neglect Giving of Our Time and Money

A FAITH THAT STANDS
Produces Selflessness and Generosity

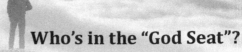

Who's in the "God Seat"?

Deuteronomy 5:6–8

"You must not have any other god but me" (Deuteronomy 5:7 NLT).

In the Old Testament, Israel had a pattern of rejecting God, disobeying God's commands, and being unfaithful to Him by worshiping other gods. Even though God forgave them for all their complaining and sinfulness, He still brought consequences upon them. God wasn't out to destroy the Israelites, but He wanted them to know that He would not tolerate other things coming before Him.

We are not much different than the Israelites. Even if we do not worship statues of gold, we sometimes allow other things or people in our lives to creep into the "God seat," sneakily taking the place of God. This could be our job, children, sports events, cell phones, social media, friends, studies, material possessions, or simply ourselves. How do we identify whether something or someone has made their way to the "God seat" in our lives?

There are five key indicators that can take our temperature on what could be a potential god in our life if we don't keep our life in check. Take a moment to answer the following questions:

1. What is at the top of my priority list each day?
2. What do I think about first when I wake up?
3. What motivates me, sometimes to the exclusion of other important things?
4. What do I talk about mostly with friends and family?
5. What am I addicted to and can't live without?

Remember, Satan is subtle. Prioritizing things before God in our lives can be a slow fade to where we aren't even aware it is happening. We do not need to be scared, but we do need to be alert and recognize potential land mines!

Today, take some time to identify any potential gods in your life. Name them, confess them, and put God in the "God seat" where He belongs!

–Tammy

To Fear the Lord

Exodus 20:1–21; Deuteronomy 5:1–22, 6:13–15

In church, we often talk about God's peace, grace, forgiveness, and love. But did you know that God is also jealous?

> Fear the Lord your God, serve him only and take your oaths in his name. Do not follow other gods, the gods of the peoples around you; for the Lord your God, who is among you, is a jealous God and his anger will burn against you, and he will destroy you from the face of the land. (Deuteronomy 6:13–15 NLT)

Wow. There are strong consequences for following other gods. God's anger will burn against anyone who does so, and He will destroy us from the face of the land! In the Ten Commandments that God gave to Moses on Mount Sinai, the very first commandment is this, "you shall have no other gods before me! The second is like it; you shall not make any graven image and worship it" (Exodus 20:3–4 NIV).

Deuteronomy 5:9 (NIV) goes on to say, "You shall not bow down to them or worship them; for I, the Lord your God, am a jealous God, punishing the children for the sin of the parents to the third and fourth generation of those who hate me."

When Scripture tells us that God is a jealous God, it means He will not stand for anything or anyone to come before Him. For many of us, that person or thing can even be ourselves. Many good things can become our god(s). But His warning is clear. We should fear Him with a healthy fear, knowing that He created us for the very purpose of worshiping Him and having a relationship with Him. He will not force us to choose Him, which is why He gives every one of us free choice.

Think of it this way. God is jealous for us, meaning He wants so much to have a relationship with every person! He loves us. He will forgive us, and His mercies know no end. I am thankful for a God that is jealous for me. He is my Father, and I love it that He is my God!

–Tammy

Do the Right Thing
Luke 6:31; 1 Peter 2:21; Galatians 6:9–10

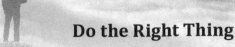

Life sometimes throws curve balls our way, making our choices to do what is right a little more challenging. I remember when my husband and I were faced with the decision to have my father-in-law, Don, come and live with us. My mother-in-law had passed away, Don had contracted Alzheimer's, and it soon became apparent that he could not live by himself in his own home. We agreed that inviting Don to live with us was the right thing to do.

Things were fine for a year or so, but after a while, Don began lashing out at me. I'm sure he didn't mean to, but the disease was taking its toll on him. After about two and a half years, we had to transfer him to a nursing home. It was a very difficult season for all of us.

Spending time and taking care of someone who may never remember it or unintentionally hurts you may seem pointless. However, Dale and I knew what God said in His Word, "Honor your father and mother.' This is the first commandment with a promise" (Ephesians 6:2–3 NLT).

Our desire to honor God outweighed any reservations we had at the onset, and we knew that God was challenging us to do what we needed to do to honor our parents. We wanted to demonstrate God's love to Dale's father the best that we could.

> So, let's not get tired of doing what is good. At just the right time we will reap a harvest of blessing if we don't give up. Therefore, whenever we have the opportunity, we should do good to everyone—especially to those in the family of faith. (Galatians 6:9-10 NLT)

Is there someone you are serving that may never fully realize or remember anything that you are doing? If so, try to see the opportunity as an amazing blessing, to be able to serve the Lord selflessly and faithfully. You will never know the impact, but you will be doing the right thing.

—Sharon

Healthy Choices
Romans 12:2–3

"Don't copy the behavior and customs of this world, but let God transform you into a new person by changing the way you think … Don't think you are better than you really are. Be honest in your evaluation of yourselves …" (Romans 12:2–3 NLT).

We all have a need to feel important, to leave the world a little better than how we found it, leaving some bit of impression on others that can be handed down to future generations. When social media became a thing, I did not feel the need to open an account at first. But then I began to feel left out of the news in everyone's lives, feeling like I was the last one to know when someone had a baby or had passed away. Eventually, peer pressure won, and I soon found myself opening a social media account that I kept for over fifteen years.

During that time, I would share with Mark the things I learned and saw on the newsfeed, some of which were concerning or negative. Like a fly in the ointment, my thinking became contaminated, causing me to view others in a negative way, instilling a judging attitude, and becoming more aware of my own self-importance. Although I was a confident adult, I began to compare myself with others, which was not healthy. After a while, Mark asked me why I was spending time on something that was stealing my joy, robbing me of precious time I could be spending otherwise? He was right. I knew I needed to make a change.

There are pros and cons to just about every option we consider in life to fill our time with. For me, this passage in Romans convicted me that my choice of social media at that time was not a healthy one for me. That's not to say it isn't a healthy choice for you or someone else.

As Christ-followers, we constantly need to reevaluate the things that fill our time daily. Do they draw us more toward Christ or more toward the world? Only we can make that change and make healthy choices for ourselves. It is only then that we will be able to allow God to truly transform our thinking into having the mind of Christ. Are there any healthy choices God might be nudging you to make today?

—Tammy

Ears to Hear

Mark 4:1—20

"Search me, O God, and know my heart; test me and know my anxious thoughts. Point out anything in me that offends you, and lead me along the path of everlasting life" (Psalm 139:23–24 NIV).

When it comes to deciphering the exact number of parables Jesus told, scholars have varying opinions of this. We know that He used over a hundred metaphors and told at least thirty-six parables that are found in the Gospels. Fifteen parables appear in Matthew, six are found in Mark (four repeats), and thirty-five occur in Luke (sixteen repeats, nineteen unique).

Parables are a distinction of Jesus' teaching, and I deeply admire how He taught practical life lessons to crowds of people at the spur of the moment. One of the most insightful parables Jesus told was the parable of the farmer scattering seed found in Mark 4. In this parable, a farmer scattered four different groups of seed, representing four groups of people who hear the message of God's Word:

1. Those who hear the message, only to have Satan come at once and take it away. (v. 15)
2. Those who hear the message and immediately receive it with joy. But since they don't have deep roots, they don't last long. They fall away as soon as they have problems or are persecuted for believing God's Word. (v. 16–17)
3. Those who hear God's Word, but the message is quickly crowded out by the worries of this life, the lure of wealth, and the desire for other things, so no fruit is produced. (v. 19)
4. Those who have ears to hear, accepting God's Word and producing a harvest of thirty, sixty, or even a hundred times as much as had been planted! (v. 20)

We all can identify with one of these groups. If we are going to give the world our best while we are here on this earth, we need to be people who have ears to hear the Holy Spirit and, after counting the cost to following Jesus, help lead others to have those same ears to hear!

—Tammy

Our Firstfruits
Proverbs 3:7–10

As a young boy, I was given the opportunity to do yardwork for my parents and my grandma. I enjoyed the work but also loved to receive the pay for a job well done even if it were small. My dad's profession as a bricklayer and home builder gave me the unique opportunity to work regularly by the time I was just entering my teens.

From the beginning, it was my mom's job to pay me. Not only did my parents talk to me about giving my first fruits to the Lord, but my mom also made sure this was practical every week. If I made a dollar mowing the yard, you can be sure I did not get a single dollar bill. I would be paid in some fashion that included either a dime or two nickels. Whatever I was paid, I could be sure that 10 percent was perfectly ready to be set aside for Sunday. That made things easy for everyone as we headed out the door on Sunday mornings to the question, "Does everyone have their Bible and tithe?"

The idea of giving our firstfruits certainly starts with our income, but it can include so much more. It can encompass our time and talents in addition to our treasures. Not only was the concept of giving my first fruits of income instilled in me early, but the idea of being a joyful giver was implanted in me as well.

However, as I think about my time and talents, there are unfortunately times when I realize that my firstfruits are going to something else. I might come home from work after a long day, certainly not ready to jump into our small group Bible study. Or I might even start my day with being so consumed with meetings I have planned that I skip my devotions and prayer.

When it comes to firstfruit giving, you might be like me and have an area you do well in but other areas that could use some development and focus. My mom realized part of the growth would come from establishing a process and setting me up for success. We can all work to establish the foundation, which leads to the joy in the process and beyond.

– Mark

Week 30 Reflections

1. After reviewing the Scriptures for each day, name three to four passages that jumped out at you this week.
2. How can you practically apply these verses to your life today and the upcoming week?
3. Who is in the "God seat" in your life?
4. What does healthy fear of the Lord look like?
5. Everyone needs to make healthy and better choices regarding obedience to the Holy Spirit and His will for us. What are some healthy choices that you might need to make so you can have peace and joy?
6. In the parable of the farmer, what group of seed are you?
7. Are you a generous person? Explain.
8. Have you ever sacrificed in giving to the point it hurt?
9. Where do your firstfruits go? Take time to pray and seek the Lord and His will in this area.

Busy as a Bee!
1 John 2:15–17

A few years ago, Mark and I celebrated twenty-five years of marriage by going to Hawaii. During our two-week vacation, we ventured to some of the most breathtaking sights we had ever seen. We spent the first morning awaking at three thirty to experience the sunrise from the top of Mt. Haleakola and then later to bike down the mountains through the clouds. The sites were surreal.

Even with all of God's beauty to admire, the Bible teaches us not to love the world or anything in it, not just the physical beauty of God's creation, but the "craving for physical pleasure, for everything we see, and pride in our achievements and possessions ..." (1 John 2:15–17 NLT).

We are instructed not to love this world because the many things that people crave will fade along with it. Sometimes we don't even realize the things we crave until we take a step back to analyze what we are so busy doing every day. Our schedules say a lot about our cravings!

I have always been a busy person. College life was particularly hectic for me, as I had every minute of every day scheduled from 7:00 a.m. until 10:00 p.m. I thrived on a busy schedule. However, as I married, had children, and, for a time, was a stay-at-home mom, I soon discovered how many choices in life there are to make all the time. Whether it be extracurricular activities with school and church, our jobs, hobbies, or simply projects around the house, our schedules soon became very complicated. Thankfully the chaos did not last forever.

Mark and I soon found that being overly busy was a measure for gauging what was most important to us. We were exhausted, easily perturbed, and not giving God and family what they deserved. Changes were inevitable, and we desperately needed God's wisdom and guidance.

We all have endless opportunities and activities to choose from, many of which are wonderful things. But God gives us red flags as we check our spirits to choose the very best things that balance and stabilize our homes. I no longer want to give God and my family my leftovers. I want to give them my best. Ultimately, Mark and I have both learned that being a busy bee isn't all that it is cracked up to "bee."

—Tammy

First Things First
Isaiah 26:8–9

"But as for me, I will sing about your power. Each morning I will sing with joy about your unfailing love. For you have been my refuge, a place of safety when I am in distress" (Psalm 59:16 NLT).

My mornings are very precious to me. From the moment I rise out of bed, feed the cat, eat breakfast, and drink my coffee, I am reminded that God has given me a new day with a blank slate. I haven't always felt this way about mornings, especially with other mouths to feed and get ready and the hustle and bustle that goes with having a family. Any time I did sit quietly with God was often before bed or midday. But as I've gotten older, I have learned to appreciate beginning my day with the Lord, spending time with God first.

My time goes a little like this: I close my eyes to settle my mind, I get on my knees, and I praise God and thank Him for who He is and has been in my life. I pray that God searches my heart, to show me if there is anything I need to repent from, and I ask Him for His mercy and forgiveness. I pray for others, and I read Scripture, trying to memorize at least one new verse. There is a peace that falls over me that gives me strength to face the day when I focus my eyes upon Jesus. He allows me to forget the yesterdays in my mind so I can move on to today.

There is power in prayer, even in the middle of the night! Do you ever have a hard time sleeping and your mind just spins with all the issues at work, conflicts at school, or relationship trouble in the family? During nights like these, I have learned to get up, get on my knees, and pour out my heart to God, telling Him everything that is keeping me awake. I pray for His peace, direction, and wisdom, knowing that He hears me.

God is a faithful God. I can't tell you the number of times I have desperately gone to God in the morning (or middle of the night), desperation filling my heart and mind. But when I meditate on all that God has done or praise Him while I play the piano and confess my anxiety to Him, I trust Him to give me a fresh start for the day. When I rise, give me Jesus, and my day will be set on the right path!

—Tammy

If I Don't Have Love

1 Corinthians 13:1–13; 1 John 4:8

There's this thing called love. Ever heard of it? Love appears 551 times in the NIV, so it must be important, don't you think?

What exactly is love? The Bible defines it with one word, God. (1 John 4:8) He is also holy, righteous, gracious, merciful, forgiving, powerful, and pure. If you want an even more in-depth definition of love, look no further than 1 Corinthians 13. If you've ever been to a wedding, you've probably heard the passage. And while it certainly can be applied to marriage, the passage speaks about the fullness and overall definition of godly love.

> Love is patient, love is kind. It does not envy, it does not boast, it is not proud. It does not dishonor others, it is not self-seeking, it is not easily angered, it keeps no record of wrongs. Love does not delight in evil but rejoices with the truth. It always protects, always trusts, always hopes, always perseveres. Love never fails. (1 Corinthians 13:4–7 NIV)

When I was a boy in Sunday school, our teacher had us do an exercise with this passage. Instead of the word *love*, we were to insert our own name. The challenge was to see if our name could honestly go before any of those statements.

Next, we were to replace the word *love* with *God*. In accordance with the rest of Scripture, God's name obviously fits and works with every statement. Now here's what's interesting. The passage just before this one explains that, if we don't have love, we are worthless and amount to nothing. Yikes. I don't want to live contrary to how God designed me to live. I want to love other people well.

If I may be vulnerable, I fear I sometimes get caught up with society's twisted versions of love instead of functioning properly within the context of God's definition of love. I desire to be genuine with pure, unadulterated love for others. I don't want to be a clanging gong!

—Scott

Reprioritizing
Psalm 119:33–40

Life has a funny way of showing us where our priorities lie. When Scott and Matt were in high school, I had a full-time job, and Mark was traveling a lot. The boys were in baseball, music, and basketball, and I had lots of rehearsals and events I had to be at. We were a busy family. But like many families, we reached a crisis point with our priorities. We were all running ragged and didn't seem to have much time left over for other people, much less quality family time. Mark and I realized if we didn't seek the Lord and His counsel, we would continue spiraling down this never-ending tunnel.

Americans are busy people … too busy. We sign our kids up for everything under the sun, all of which require transportation. We want to do it all, and our motives are good! We begin to think we are making the most of our days and time, but we are burning the candle from both ends.

God never intended us to be able to sustain that kind of living. As you read and meditate on the following passage, identify key action words where God might be speaking to you. For those who need to reprioritize, this Scripture might jumpstart a prayer toward a new beginning!

> I told you my plans, and you answered. Now teach me your decrees. Help me understand the meaning of your commandments, and I will meditate on your wonderful deeds … encourage me by your word. Keep me from lying to myself; give me the privilege of knowing your instructions. I have chosen to be faithful; I have determined to live by your regulations. I cling to your laws … I will pursue your commands, for you expand my understanding … Give me understanding and I will obey your instructions; I will put them into practice with all my heart. Make me walk along the path of your commands, for that is where my happiness is found … Turn my eyes from worthless things and give me life through your word … Renew my life with your goodness. (Psalm 119:26–40 NLT)

Life Is Too Short
Psalm 39:4–5

I was sixteen years old sitting in a pew at a Wednesday evening prayer service at my home church in New York. I listened to a thirty-year-old husband pleading for prayer for his twenty-nine-year-old wife who had collapsed in the grocery store with her four young children in tow. She was in the hospital in a coma and was in critical condition. I remember leaving the building that night disregarding the urgent request to pray. After all, she was twenty-nine. Who dies at twenty-nine from an unknown cause? But the deeper issue that came to the surface was my skepticism about prayer itself. Did it work? Was it real? Did it make a difference?

Four days later, Patty passed away. The knowledge and pain of the news hit me right between the eyes. I didn't pray for her. I didn't believe. Would she still be alive had I prayed?

We all go through crisis points in our faith. But sometimes we can linger in those crisis points for years, wasting precious time. When Patty passed away, I began to pray. I asked God to help me believe because, although I was a Christian, I didn't know if I believed in the power of prayer. If a healthy, strong mother of four could pass away at twenty-nine, I could pass away unexpectedly as well. I needed to make a choice to either be all in for God or forget it altogether. Life is short, but eternity is forever.

Where are you struggling in your faith walk? Are you skeptical? Shallow? Too comfortable? Self-centered? Unforgiving? Too busy?

As you take time to meditate and pray today, may the words of Psalm 39:4–5 reach down into your soul and encourage you to make things right with a God who is real and all-powerful, our Healer, our Provider, Redeemer, and Transformer.

—Tammy

> Lord, remind me how brief my time on earth will be. Remind me that my days are numbered—how fleeting my life is. You have made my life no longer than the width of my hand. My entire lifetime is just a moment to you; at best, each of us is but a breath. (Psalm 39:4–5 NLT)

Concrete Heart
Matthew 11:15, 13:11–15

Early in my career, I was given the opportunity to learn about lean manufacturing from a Japanese sensei. This was often a very intense process, as he pushed me and others to do things we did not even think possible. Personally, I enjoyed the challenges. Part of that enjoyment was from the learning itself, but seeing the results that came from implementing the lean tools was particularly rewarding.

Nevertheless, there were times that one of my team might not be learning or implementing the tools properly and the sensei would call us a "concrete head." Not the most endearing term, but it certainly got the point across. The sensei told us over and over that we were just not paying attention or we were too stubborn to act on the training.

In the book of Matthew, Jesus explains the parable of the four soils. He explained that for those that were listening, more understanding would be given. In fact, they would have an abundance of knowledge. But for those not listening, even what little understanding they had, would be taken away from them.

This parable played out in the times with our Japanese sensei. He would share his teaching with us, and those who truly listened would gain understanding. Still, those that would not listen he called "concrete heads," but even worse, there were some he told that they were not worthy of his training. Thus, he moved on to other students. What a terrible thing when that happened as the leadership in our company often gave up on these people too.

Being a "concrete head" at work can lead to less promotion or even a job loss. But how much worse to fall into the category Jesus describes as not a "concrete head," but a concrete heart. This only happens when someone closes their eyes and shuts their ears, tuning out God and His Word. As a result, their hearts are concrete and are unable to turn to God to let Him heal them.

As Jesus concludes this parable, may we learn and seek to be fertile soil in every part of our lives, but especially in hearing God's Word.

-Mark

Week 31 Reflections

1. After reviewing the Scriptures for each day, name three to four passages that jumped out at you this week.
2. How can you practically apply these verses to your life today and the upcoming week?
3. What are you craving in life? How are your cravings reflected in your busy schedule?
4. What are the first things you do in the morning? How can prioritizing God time in the morning help with being fruitful the rest of the day?
5. God looks at the individual heart when it comes to loving others. Love crosses the bridge of race, gender, and socioeconomics. How can you demonstrate more love for others right where you are?
6. Do you think God wants you to reprioritize anything in your life? Explain.
7. Are you struggling with skepticism? Doubt? Write them down. Then meditate on faith and what that means. What is God saying to you?
8. Are you teachable? On a scale from one to ten, how teachable are you?
9. What is God teaching you this week about His Word?

The Rich Man (Are You Willing?)
Matthew 19:16–24

I have always empathized with the rich man in Matthew 19:16–24 because I think he was caught off guard with Jesus' response when he asked Jesus how to attain eternal life. I envision this man living in a palace surrounded by treasures of gold and silver, owning acres of land, and managing and employing many servants. He seems moral enough, indicating that he followed the law diligently. But he also seemed to sense that there was something lacking, now seeking to fill the void that his treasures could not fill. I can only imagine the shock and sadness the rich man felt when Jesus answered him, instructing him to sell everything he had and then come and follow. Sadly, the man was unwilling to do that and consequently walked away defeated.

I have often wondered how I would have responded to Jesus. Would I have jumped for joy with eagerness to go and sell all my property, my possessions, letting go of every servant I had and then coming to follow Jesus? Or would I have walked away defeated like the rich man? Jesus didn't even clarify with the man what following him would entail.

The lesson in this story is clear to me. Jesus wants to know what is truly in our hearts. God will not compete with anything else that has the potential to be all-important to us. He doesn't want us to merely live moral lives and do good works. He wants to be Lord of everything we have and all that we consider important.

I believe that a person can be monetarily rich and still follow Jesus. However, the more a person has, the harder it is to give up. We need to hold on to things loosely when we choose to follow Jesus.

Is there anything in your life that would sting if God asked you to surrender it to Him? Perhaps your bank account, status, phone, social media, job, or even family. Whatever that thing is that you don't think you can live without is exactly the thing that God wants you to surrender to Him.

Be honest with God. He knows our priorities before we admit them. Jesus knew that the rich man was wrestling with other gods in his life and confronted it. What are you willing to surrender to Jesus today?

–Tammy

Bible Baseball
Matthew 7:21; Colossians 3

"SAFE!" the umpire shouted as the winning runner slid into home plate. The catcher, bewildered at how he missed the tag, stood with his mouth gaping open, angry with himself thinking, *I had the ball in my hands! How did I miss him? I thought for sure I had him ...*

To a catcher, that moment is arguably one of the most intense pressure points in the whole game. The runner? He was too fast for the tag. The runner didn't merely jog around the bases when the ball was in play. He sprinted as fast as he could to the next bag.

If people run that hard for a simple game, I wonder how hard we should be running for our faith. Are we walking, jogging, or sprinting around the bases? In 1 Corinthians 9, Paul explains that we are to be running the spiritual race marked out for us as though we are running for first place. And while there aren't any direct baseball metaphors in the Bible, we can understand the remaining principle from other parts of Scripture, which is doing everything we do with the understanding that we're doing it first and foremost for God (Colossians 3). Jesus taught us, "Not everyone who calls out to me, 'Lord! Lord!' will enter the Kingdom of Heaven. Only those who actually do the will of my Father in heaven will enter" (Matthew 7:21 NLT).

I know the opening sentences posed a trivial metaphor, but if God is the umpire, Satan is the catcher, and people are the runners, we learn that if we are not running fast enough, we might get caught. While I wouldn't suggest we think of God standing there making stark judgment calls on who's safe and who's not, I would remind us that salvation is no joking matter. "Since we are receiving a Kingdom that is unshakable, let us be thankful and please God by worshiping him with holy fear and awe. For our God is a devouring fire" (Hebrews 12:28–29 NLT).

God wants to consume us with His fire, causing us to run with fervor and passion so as not to get caught by the snares of this world!

—Scott

Selfish Thinking

Haggai 1:1–15

Haggai was one of the twelve minor prophets who lived in sixth-century BC and wrote the thirty-seventh book of the Old Testament. The theme of the book of Haggai is one that very easily applies now in the twenty-first-century church, especially in the area of priorities.

Following the Babylonian exile, the remnant of Judah was not prioritizing obedience to the Lord. Haggai was a prophet who encouraged the returned exiles to rebuild the temple as God desired. His words to the people clearly show the consequences of their selfish thinking. They were living well and affluently while God's temple lay in ruins. As you read this passage in Haggai 1, look for some parallels from the remnant people of Judah and the people of today. Haggai teaches us that when people give priority to God and his house, then they will be blessed.

As I examine my own priorities, I have been challenged by a good friend about the way I spend money. She told me about the awesome habit that both she and her husband have developed regarding their finances. They added a new "food rule" to their budget when they eat out. The "food rule" holds them accountable to match any dollar amount they spend out to eat (coffee, lunch, dinner, and snacks) and put it toward the child that they sponsor in Rwanda. God specifically pointed out to them that if they had enough money to spend $100 on a nice dinner, they could give $100 to a family in Rwanda that would feed them for three months.

About ten years ago, our pastor asked the congregation if they considered themselves rich. Only a handful out of a thousand raised their hands. But then he changed it to asking how many people made more than $10,000 a year or higher. Almost everyone raised their hands. Meanwhile, the median worldwide family income is less than $10,000!

I want to change and have eyes to see the suffering world around me, acting on what I know God wants me to do. Let's heed the words of Haggai and listen to what God might be saying to us about our priorities and selfish thinking today!

—Tammy

Excuses, Excuses, Excuses
Luke 14:15–24

Parable of the Great Banquet

While I was in college, I was asked to play for a wedding of an acquaintance in another state. At the age of nineteen, I didn't have the greatest skills in saying no, but for some reason, I felt like my reasons were not good enough. So what did I do? I said yes to playing! That's right. I said yes. Embarrassingly, when it got to be about two months prior to the wedding, I started the attempts to back out of my commitment, making one lame excuse after the other. I said I couldn't afford it or I didn't have a car. You get the point. But the bride and groom kept offering to help, shutting down my excuses. Eventually I realized I was not being honest with them or myself, so I finally got the nerve up to say, "I'm sorry. I should have said no to begin with, but the timing is just not good with school and my job."

Just retelling this story makes me cringe about what I did and how I handled myself. However, I learned a great lesson from the turmoil it put me through. Giving excuses only prolongs the inevitable.

In the parable of the great banquet in Luke 14, there is a seat for us at the table, meaning there is an open invitation to dine in the presence of the Lord for all of eternity. This invitation is open to everyone, favoring no one, not rich or poor, Jew nor Gentile, or slave nor free. We can either accept this invitation or decline it. But God does not want excuses from us that only prolong the inevitable, which is our "no" to his invite. He wants our yes to be yes and our no to be no. We either accept the invitation or we reject it. There is no middle ground.

Have you accepted God's invitation to His banquet? If not, why not? What are your excuses? Sometimes the thought of giving up control of our lives to God is unappealing because we are used to being our own master and doing as we please. As a Christ-follower myself who is free-spirited and strong-willed at times, I can tell you this: allowing God to be Lord over my life is the best decision I ever made. I have never felt stifled. I have found freedom and peace through Christ that I never expected.

If you find yourself making excuses, stop wavering and consider all that you have to gain through God. Eternity is a very long time!

–Tammy

Generosity
2 Corinthians 8:1–7

Today's topic recalls for me one of the deepest and longest-lasting lessons my parents taught me, the lesson of generosity.

As you read 2 Corinthians 8:1–7, the people in Macedonia did not have much. Likewise, my parents did not have much in terms of what society would define as riches. But while I was a young boy my dad (and truly our family) was called to be a lay pastor. In addition to his full-time job as a bricklayer, he would also take on the role of pastor for a new church plant. God blessed this church, and eventually my dad was led to build a new church building for this young congregation. While my parents gave financially as best they could, the part of this story that truly made the lasting impact on a young boy was the time and energy commitment they made. For nineteen months, my dad (and family) went from his physically demanding job straight to the new church location to work until bedtime. The exceptions were Sundays, which were filled with services and visitations, as well as Wednesday night prayer meetings. Each day I saw firsthand the personal sacrifices my parents so generously made.

In verse 5 today, we see that the people gave themselves first to the Lord and then to others. In verse 7, Paul highlights that they excel in everything but takes the opportunity to exhort them to excel in the grace of giving. I was able to see this as a young boy played out in front of me. My parents loved the Lord, and I saw this in many ways such as their Bible reading and prayer time. But they also took that next step and loved others, and this is where I truly learned about generosity.

Often I read the Bible and find something new that God is teaching me, and I work to apply it. Today's verses were not a new concept as my parents taught me this lesson long ago. Their generosity of time, money, and energy given to the church in Ohio certainly impacted that community, but possibly the greatest impact it had was on their own son. As we work to excel in everything, let each of us not forget to also excel in the grace of giving. You may never know the impact your generosity has on those around you directly, indirectly, or yourself.

–Mark

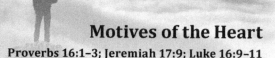

Motives of the Heart
Proverbs 16:1–3; Jeremiah 17:9; Luke 16:9–11

"All a person's ways seem pure to them, but motives are weighed by the LORD" (Proverbs 16:2 NLT).

Humans are intelligent creatures. Over the course of many generations, we have devoted countless hours to bettering our minds and strengthening our educational development so we can be the very best humans we can possibly be. We've even developed a measurement for intelligence with tests, more readily known as IQ (intelligence quotient). In our history, we have celebrated those with high IQs, whose minds have led to innovative inventions, engineering feats, computer systems, and the discovery of cures and vaccines for diseases.

But how do we measure the motives of one's heart? Proverbs tells us that our motives, or reasons behind what we do, are measured by the Lord. Although accomplishments are to be celebrated, the reasons behind what we do are more important to the Lord. Why do you think motives are so important to God?

Jeremiah 17:9 answers that for us by telling us that our hearts are very deceitful, and we can easily fool even ourselves about the reasons behind our actions. We can pretend that we are choosing good actions for God, perhaps fooling everyone around us, when we actually have ulterior motives. God is not fooled by our deceitfulness and is "a discerner of the thoughts and intents of the heart" (Hebrews 4:12 NLT).

Sin nature leads to negative motivations like revenge, pride, the need for approval, self-righteousness, or a sense of entitlement. Any motivation that derives from the flesh is not pleasing to God (Romans 8:8). There is no real test to take to determine what lies deep in our hearts; however, God has a way of revealing to us our impure motives by speaking to us through His Word. Accountability by other Christians can help detect sinful motives in us as well.

Questions to ask ourselves: Why do I give? Why am I making this decision? Why am I befriending this person? Why am I serving? Let us ask God today to search our hearts and reveal to us any deceitful way in us. Let Him purify our motives so that His will becomes our own.

—Tammy

Week 32 Reflections

1. After reviewing the Scriptures for each day, name three to four passages that jumped out at you this week.
2. How can you practically apply these verses to your life today and the upcoming week?
3. What, if anything, in your life would sting if God asked you to surrender it to Him?
4. We can easily become sluggish in our faith. What is the challenge and benefit to sprinting in the Christian faith?
5. We do not always see selfishness in ourselves. Ask a family member or friend if they see selfishness in you and write down what you think as well.
6. God has invited you to His banquet. Have you accepted, or are you making excuses? If so, what are they?
7. What is more valuable to you, time or money? Explain.
8. What does God require of you in the areas of time and money?
9. Have you ever caught yourself having an ulterior motive in giving? Explain.

Healthy Boundaries
Mark 6:1–12

Have you ever had an unhealthy relationship or job that slowly brings you down? Some days you may feel as though you are banging your head against a wall, trying everything on your end to make things work, but the anxiety and stress is growing? I compare the experience to a frog being put in a pot of water, not realizing the water is slowly beginning to boil. The environment has grown toxic, and putting some healthy boundaries in place would help.

In Mark 6, Jesus found it difficult, if not impossible, to teach and perform miracles in His hometown of Nazareth. They knew Him as Mary's son and the brother of James, Joseph, Judas, and Simon. They skeptically questioned him where He got His wisdom and the ability to perform miracles. The crowd of people was offended by Jesus, and He knew He needed to move on because of the disbelief. This was His hometown!

> Then Jesus told them, "A prophet is honored everywhere except in his own hometown and among his relatives and his own family." And because of their unbelief, he couldn't do any miracles among them except to place his hands on a few sick people and heal them …
> (Mark 6:4–6 NLT)

Boundaries are like our psychological immune system. Healthy boundaries act like a filter, letting good influences into your life and keeping not-so-good influences out. Poor boundaries, on the other hand, lead to vulnerability, chaos, and stress. God wants more for you.

Boundaries are essential to healthy relationships and really a healthy life. But setting and sustaining boundaries is a learned skill. Recognizing when to stay put or move on can be a blurry line, but God gives us direction when we seek Him.

How might God be trying to get your attention to make some changes in your life? Has your environment grown toxic? Remember, there is a time to persevere, a time to discern healthy boundaries, and a time to open a new chapter. Seek Him and you will find Him!

—Tammy

Be a Difference Maker

Daniel 6; Matthew 10:37–39

"If you refuse to take up your cross and follow me, you are not worthy of being mine. If you cling to your life, you will lose it; but if you give up your life for me, you will find it" (Matthew 10:38–39 NLT).

The prophet Daniel was a difference-maker. As you read the Scripture passages for today, I've included some fun facts about this bold prophet:

1. Daniel lived around 620–538 BC.
2. Daniel comes from the priestly line of David, ultimately in the lineage of the Messiah.
3. Daniel was handsome, intelligent, and wise, being chosen by King Nebuchadnezzar to serve him at around age fifteen in 605 BC.
4. Daniel had unwavering faithfulness to God.
5. God gave Daniel the ability to interpret dreams because of Daniel's dedication and faith in God.
6. Daniel was probably in his eighties when he was in the lion's den.

Daniel's faith was unusual, and God set him apart from everyone else. Daniel never used the power of God for his own gain; rather he was an upright man, filled with integrity and divine wisdom. His unwavering faith was demonstrated when Daniel's jealous adversaries tricked King Darius into issuing a decree that for thirty days, everyone was to offer prayers to king Darius alone. If anyone disobeyed this command, they would be thrown into the lion's den. Daniel, being the man that he was, absolutely refused to pray to anyone other than his God, and so they threw him into the den of lions. Miraculously, God closed the mouths of the lions, and Daniel was unscathed.

What is the application for today? We live in a culture where moral integrity has broken down in our families, schools, and even churches. What if we had a faith like Daniel and stood up for God to be a difference-maker? The challenge is, are we willing to be thrown into a den of lions? Are we willing to be persecuted for the sake of Christ? As Christ-followers, staying silent, compromising our beliefs, or normalizing sin is wrong. Are you ready and willing to be a difference-maker today?

—Tammy

When is Enough Enough?

John 8:31–32

All the while I was growing up, I had a vague sense of feeling guilty. I couldn't pinpoint why, but it dominated my thoughts and actions. I had one sibling, a sister five years younger than I was. She had several special needs, but being raised in the 1950s, these problems were never diagnosed, and there weren't special services for children like my sister. I grew up always thinking, *Poor Janeen, poor, poor Janeen.* I continually tried to help her, especially into adulthood, but it was never enough. And so, I felt guilty that I was letting her down. "Jesus said to the people who believed in Him, 'You are truly my disciples if you remain faithful to my teachings. And you will know the truth, and the truth will set you free'" (John 8:31–32 NLT).

I had not yet accepted Christ or trusted Him as my Savior, even though I went to church and Sunday school every week. Then at the age of thirty-three, I trusted Christ. What an overwhelming change it made in my life! As I learned the truths from God's Word, I had the wisdom to see things more clearly. I could not fill my sister's needs, but God could. I needed to allow others to care for her in their way and trust that God would fill the voids that were missed. I was able to love her in a much healthier way by doing what I could and allowing others to do what they could.

A few years later, Janeen made the decision to follow Jesus at a Billy Graham crusade. After that, our relationship began to improve. Not long after that, Janeen passed away, but I know she is in heaven and I will see her again someday.

Thank You, Father, for Your Word and for freeing me from false guilt. I am grateful that Your resources are limitless and that I am able to continually glean new truths that help me in my daily walk with You. Amen.

—Sharon

Who's in the Mirror?

James 1:19–25

In 2009, our family took a church mission trip to the Dominican Republic. One of the duties I had was to create and teach a VBS to the village children there. I taught them Spanish Scripture songs, played games, taught Bible lessons, made animal balloons, and did face-painting. I can't say I was necessarily qualified for all of this, but God equipped me to serve in this way, and it brought me so much joy.

On the day of face-painting, I painted different pictures on my arm that they could pick from to have on their hand or face. After painting their cheeks, I would then show them what they looked like in the pocket mirror I brought with me. The expressions I saw from that simple act revealed to me that these children had never seen themselves in a mirror before, and I was witness to them seeing themselves for the very first time!

> For if you listen to the word and don't obey, it is like glancing at your face in a mirror. You see yourself, walk away, and forget what you look like. But if you look carefully into the perfect law that sets you free, and if you do what it says and don't forget what you heard, then God will bless you for doing it. (James 1:19–25 NLT)

I am sure those children who looked at themselves for the first time never forgot what they looked like. The image was permanently engraved into their minds. This was a humbling experience for me, but a very impressionable visual of obeying the Word of God.

We can learn all we can and read as much as we can, but if we don't do what it says, it is pointless. The easy thing to do is read. The harder thing is to obey. As Christ-followers, we benefit from having partners or groups to hold us accountable to God's Word. Obedience is hard, but through the Holy Spirit's help, we can be victorious.

Let us move forward with new vigor, showing ourselves obedient to Christ and following His leading in our lives. Let's not ever forget what we look like in the mirror!

—Tammy

We Are Exposed!
Ephesians 5:8–14

A few months ago, Mark and I awoke at 4:00 a.m. to a loud tumble on the roof. At first, we thought it was thunder, but then woke up enough to realize it was not like any kind of storm we had heard before. I got up out of bed to look out the window, but as I peered out, I was unable to decipher the large, dark image on our back patio. The moon glimmered, exposing some slight shadows, but a flashlight later revealed two great-horned owls, one of which appeared to be stunned and lifeless on the patio floor with his full wingspan stretched out. His mate sat next to him, hooting continuously, trying to awaken his friend. The majestic owl stared directly at Mark and me, and we reveled in this amazing and unforgettable sight. Gratefully, twenty minutes later, both birds flew away, and we celebrated the rare event we had just seen.

This is a simple analogy of how it is when we hear rumblings of "worthless deeds of evil" (Ephesians 5:11 NLT). We hear things, but we don't know how to help or what to do about them. "Jesus spoke to the people once more and said, 'I am the light of the world. If you follow me, you won't have to walk in darkness, because you will have the light that leads to life'" (John 8:12 NLT).

Our world has many dark places. Sin has become acceptable with no clear line of right and wrong. As Christ-followers, we have the light of Christ that shines out from us. Evil cannot coexist with that light. Light will expose the darkness, and darkness will flee in the power of Jesus' name.

Scripture tells us that in the last days, pastors and leaders will tickle the ears of the people, giving them what they want to hear. Accountability will be seen as overbearing and judging, and Christians will become immune to the evil right before their eyes, desensitizing them to truth. As we pray and seek God today, reflect on the things in your daily life that Jesus wants to shed light on. Be proactive! The truth will shine on all the dark places and be totally exposed.

—Tammy

Make the Most of Each Day
Ephesians 5:15–20; James 4:13–17; Revelation 21:4

"So be careful how you live. Don't live like fools, but like those who are wise. Make the most of every opportunity in these evil days. Don't act thoughtlessly, but understand what the Lord wants you to do" (Ephesians 5:15–17 NLT).

On Tuesday, September 11, 2001, nobody who worked in the New York Twin Towers that morning expected it to be their last. Some had just dropped their children off at daycare, not knowing they were kissing their son or daughter for the last time. Others had lunch meetings planned later in the day with clients that would never happen. Life is unpredictable. That is just a fact. We can't count on tomorrow, but we also cannot live in fear. God desires all of us to make the most of every day.

When it comes to having this mindset, Mark and I make a good team. Mark is much more of a planner, yet I am the more spontaneous one, who sometimes likes to fly by the seat of my pants! There is no right or wrong to either way, but we have learned to join the two mindsets into how we can serve God best and make the most of every day. This means that overall, we have chosen mission fields where we want to give of our time and resources. But we have also left the door wide open for the Holy Spirit to move spontaneously in case there is a sudden need.

> Look here, you who say, "Today or tomorrow we are going to a certain town and will stay there a year. We will do business there and make a profit." How do you know what your life will be like tomorrow? Your life is like the morning fog—it's here a little while, then it's gone. (James 4:13–14 NLT)

The main thing that Mark and I have learned together is that we want to make the most of every day when it comes to our schedules and finances. We don't want to be so planned out that we miss opportunities that come up right in front of our eyes. But we also don't want to overlook the importance of careful financial planning and time management in our generosity. We want to be ready for both.

—Tammy

Week 33 Reflections

1. After reviewing the Scriptures for each day, name three to four passages that jumped out at you this week.
2. How can you practically apply these verses to your life today and the upcoming week?
3. Name a situation in your life that requires healthy boundaries.
4. What hesitations do you have in placing healthy boundaries in your life? What does God want you to do?
5. Is your faith making a difference in your daily life? Explain.
6. Do you suffer from false guilt? What does God's Word say about that?
7. When it comes to generosity, are you more of a planner, or are you more spontaneous? How can God use that but also stretch you in one area or the other?
8. Has Jesus shed light on a dark spot in your life? If so, write down what it is. Pray for Him to completely light it up and expose it.
9. Our lives are but a breath. Every day is precious to God. What will you do to make the most of today so that you are pleasing God?

MONTH 9
Trials We Encounter May Cause Worrying and Complaining

A FAITH THAT STANDS
Produces Peace, Contentment, and Gratefulness

Peace: the Real Thing

Romans 15:13; Philippians 4:6–8

Mark and I have learned some very funny things about men's and women's brains that have shed light on some of the things we quarrel over. I think one of the funniest things I have learned about men is that they have little compartmentalized boxes of their lives and the boxes do not touch! A woman's brain, however, is like a ball of wire, seamlessly connecting all things into one endless piece of information!

A strategy I have found that helps me communicate to my husband and two sons is taking my emotion out of what I am trying to explain. In turn, I try to communicate like a logic problem does, so that what I'm saying will compute with them more with facts than with feelings. This approach probably helps me more than it helps them!

For example: **IF** you watch football all day, **THEN** I will feel neglected. **IF** I feel neglected, **THEN** I will be upset. **IF** I feel upset, **THEN** I will not feel like making you brownies! The conclusion? **IF** you watch football all day, **THEN** I will not feel like making you brownies!

Let's use this same concept to apply the Scripture readings for today. **IF** I am anxious, **THEN** I should pray, trust, be thankful, and present my requests to God. **IF** I pray, trust, am thankful, and present my requests to God, **THEN** I will have a peace that transcends all understanding. **IF** I have a peace that transcends all understanding, **THEN** God will give me abundant joy to think about what is true, noble, and praiseworthy. The conclusion? **IF** I am feeling anxious, **THEN** God will be my source of abundant joy to think about what is true, noble, and praiseworthy through the Holy Spirit.

God is our only source of peace. Often we must break a passage of Scripture down, taking one step at a time as in a logic problem. Separating the verses out and praying for Him to wash over us with His peace can help us understand how to achieve what is in the text.

When you are feeling anxious, reach up to Him! Tell Him what you are thankful for and pray for His peace, joy, and hope because it is **THEN** that you will be able to think about what is true, noble, and praiseworthy through the power of His Holy Spirit!

–Tammy

God's Purpose for Us

Jeremiah 32:38–40

When Scott and Matt were in first grade and kindergarten, respectively, we moved in the middle of the year from Ohio to Pennsylvania. I felt very sad to move Matt particularly because he loved his teacher. She was young, loving, kind, and nurturing, and I thought she had hung the moon! When we moved, Matt got an older, firmer, no-nonsense teacher that did not seem as nurturing (at first). I remember after dropping Matt off, I called my mom crying. Matt's kindergarten year was going to be ruined! My emotions had certainly gotten the best of me.

Then the unexpected happened! When I picked Matt up from school that day, I asked him how it went, and he said, "Great! I really like my teacher!" I asked him why, and he said, "Her name rhymes with tiger, and she has control of the whole class! She told me where I should put my bag, and she let me be the line leader because I was quiet."

At that moment, I realized that Matt thrived under a strict teacher with firm guidelines because he could trust that rules would be followed and boundaries would be clear. For the rest of his school career, I requested teachers like this one, and Matt excelled under their direction.

Like Matt's teachers, sometimes God can seem insensitive, especially when we look at the Israelites, their rebellion, and how God punished them. I have often pondered the wrath of God because He is also a loving and merciful God. But when I read through the first five books of the Bible, God was not getting through to the Israelites. He created humans to worship Him, and yet they continued to turn their backs on Him. God needed to be firm, giving them firm guidelines and using Israel as an example to all nations what He desired from His people. "They will be my people, and I will be their God. And I will give them one heart and one purpose: to worship me forever" (Jeremiah 32:38–39 NLT).

God wants a relationship with us! Today let us thank Him for His clear guidelines, for if we follow them, there is so much to be gained.

—Tammy

The Lord Is Good

Philippians 4:6; Hebrews 4:16

It never hurts to ask, right? Or so they say. But perhaps it depends on what and whom we ask. And what if the answer is no? There are times when asking is easy, when a no answer might provide a minor inconvenience or temporary disappointment, but it's a different story when it feels like a no answer just might crush you.

Is this true in your relationship with God? Does fear keep you from praying big, bold prayers? How do we wholeheartedly present our requests for the things that seem so right and so necessary to us, but then also pray "Thy will be done"? How do we ask in full faith, truly believing for the impossible and simultaneously accepting that the answer may be no?

Even with our greatest desires and perceived needs, it can feel easier to believe that He can and simply not ask than to ask and find out that He won't. It can feel easier to pray about it and around it, without ever really asking for it. It can feel easier to remain stuck than to risk a no answer. This, however, is only true when we focus solely on the ask itself and forget the goodness of the One we ask, the One who sees the big picture, knows our hearts and wants what's best for us, and loves and cares for us beyond what we can fathom.

> Taste and see that the Lord is good. Oh, the joys of those who take refuge in him! Fear the Lord, you his goldy people, for those who fear him will have all they need … but those who trust in the Lord will lack no good thing. (Psalm 34: 8–10 NLT)

If we are to pray boldly and confidently, we must not only believe in God's power but also remember His goodness. We must put our trust in the character and the will of God. When we do so, we can pour our hearts out to Him over all things big and small, and we can praise Him no matter the answer.

-Kara

Kristin in the school's communications office called the paper. A day later my office squeezed in David Sedeno, executive editor of The Texas Catholic; Seth Gonzalez, a videographer; Michael Gresham, managing editor; and Jenna Teter, a photographer. More than a single article, David wanted to document our pregnancy journey. To my surprise, he was saying he wanted to film it. *Whoa.* For that answer, I said, I'd have to talk to my husband.

That evening at home, from up, down and sideways, Jonas and I debated what it would look like to give a newspaper, or anyone, unguarded access to our lives. Jonas values privacy. I was okay with a crew at my elbow, and we came to a compromise: full access to me, limited access to him. When the baby came, no crew or cameras. The next day I gave The Texas Catholic our ground rules, and they asked to start right away.

One week later, our varsity volleyball players, coaches and managers boarded a bus to our start-of-season bonding retreat on Lake Texoma. The Texas Catholic crew would meet us there. The annual getaway sets the tone for the season, and I was excited to leave town with the girls.

Why Lake Texoma for this all-important annual launch? Because I had lived there. In the early nineties when my parents divorced, my mom moved my sister and me from the North Dallas suburb we'd always known to a middle-of-nowhere town called Pottsboro, Texas, which in winter tops out at 1,200 people. Come summer, though, with its cheek-to-jowl proximity to Lake Texoma, the area draws thousands of people with boats and jet skis in tow.

Water sports meant nothing to my sister and me when we had to trade our father and our Dallas friends to live where a grocery run is a half-hour drive. For a while we drug our feet. Then we accepted what we couldn't change. And then our classmates became our friends, and school sports opened our worlds.

Now a former classmate of mine ran a retreat center on a peninsula next to the water, a setting of cabins with a small hotel and a main building with a dining hall and large common room.

From the hill a path led to a lake with a beach and a swimming pool. Every year I'd point out my high school and my childhood home to girls who live where convenient gas and groceries are birthrights. To build the trust here that could take us through the rough year ahead, my own candor would be necessary to encourage theirs.

At the main office, I checked in for everyone. The girls dashed to their cabins to change into bathing suits for our first meeting, which was near the lake. I left the office just as the car with our two-person crew from The Texas Catholic rolled across the parking lot gravel.

Jenna, our photographer, enthusiastic and gifted, was in her late twenties, a Bishop Lynch grad herself, already a veteran of dozens of assignments at our school. Our videographer, Seth, matched her in high spirits. Climbing out of their car, where the rest of us saw scenery, they knew to scan for interview backdrops and b-roll. They wanted to be flies on our wall, meaning they wanted us to go about our lives ignoring the large cameras at the fringes of all we did. For every shoot I'd be mic'd. On occasion, coaches and players would also wire up. I felt like the lead in a reality TV show, and when I thought about it too long, I grew anxious. But I'd agreed to the coverage. I believed in the value of banking these moments, and I trusted the process.

> I felt like the lead in a reality TV show, and when I thought about it too long, I grew anxious.

Our girls met up with Josh and me at the main building. From there, we walked together to the beach where we settled in under a weeping willow, shallow waves lapping against the nearby shore. When Jenna and Seth found us, they seized the moment to ask us to help keep their work true. "Pretend we're not here," Seth directed. "Never look directly into the camera."

For the next hour each girl in the circle introduced herself and her hopes for the season. When my turn came, I described my upbringing in Dallas and Pottsboro, college at Baylor University

Grateful for the Losses
Ecclesiastes 3:1–8; 2 Corinthians 12:9; Philippians 4:19

Loss is difficult to manage. Loss makes us feel weak. Loss makes us feel hopeless. In minor cases, we lose our keys, our train of thought, and our place on a page. In more severe instances, we lose our jobs, our joy, and our loved ones. Somewhere in the middle of that spectrum, I find my current loss, my ability to smell and taste. Thirteen months ago, I lost this ability from an all-too-familiar virus, and while this loss may end up being temporary, it brings hundreds of despairing thoughts to my mind. Almost always, the loss we experience transitions into feelings of weakness.

But Paul's words to the Corinthians ring true each day that I go without smell and taste, and they should ring true to everyone regardless of what loss or weakness they may be experiencing. The truth of humans having weakness is exactly that, truth. Try as we might, we will never achieve any feat on Earth that will impress God to the extent that He grants us special access into heaven. That special access is given to all who believe in Him! This truth is one of the greatest gifts of encouragement given to us, as it gives us both the freedom to fail and the assurance of hope in times of seeming hopelessness.

> But he said to me, "My grace is sufficient for you, for my power is made perfect in weakness." Therefore, I will boast all the more gladly about my weaknesses, so that Christ's power may rest on me. (2 Corinthians 12:9 NLT)

Reflect on a time when you experienced loss or weakness. Did you turn to the Lord for hope and strength? Now consider the loss you may be experiencing right now or perhaps at a future time. Turn to the Lord for His strength. The Lord works marvels in our lives to bless us in the ways we need to be blessed, and we can be grateful for the losses.

—Matt

> And my God will meet all your needs according to the riches of his glory in Christ Jesus. (Philippians 4:19 NIV)

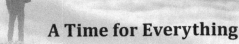

A Time for Everything

Ecclesiastes 3:1–8; 2 Corinthians 12:9; Philippians 4:19

"For everything there is a season; a time for every activity under heaven. A time to be born and a time to die. A time to plant and a time to harvest. A time to kill and a time to heal. A time to tear down and a time to build up. A time to cry and a time to laugh. A time to grieve and a time to dance. A time to scatter stones and a time to gather stones. A time to embrace and a time to turn away. A time to search and a time to quit searching. A time to keep and a time to throw away. A time to tear and a time to mend. A time to be quiet and a time to speak. A time to love and a time to hate. A time for war and a time for peace" (Ecclesiastes 3:1–8 NLT).

King Solomon penned these words in the tenth-century BC that became famous in a song, "Turn, Turn, Turn" by the 1960s band, The Byrds, after Pete Seeger put them to music in 1959. The song became number one in December 1965 when American ground troops landed in Vietnam. Although the song is a secular song, the words are straight from Ecclesiastes 3:1–8.

Ecclesiastes can leave a person feeling dreary, as Solomon recounts the cycles of life through human reason, personal experience, and pleasure-seeking. He sees life as a random repeat of events, seemingly meaningless. However, he changes his perspective when he sees life through the lens of faith, recognizing that life without God is what is truly meaningless. Life with God gives purpose to everything.

With faith in God as the foundation for understanding, he recognizes that all the cycles of life are part of God's timetable and perfect plan. The latter use of the phrase "under heaven" instead of "under the sun" earlier in the book suggests his new divine perspective. Likewise, although we can't control what life brings us, we can choose whether to live life without God or for God, trusting His purpose for every season.

Life is hard. But I can't imagine going through life's many seasons without faith and without God. The Lord brings purpose through every change, every transition, and every time, which in turn aligns our purpose with His!

–Tammy

The Voice of the Lord
Psalm 29, 33:6; Romans 4:17

"The Lord merely spoke, and the heavens were created. He breathed the word, and all the stars were born" (Romans 4:17 NLT).

The word *powerful* can be used to describe many different things. If I eat something powerful, it usually means the food is very spicy or flavorful. If I am watching an Olympic gymnast, I would say that their performances are strong and powerful. If there is an odor that is extremely strong, I refer to the smell as powerful. If I hear a great song with musical and spiritual depth, I will identify that song as powerful.

When it comes to describing God, how do we even begin to describe Him? The use of the word *powerful* seems to be so often minimized in our language, just like the word *love* is minimized when we say we *love* ice cream or we *love* the color on the walls. But we also love our families, our friends, and God. So how do we give the proper value to the word *powerful* when it comes to describing God?

Psalm 29 is a beautiful metaphorical illustration describing one aspect of His power in particular, His voice.

> The voice of the Lord echoes above the sea. The God of glory thunders. The Lord thunders over the mighty sea. The voice of the Lord is powerful; the voice of the Lord is majestic. The voice of the Lord splits the mighty cedars; the Lord shatters the cedars of Lebanon ... The voice of the Lord strikes with bolts of lightning. The voice of the Lord makes the barren wilderness quake. The voice of the Lord twists mighty oaks and strips the forests bare ... (Psalm 29:3–5, 7–9a NLT)

God spoke to Moses in a burning bush. Jesus spoke, and people were healed, demons cast out, and hope restored. God speaks to us today. Whether in a still, soft voice or a voice that "twists the mighty oaks," there is power in the voice of the Lord.

—Tammy

Week 34 Reflections

1. After reviewing the Scriptures for each day, name three to four passages that jumped out at you this week.
2. How can you practically apply these verses to your life today and the upcoming week?
3. Pursuing God's peace goes hand in hand with renewing our minds. What should you ask for and think upon?
4. What is God's purpose for you considering Jeremiah 32:38–40?
5. When has God given a clear no to something you have pleaded with Him for? What was your response? How did it affect your faith?
6. What losses have you experienced lately? Reflecting on them, what is God teaching you through those losses?
7. How does the Psalmist describe God's Word in Psalm 19?
8. Describe the voice of the Lord.
9. The Lord is powerful. What does that mean for you?

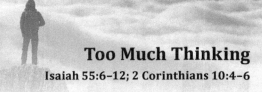

Too Much Thinking

Isaiah 55:6–12; 2 Corinthians 10:4–6

"'My thoughts are nothing like your thoughts,' says the Lord. 'And my ways are far beyond anything you could imagine. For just as the heavens are higher than the earth, so my ways are higher than your ways and my thoughts higher than your thoughts'" (Isaiah 55:8–9 NLT).

I am an overthinker. Sometimes I exhaust myself with the amount of thinking I do in a day. My friends laugh with me at times because I'm not only thinking creatively, but I rehash conversations and events that already happened. By the time I am done thinking, I've gotten myself worked up to assume the worst, often leading me to worry. This overthinking is damaging to me emotionally and spiritually, leading to the sin of worry and negative thinking.

Isaiah reminds us that our thoughts are not like God's thoughts and that His ways are so much higher than our ways. God wants to get a hold of our thought life and has a plan to help us with that. Just like the "stop, drop, and roll" training we are taught to do in a fire, it would be good if we could recognize the warning signs of overthinking with a similar reminder to focus on God. Perhaps something like, "stop, drop it, and move forward" " … and we take captive every thought to make it obedient to Christ" (2 Corinthians 10:5 NIV).

Since I'm visual, I have this image in my head of taking my thoughts that are not of God and putting them in a metal box with a huge lock on it. Then I ask God to fill those empty spaces in my head with His thoughts that include love for others, forgiveness, grace, peace, hope, trust, and purity. If I find myself thinking thoughts that are contrary to these things, I repeat the process again, "stop, drop it, and move forward."

God's thoughts are nothing like your thoughts, and His ways are more than you possibly can imagine! If you find yourself on the downward cycle of overthinking, God wants you to come to Him. He promises to give you His peace.

–Tammy

Tornado Thinking

Psalm 13

I was flabbergasted the day I learned that men can actually think about absolutely nothing! For years, I asked my husband and sons what they were thinking about, and they would sometimes reply, "Nothing." I thought they just didn't want to talk. But no, men have this uncanny ability to block everything else out and think about absolutely nothing!

I cannot relate to this. I describe my thinking as tornado thinking. If you've ever seen or been a part of a tornado, you know that when the opposing air currents collide, they begin to spiral, picking up debris and speed, destroying everything in its path. The tornado doesn't come out of nowhere, for the conditions can be tracked beforehand, warning people to take shelter. For women especially, our pattern of thinking is much like a tornado. Negative thoughts that once start small begin to pick up other thoughts, spiraling into much bigger and broader negative thoughts, destroying our peace, our confidence, and our hope.

In Psalm 13, David demonstrates how negative thoughts can bring us down as he questions God, feeling utterly defeated and forgotten. He's letting God know that he is at his wit's end. "Turn and answer me, O Lord my God! Restore the sparkle to my eyes, or I will die" (Psalm 13:3 NLT).

Two verses later, David uses the word *but*, indicating a change in his thinking. He says, "**But** I **trust** in your unfailing love. I will **rejoice** because you have rescued me. I will **sing** to the Lord because he is good to me" (Psalm 13:5 NLT).

These bolded words give us action items to trust, rejoice, and sing when our thoughts begin to spiral. God is a faithful God, and when we offer Him praise as in these two verses, He inhabits those praises and renews our minds. When our thoughts begin to swell with negativity, let's remember the tornado and seek God with praise before they destroy us and everyone in our path!

—Tammy

Get Off the Merry-go-round!

Colossians 3:1–11

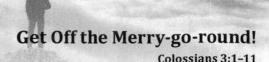

I was hiking in the hills of Kentucky with friends during college when we got ourselves lost. We thought we had stayed on the marked trail, but somehow we lost it. At six thirty in the evening, we knew we didn't have many hours of sunlight left, so we began to walk faster, desperately seeking the trail exit. An hour later, to our dismay, we found ourselves right back where we had been hours earlier. We were going in circles and didn't know how to get back on the marked trail. So we split up for five minutes, and all five of us went in different directions, hoping to find the yellow markers. Miraculously, we were only about a hundred feet off the trail, and we all ran the rest of the way before nightfall hit.

I remember the fear I felt, wondering how we were ever going to get off this path that seemed to go nowhere but in circles! There is a saying that if you do the same thing over and over, you will get the same result over and over. If you want change, you need to do something different to get a different result!

Spiritually this concept applies to all of us. We want the Holy Spirit to change us, yet we keep going to the same bars, exposing ourselves to the same bad influences, keeping a hidden stash of supplies "just in case," and putting off church "just one more time." Our first step is to recognize that we are on a merry-go-round, a never-ending cycle of repeated behavior resulting in destruction.

Once we realize we are on the wrong path, the next step is to repent and ask God to help us get off the merry-go-round with a desire to be put back on the trail with the yellow markers. He will help us find the way out and sustain us on the proper path.

As you read Colossians 3, I encourage you to read it once, meditate on it, and read it again. Let the words encourage you to get off the merry-go-round yourself or to encourage a fellow brother and sister to do so. God is for you, not against you. His plans far exceed anything you could ever imagine!

–Tammy

Lead Me to the Rock
Psalm 61, 121

"From the ends of the earth I call to you, I call as my heart grows faint; lead me to the rock that is higher than I" (Psalm 61:2 NIV).

I was Googling pictures of scary fish that live in the deepest, darkest places of the oceans. Many of them look like they were created for a horror movie with no eyes, exhibiting huge mouths, unusually long fangs, and other features that could give you nightmares if you stared at them too long! These fish never see sunlight. They are bottom-dwellers, living in the dark, cold waters, and for the most part, they are unseen by the rest of the world.

Sometimes I feel like one of these fish. I'm alone, trying to function in the dark while surviving the icy waters that surround me, and my perspective is bleak and small. I can barely see what is in front of my face, much less see what is ahead. Hope is difficult to cling to in times like these. Unlike the bottom-dweller fish at the bottom of the ocean, I was not created to live in the dark, especially days, weeks, and months on end. As human beings, we need light, warmth, fellowship with others, and a closeness to our Savior. Many times, we need to have a new perspective through the eyes of Christ so we can take our eyes off ourselves.

> I lift up my eyes to the hills. From where does my help come? My help comes from the Lord, who made heaven and earth. He will not let your foot be moved; he who keeps you will not slumber. (Psalm 121:1–3 NIV)

We can't see the mountains when we are in the ocean depths, but God knows we cannot live at the cold bottom for long. Psalm 61 takes us on a spiritual flight to soar above our problems and our situations. It is a heartfelt prayer for God to lead us to a supernatural place! He wants to take us there on wings like eagles, to gain fresh eyes on our situations, and to recognize that the God who created all of creation has the power to help us in times of trouble. May He lead us to the Rock so we can rest in the shadow of His wings and soak in every part of who He is.

—Tammy

Planning for Tomorrow
Matthew 6:33–34

My wife has an uncanny ability to see all the things that could go wrong in a situation. At times she can see all the details of what might happen when nothing has even begun to play out. If only the military leaders knew of her great skills, they could use her for their strategic planning on the largest battlegrounds. Every potential bad outcome would be seen and discussed prior to it happening.

Of course, her thought process, like many humans, takes her to the worst-case scenarios that lead to unnecessary worrying. For Tammy and everyone, if we are not careful, we can spend lots of time and energy worrying about things that never happen.

As part of Jesus' Sermon on the Mount, he taught about worry. He taught us not to worry about everyday things like what to eat, drink, or wear. Even better He gives the steps to take to avoid worrying about our daily needs.

> Seek the Kingdom of God above all else, and live righteously, and he will give you everything you need. So do not worry about tomorrow, for tomorrow will bring its own worries. Today's trouble is enough for today. (Matthew 6:33–34 NIV)

We will have troubles on this earth. Jesus is very clear about this, and so we should not expect less. We need to stay focused on the present. Much like the best military planning, some future thinking about possible scenarios is necessary to prepare for upcoming events and situations. Preparation is a good thing when done in the right context, but worrying about the future only eats away at us.

Again, we will have troubles on this earth. However, when we allow ourselves to begin worrying about the future, let's take a step back and start by seeking the kingdom of God above all else and surrendering those worries to Jesus for Him to take care of. God's promise is to give us everything we need. That is the best planning ever.

—Mark

Toxic Thinking
Romans 8:5–8, 12:2

Social media and the need to find our place in this world is rampant. We want to leave a legacy. We want to make a difference. Though these are wonderful aspirations, we can quickly fill our minds with toxic thoughts that turn our eyes to the things of this world instead of having the mindset of our heavenly Father. Some of those toxic thoughts are:

1. Allowing others' opinions of us define who we think we are
2. Putting value on things that are temporary and not eternal
3. Not accepting that some things in life are just what they are and that we cannot change others' actions and words
4. Worrying about the future
5. Living our lives as a victim instead of an overcomer
6. Believing that the past defines our future
7. Replaying negative thoughts over and over in our mind, consuming our thoughts with bad feelings about ourselves

> Those who are dominated by the sinful nature think about sinful things, but those who are controlled by the Holy Spirit think about things that please the Spirit. So, letting your sinful nature control your mind leads to death. But letting the Spirit control your mind leads to life and peace. (Romans 8:5–6 NLT)

Letting the Holy Spirit control our mind is key to allowing the Spirit to change and renew our thinking in general. I have struggled with toxic thinking, causing me to feel defeated before I even begin to move forward. Negative thoughts are not from God, yet we allow them to play out in our minds. The key is to nip them in the bud.

> Don't copy the behavior and customs of this world, but let God transform you into a new person by changing the way you think. Then you will learn to know God's will for you, which is good and pleasing and perfect. (Romans 12:2 NLT)

—Tammy

Week 35 Reflections

1. After reviewing the Scriptures for each day, name three to four passages that jumped out at you this week.
2. How can you practically apply these verses to your life today and the upcoming week?
3. Do you think too much? How does your thinking draw you closer to God or away from God?
4. God wants to intervene on our thoughts, especially when they begin to snowball and spiral. What is your plan with Jesus the next time you fall into this pattern of thinking?
5. In what areas in your life do you notice that you are still on the merry-go-round, going down the same path and getting the same results?
6. I love the visual of looking up, leading us to the Rock that is higher than we are. Write out a simple prayer, asking God to do just that.
7. Has worrying ever helped you? Has it ever hurt you? Explain. How is worry a sin?
8. Toxic thinking can invade our relationships and our ability to discern what is really true. What toxic thinking do you need to confess and let the Lord transform?
9. Overall, what is God speaking to you about this week?

Do You Stink?
Numbers 11:1–10; Ecclesiastes 10:1–2

Growing up, my family had a full house of animals that included a dog, cat, bird, guinea pig, rabbit, turtle, hamster, and fish. Let's just say I was used to a variety of smells simply because of the number of living creatures that inhabited our house.

Years later when I was married with two middle school–age boys under our roof, I realized the word *smells* took on brand-new meaning, from the stinky shoes in the hallway to the week-old uneaten turkey sandwich found in their hall cubby.

The sense of smell is a powerful tool God gave us to identify what is around us, some of which is beautiful and some of which is simply not so good. Smells can also indicate warning signs, such as a plugged toilet, spoiled food, or a gas leak in the home. Some odors indicate potential behaviors that need to change, such as poor cleanliness and hygiene.

We are all smelly people. Some of our stink can be smelled with our noses, yet other odors are given off through our behaviors. In the Old Testament, God was very frustrated with the Israelites because of all their complaining. The stink of their ungratefulness of all God had done for them led them to worship other gods and to complain about their circumstances.

Do you give off any smells that indicate something needs to change? Perhaps it's the smell of gossip or negativity? Or maybe pride or stubbornness have taken root and give off an odor that other people are beginning to smell. We can't hide odors for long. We may mask the odor with a smile (or a little too much cologne) or by simply saying the right things. But if the human heart is contaminated with a stench that is not pleasing to God, there is a need to repent.

My prayer is that if I begin to stink in my behavior or attitude, someone I trust will bring it to my attention. After all, I don't want to stink! There are enough bad odors in this world. "As dead flies cause even a bottle of perfume to stink, so a little foolishness spoils great wisdom and honor" (Ecclesiastes 10:1–2 NLT).

—Tammy

Israelite Thinking
Exodus 16

Allow me to take you back to a time in ancient Israel when God had recently brought the Israelites out of Egypt, out of the land of slavery. This major event in biblical history happened just one month prior to the events in Exodus 16, our passage for today. As we read through the story, the historical context to this chapter enlightens us to what God was doing with the Israelites and how they were responding to God. The Israelite's thinking was off, and God was losing His patience.

Moses and Aaron were the vessels God used to lead the people out of Egypt, but they now found the Israelites wandering in the wilderness, tirelessly complaining. The joyful singing that had been filling the camps had quickly turned to grumbling out of anticipation of starving with limited food supplies. Notice, they were not starving at that time. They were simply grumbling out of anticipating the worst, even after all that God had done for them.

The story continues as the Israelites accuse Moses and Aaron of evil motives by taking them out into the wilderness to kill them. Instead of having a spirit of gratefulness to God and their leaders, they quickly turned to bellyaching, attacking the very people who were helping them and communicating with God on their behalf.

As the story goes, God continued to show His mercy by providing for the Israelites in a very unexpected way. He showered bread from heaven (manna) for them each morning and provided meat in the evenings. But you'll have to read the rest of the chapter to learn how they further disobeyed!

Frustrating behavior, isn't it? But how often do we also fall into this same trap? God provides for us, rescues us, and guides us, but we quickly forget all of that and go back to not trusting Him. We start to complain. We begin to worry and anticipate the worst in others and in God.

One thing I know for sure: we can all learn from the Israelites' missteps that God can be trusted, and He will always provide for us! Let us not have Israelite thinking, but instead be grateful and anticipate all the good things He is already and will continue to do in our lives.

-Tammy

Just Say Thank You
Luke 17:11–19

Ten Lepers

Saying "thank you" means a lot. When Mark and I became parents, we both wanted to raise boys with good manners, appreciating what God and others had given to them, saying "please" and "thank you." For all of you first-time parents reading this, please know that this didn't happen overnight! This was a constant endeavor, always at the forefront of behavioral teaching.

Sometimes we forget to say "thank you" far into adulthood. We might ask God for something for so long that when it finally happens or is given to us, we almost feel like our "thank you" is not enough. We also can take for granted that God has bestowed Himself on us again, so we forget to say those words of thanks. Lastly, we can find ourselves so focused on ourselves that we aren't even thinking about the Giver.

I remember in my teen years I would play piano for church, concerts, or competitions. Since I was a perfectionist, this resulted in a sour facial expression if I made mistakes, almost making it impossible to respond properly to compliments from people with the words "thank you!" In my mind, I thought if I said "thank you," I was saying that I believed it was a stellar performance and it would impact my image. Not sensible, right? Prideful, no doubt. But then a mentor and teacher told me that responding in true thanks was appreciating the person who gave the compliment. It was acknowledging that they went out of their way to encourage me and that it was polite to smile and be gracious.

In Luke 17, Jesus tells this story of when he healed ten men from leprosy. As they walked away, only one man came back to say "thank you." One man out of ten! Because of the man's gratefulness and appreciation toward Jesus, Jesus told Him that the man's faith had healed him! He was then referring to his inner soul in need of healing.

What can we glean from this story of the ten lepers? Awareness, love, and appreciation of others, even if it means going out of our way to show our gratefulness. Whether it's writing a card, sending a text, or picking up the phone, your "thank you" could be the bright spot in someone's day.

—Tammy

Soar Like an Eagle
Isaiah 40:25–31

I had never seen an eagle in flight until a few weeks ago when one flew directly over my house. It was low enough where I could see the details of its wings and the white tips of his tail and head, a spectacular sight. Did you know that the eagle is mentioned throughout the Bible in thirty-three different verses? For ancient writers, the eagle was a symbol for freedom, strength, and power. In fact, the bald eagle was adopted as the national bird in the United States in 1792 because of its majesty, large wingspan, and long life span.

When I saw that eagle, I thought about what God's perspective is like. He sees it all. He is not limited in His understanding and never grows weary. Isaiah uses the eagle to symbolize God's perspective. "But those who trust in the Lord will find new strength. They will soar high on wings like eagles. They will run and not grow weary. They will walk and not faint" (Isaiah 40:31 NLT).

Our view is very limited. We see a very small glimpse of what God sees. To us, we can grow tired quickly, get discouraged easily, and feel hopeless when the familiar falters around us. God's view is vast, which is why we need to trust the God who sees. God wants to show us His perspective, but more than anything, He wants us to trust Him with it.

Why is it so hard sometimes to trust the Lord and commit our daily routines and relationships to Him? How different would our day, our week, or our year be, if we were to look up to God in full recognition of His majesty, strength, freedom, and perspective? We may see a breakthrough in our marriage! We may discover that the very thing we have been holding on to so hard is the very thing God wants us to let go of! God sees it all. You can't hide anything from Him. "He never grows weak or weary. No one can measure the depths of his understanding. He gives power to the weak and strength to the powerless" (Isaiah 40:28–29 NLT).

—Tammy

Perseverance in Marriage
Isaiah 43:1–2; John 8:32; 1 Corinthians 13

My husband died nine years ago of colon cancer. I truly miss my husband, but I could not always say that. When coming into a marriage, everyone has baggage, and when two people unite in marriage, they bring their baggage with them. I was an introvert and brought extreme shyness with me; my husband brought tremendous anger. This anger didn't rear its ugly head at first, but as the years went by, his anger exploded. It was horrible for our two daughters and me. There was much yelling and throwing things, instilling much fear in all of us. This really led me to seek professional help from a Christian counselor, where we learned how vital it was to communicate with each other and persevere. Was it hard work? Yes. Had we not found Christ, we never would have made it through.

After three and a half years of Christian counseling, through many tears and anguish, we got to the truth (John 8:32), and honestly, that set us free! It was a long process. We realized that we could not do it without the help of God. We had to seek Him, moment by moment of every day.

The latter years of our marriage were beautiful. I had always known deep down inside that my husband had a very tender, loving heart toward the girls and me. Perseverance had developed character, and the outcome was a deeper love than we had at the beginning of our marriage.

While doing a scrapbook of his life a short time ago, I came across a love letter he wrote to me the first year we started dating. Every time I read it, I can't stop crying. In a nutshell, he wrote, "You have taught me to care and love. But most important, you have let me love you, and you have let me take you into my heart, where you will remain forever. I love you very sincerely, and may God always bless you."

I have a lot to thank God for. I stuck with the process of healing, even though it was long and painful. What Satan intended for evil, God intended for good. We began well, and we ended well. Love never fails (1 Corinthians 13).

—Sharon

Let's Be a Honeybee!
Psalm 19:1–10

The Bible uses honey as a metaphor for delight, God's abundant provision, and sweetness. Mentioned over sixty times in the Bible, honey from a honeycomb is often compared to the Word of God, but it also refers to the Promised Land as the land flowing with milk and honey. Psalm 19 says this about God's Word and teaching:

1.   His instructions are perfect.
2.   They revive one's soul.
3.   His decrees are trustworthy.
4.   His commandments are right and bring joy to the hearts.
5.   God's commands are clear and give insight for living.
6.   Reverence for God is pure and lasts forever.
7.   God's laws are true and fair.
8.   The Words of God are more desirable than the finest gold.
9.   The Words of God are sweeter than honey dripping from a comb.

The Word of God sounds ideal, don't you think? And yet we spend so many hours of our lives searching for other ways to fill the voids in our lives, to heal our broken hearts, and to give us insight and direction, forgetting that we have access to the sweet honey from God Himself!

I need Jesus! You need Jesus! Our world needs Jesus! Our culture needs revival, and it will take a swarm of human honeybees to spread this honey to the rest of the world. We don't need to go far to be a honey-giver. For many of us, we can start right in the home, our place of employment, our neighborhoods, our churches, and our cities.

If followers of Jesus stop giving and speaking the Word of God to the world around them, what will happen to future generations? It's a scary thought, but I'm sure God would have that figured out too.

When all is said and done, when I reach the gates of eternity, I hope to be an exhausted honeybee who kept going until the very end to spread God's love, the healing balm to our souls. Let's all be honeybees together!

—Tammy

Week 36 Reflections

1. After reviewing the Scriptures for each day, name three to four passages that jumped out at you this week.
2. How can you practically apply these verses to your life today and the upcoming week?
3. What are some of the odors people may notice from you?
4. Complaining can turn into a habit if we are not careful. How often do you complain? What do you typically complain about?
5. How can God turn complaining into gratefulness? Be specific.
6. We all need God's perspective that soars above our circumstances. Write a prayer asking God to give you His perspective on _____.
7. What is more valuable to you, time or money? Explain.
8. Whether you are married or unmarried, what are you persevering through right now? What do you need from God to help you?
9. How can being a honeybee bring healing to our society? How specifically can you be a honeybee this week and to whom?

Worry and Anxiety at its Finest
Psalm 9:10; Matthew 6:25–34

When I was in first grade, our family was involved in a car accident coming home to Syracuse, New York, from Disney World in Florida. The snow blizzard swept across New York and Pennsylvania, and before we knew it, we had spun around several times, colliding with a guardrail, towing a twenty-foot camper on the back. We were stuck in a huge snowbank, but we were safe. When my parents got out of the car to evaluate the situation, the guardrail we collided with overlooked a deep, rocky ravine that if we had gone over, we would not have survived. After rescue workers came to help, they informed us that we were spared because a mile up the road was a twenty-two-car pileup with several fatalities.

There is so much in life we have absolutely no control over. The sooner we come to grips with that, the better we will be able to experience God's peace. We worry and are anxious because of things we have no control over, such as weather, disease, death, the economy, and decisions that other people make. We make plans but then worry whether they will come to pass because of life's unpredictability.

If we know all of this, why do we worry? Why do we stress ourselves, battling for control over what we know we don't have any? The Bible says that in this world, we will have hardship, but Jesus has overcome the world as we know it. This means we will suffer. There will be times of grief and challenge. However, God can give us the ability to handle anything we may go through when we seek Him with all our heart. "Those who know your name trust in you, for you, Lord, have never forsaken those who seek you" (Psalm 9:10 NIV).

God may not spare us from disease, death, or accidents, but He will prepare us for those times as we seek Him daily. Amid our anxiety and stress, may we learn to empty ourselves out and place our trust in Jesus. He will replace every worry with His peace, hope, and strength, and we will see His faithfulness unfold before our very eyes. Keep your eyes on Jesus! "Each day has enough trouble of its own" (Matthew 6:34 NIV).

—Tammy

Whose Standard of Measurement?

2 Corinthians 10; Galatians 1:10

Christ followers are set apart to be different by the world's standard of measurement. In 2 Corinthians 10, Paul is responding to the church in Corinth because they have accused him of being too timid in person but then too bold in his letters. He responds to them,

> We are human, but we don't wage war as humans do. We use God's mighty weapons, not worldly weapons, to knock down the strongholds of human reasoning and to destroy false arguments. (2 Corinthians 10:3 NLT)

He explains that the authority of Christ in his life sets him apart to be different. He isn't going to wage war or use force on people to obey Jesus. However, he will always speak truth in love and boldness. He cannot be compared with the world or anyone in it.

> Oh, don't worry; we wouldn't dare say that we are as wonderful as these other men who tell you how important they are! But they are only comparing themselves with each other, using themselves as the standard of measurement. How ignorant! (2 Corinthians 10:12 NLT)

Comparing ourselves to others is dangerous, as this can foster discontentment in one's soul. Yes, we often compare our occupations, talents, children, homes, or friends with those around us. But when our eyes are on others, our eyes are not on Jesus. "Obviously, I'm not trying to win the approval of people, but of God. If pleasing people were my goal, I would not be Christ's servant" (Galatians 1:10 NLT).

Whose standard of measurement do you measure yourself by? Remember, you will never please people. You, too, are Christ's servant.

—Tammy

Made to Be Different

Mark 1:1–8

Normal. What exactly is normal? I like extra pickles on my chicken sandwich. Is that normal? I enjoy doing laundry. Is that normal? I could sit and play the piano for hours and never feel the time pass. Normal or abnormal? Normal seems to be a word we attach to something, someone, or behavior that we can personally identify with and find common ground with. Regardless, normal is a subjective term and has absolutely no relevance in describing people.

One of the most abnormal people in the Bible (remember, this is subjective) is John the Baptist. Of all the men and women in the Bible, I find John, not to be confused with the disciple John, to be a most interesting person. This is how Mark describes him, "His clothes were woven from coarse camel hair, and he wore a leather belt around his waist. For food he ate locusts and wild honey" (Mark 1:6 NLT).

John was also bold, wild in nature, and unsophisticated. I have often wondered that if I had lived back then, would I have taken John seriously? In my limited mindset, the description that the Bible gives of John the Baptist describes someone I naturally may not have gravitated toward. But knowing that John was set apart by God to be the prophet who would prepare the way for Jesus to come intrigues me.

I believe that God had a very special reason for using a unique individual to prepare the way for the Lord's coming. Think about it. Jesus was radical! He did not fit the mold in any sense of the word. Yet both men drew large crowds, and God made His way into the hearts of men and women through them.

God has created each of us to be different. However there is a caution that goes with being different. We should never use our uniqueness to rationalize a sinful lifestyle. What we feel is not always from God. We must be discerning as to not misinterpret something in ourselves to be from God when it is from the enemy. God created every human being to be a unique man or woman who lives within His parameters of holy living. His Word clearly defines His love for you when He created you, and He made you to be different in order to fulfill His purpose in your life!

—Tammy

The Comparison Trap
Psalm 139:13–18

I've always been told by my mom that I was unique. To be honest, I didn't interpret the term *unique* as being a good thing. I misconstrued my mother's words to take them in a bad sort of way, thinking that I was weird and not normal. However, as I grew older, I accepted that being unique was not a bad thing at all! Yes, I was different. Yes, I was creative, and yes, I was strong-willed. But God created me the way I am for a purpose, crafted in His fingers, and uniquely inspired to reflect His glory! I am a person with a blueprint designed by God Himself, and I am not to compare my blueprint with anyone else's.

This leads to an epidemic of humanity, the comparison trap. Many people struggle with low self-esteem, falling into the trap of comparing themselves to others, everything from physical appearances to handicaps, intelligence, possessions, talents, and popularity. Value in a person does not come from other people. It only comes from God.

Why do humans compare? Most often the need to feel accepted by others trumps the fact that God did not shortchange us. Perhaps we value too highly the worldly view of what is normal, good, and acceptable in the eyes of man. But He didn't create us for other people's approval. He created us to reflect Himself.

When my boys were young, they would often make and bring home crafts they made with specifically Mark or me in mind. When we opened their projects, our faces beamed, and we displayed their gifts of creativity for all to see, remembering the boys with fondness every time we saw their projects. We never once compared their projects to each other's. After all, their works were reflections of their hearts and love for us. They were proud of them and were made for very specific purposes.

That is how God is. He is the master craftsman. He never intended for any person to be like someone else. He delights in His creation, and so should we! When we do so, God will be seen in and through us, which is our greatest purpose of all.

—Tammy

Cast All Your Cares
1 Peter 5:7

I remember as a little girl my mom sang this song to me, "Cast All Your Cares," by Kelly Willard, "I cast all my cares upon you, I lay all of my burdens down at Your feet …"

The song gave me comfort any time I was worried about something. But the older I have gotten, the more life has started throwing more burdens my way. As a student, I remember being burdened with chasing grades or social acceptance. As a young adult, I felt pressure to perform at work. When starting a family, I have had the extra blessings and responsibilities of caring for John, meeting household demands, and providing constant care for our children. And then, as our children have grown, I find myself taking their burdens on as my own, not to mention unpredictable health concerns or financial burdens.

When not properly dealt with, our cares seem to only deepen over time. As the song goes, "Any time I don't know what to do," any time the burdens reach a boiling point, any time the stress seems overwhelming, or any time the what-ifs seem too much to handle, we should cast all our cares upon Him.

As a child, I understood the truth behind this verse. Jesus was constantly reminding us how much His Father cares for his creation. What we overlook or overcomplicate, Jesus brings back to the simple truth: God cares for us. Does the bird not find food? With relatively few burdens, this was an easy realization. As the burdens stockpile and become more serious, it seems more critical to keep laying down our burdens at His feet over and over. We cannot shoulder them ourselves. We cannot dump them onto others. We need to let go of our anxieties, worries, and burdens. Because He cares for us, He wants better for us.

Nowadays I am raising two young children of my own. When they were babies, I enjoyed rocking them and singing the same song my mother sang to me. It is reassuring to cast all my cares upon Him.

—Ashley

Jesus Walks on the Water
Matthew 14:22–36

I see a lot of myself in Peter, mostly in my faults. The story of Jesus walking on the water is one of those examples. Jesus had sent his disciples into the boat to return home while he went alone to pray. During this boat ride, a storm kicked up, and they were fighting heavy waves. I can imagine them doing everything possible to navigate this storm based on their own experiences and skills. But that is usually my first response to the storms in my life as well. I am a problem-solver by nature and am all too quick to jump in to fix things myself.

Next, Jesus shows up to the disciples walking on the water. They are terrified, believing Him to be a ghost. While not often terrified, I do share with them the doubt. Often while I am frantically trying to fix things on my own, I later find that Jesus has been there waiting to help me.

Peter takes the incredible step to ask Jesus to let him come to Him by way of walking on the water. This is still in the middle of the horrible storm. This is an area I want to develop further like Peter. Too often I cannot stop my frantic and feeble efforts to calm the storm or navigate through it. I want to be like Peter and put my focus on Jesus.

In those storms where I have been able to stop to focus on Jesus, my next steps often do imitate Peter's next step. First Peter so boldly goes over the side of the boat and starts to walk on the water to Jesus. He is laser-focused on Jesus, and he is able to walk on the water.

Back to where I relate to Peter so well, he now feels the wind and waves, which terrify him, and he starts to sink. Too often even when I feel and see Jesus, I look back to my struggles and storms. Oh, that I could keep my focus on Jesus.

Finally though, as Peter is sinking and terrified again, he still knows to place his trust in Jesus. As I can take my eyes off Jesus in life's storms, I am reminded by Peter that Jesus is there for me every time. God's Word is clear that we will experience trials in our lives. But it is also clear that we should reach out to Jesus. We can be sure he is aware of our storms and will either calm these storms or calm us during the storm.

-Mark

Week 37 Reflections

1. After reviewing the Scriptures for each day, name three to four passages that jumped out at you this week.
2. How can you practically apply these verses to your life today and the upcoming week?
3. Name the worries that plague your mind and heart. Write a prayer asking God to take control of every single worry. Surrender them.
4. Who are you most tempted to compare your life to? Why? What are God's thoughts on that?
5. What unique qualities did God give to you? How can you use those to glorify Him?
6. Make a list of the cares you carry. Commit each care to God. Expect Him to take them from here as you surrender them.
7. If Jesus could walk on the water, He certainly can handle your burdens. Take a moment and reflect on God's faithfulness in your life and thank Him for His presence.
8. Are you a people-pleaser? Explain.
9. What is the first step you need to take to allow God to instill in you a heart to please Him first and foremost?

God Is in Our Prison (Joseph)

Genesis 39:20–23

"Joseph's master took him and put him in prison, the place where the king's prisoners were confined. But while Joseph was there in the prison, the Lord was with him; he showed him kindness and granted him favor in the eyes of the prison warden" (Genesis 39:20–21 NLT).

I would not do well emotionally in an ancient prison. Our prisons today are luxuries compared to what they were in the time of Joseph, who describes his prison as a dungeon (Genesis 40:15). For thirteen years, Joseph remained in this prison, located in the lower levels of the house that Potiphar lived in as captain of the bodyguard. But Genesis 20–21 tells us that the Lord was with him in his prison. Similarly, God is in our "prison" or a prison of sorts.

In 2008 our family moved from Michigan to Wisconsin, which I often describe the move as an arranged marriage. I had left a job and friends I loved, causing my heart to grieve severely. For the first time in my life, I experienced depression. After several months of hopelessness and feeling like the walls were caving in on me, God met me right where I was at.

God was close to me in a way I had not experienced before and succeeded in bringing me out of my prison of depression. In turn, He softened my heart to have more compassion on those that are suffering around me. He gave me new music to write in the pit of my despair, and He showed me that He was with me. Looking back, I see His faithfulness and love all over the situation, in that He gave me a caring husband, friends who reached out, and prayer times that reached the depths of my soul that I didn't know existed.

Yes, God was in my prison. He gave me peace and hope and became the reason I got out of bed in the morning. I learned to praise Him through the numbness and felt His joy encompass my being, a joy that only Jesus could give in my sadness. I learned that when I feel surrounded with thick walls, seemingly with no way of escape, Jesus is there.

If you feel like you are in a prison today, you are not alone. Just like with Joseph, God is in your prison, and He will show you the way out!

–Tammy

Power in Praising
Acts 16:16–34 (Paul and Silas)

Having been a worship leader for many years, I have learned that people who come to church do not always feel like praising God. They are tired, they are worn down by life's afflictions, and they are not always in a happy mood. But does praise come from a heart of happiness? In Acts 16, we learn that praise does not always come from a happy heart, but from a heart of sorrow. How is this possible?

Paul and Silas are two of my favorite biblical role models. They were both in prison, which in the day, were horrible places. The Bible tells us that after Paul and Silas were beaten, they were thrown into the dungeon where the worst prisoners went, and their feet clamped in the stocks. The dungeons were pungent with smell where starving prisoners never saw the light of day. Unless friends brought them food and water, they would starve and die in the prison cell. That would be a hopeless feeling, don't you think? Yet we read,

> Around midnight Paul and Silas were praying and singing hymns to God, and the other prisoners were listening. Suddenly, there was a massive earthquake, and the prison was shaken to its foundations. All the doors immediately flew open, and the chains of every prisoner fell off! (Acts 16:25–26 NLT)

Wow! There is power in our praise! When we praise God out of our pure love and gratefulness to Him despite how we feel, there is no telling what God will do. In Paul and Silas' case, God created a massive earthquake, all the doors flew open, and every prisoner was set free! This imagery sends chills up my spine of the power of God. When we praise God from a place of pure adoration for Him, it is a sacrifice of praise, and He inhabits every single bit of it. There is power in praising Him!

The temptation is to praise God only when it feels right, but we'd better take heed and reevaluate the reasons behind our praise. When we praise God unconditionally, we will see His power unleash!

–Tammy

The Solid Rock

Matthew 5–6, 7:24–28; 1 Corinthians 10:1–22

The Sermon on the Mount in Matthew 5–7 is a collection of teachings by Jesus that He gave on the Mount of the Beatitudes, a hill in Northern Israel. One of His teachings speaks to two types of people: the wise person and the foolish person. He describes the wise person as the one who stands on a rock, the Rock being Jesus Himself, unwavering and rooted in truth.

> But to the fool he says, "But anyone who hears my teaching and doesn't obey it is foolish, like a person who builds a house on sand. When the rains and floods come and the winds beat against that house, it will collapse with a mighty crash." (Matthew 7:26–27 NLT)

In 1834, Pastor Edward Mote wrote lyrics to a hymn based on Matthew 7:24–28, "The Solid Rock." William Bradberry later wrote the melody to these lyrics, and the song has been arranged and used in modern songs ever since:

> My hope is built on nothing less than Jesus' blood and righteousness.
> I dare not trust the sweetest frame, but wholly lean on Jesus' name.
> On Christ the solid Rock I stand, all other ground is sinking sand,
> all other ground is sinking sand. (Verse 1, Refrain)

There is a spiritual battle going on, vying for the hearts of man every single day. My prayer is that I will "wholly lean on Jesus' name" in all circumstances without questioning. I want to be courageous and strong when the day comes when standing for my faith in Jesus may cost me my life. With Jesus at the forefront, I don't have to worry. I can be prepared for the storms that come my way because Jesus is the solid Rock I stand on and the strength of my soul!

–Tammy

God's Answers
Jeremiah 29:12–13

Scott was six years old when he expressed his desire to have a pet. I had grown up with many types of pets, but Mark did not particularly care for animals in the house. I understood his position, but also felt for Scott who greatly wanted a pet to hug and care for. We found ourselves in quite a quandary.

I am passionate about prayer, so this seemingly impossible situation seemed like the perfect opportunity to teach Scott about the power of prayer. I explained to him that in situations like these, we should pray that God would align our hearts with His, making His will become our own. This means, if God wants us to have a pet, God will change Daddy's heart. On the other hand, if God doesn't think a pet is the right thing for our family, then God will change Scott's heart (and mine). For five nights in a row, Scott knelt beside his bed earnestly praying with folded hands, talking to God as if He were sitting on the bed with us.

Later that week, a little black kitty started coming out of the woods to play with the boys whenever they were out at their turtle sandbox. This continued throughout the summer and into October, when we had a bad storm while Mark was out of town on business.

The rain poured down in sheets, hail beat at the windows, and we heard a little "meow" by our screened-in porch. I let the kitty into the porch, fed him, dried him off, and made a little tent for him with blankets. However, I explained to the boys that we could not keep him and we needed to respect Daddy's wishes concerning the cat being a pet.

When Mark returned home, I told him what happened. He went to the porch to see the kitty. When he returned, he told us that God had changed his heart and we could keep the cat!

Years later when Licorice passed away, we circled around him, crying and giving thanks to God for showing His will to us years back in a seemingly impossible situation. God's answers ... priceless!

> In those days when you pray, I will listen. If you look for me wholeheartedly, you will find me. (Jeremiah 29:12–13 NLT)

—Tammy

Staying on the Line
Ruth 1–4

Do my choices affect the fruition of God's will in my life? After all, God is sovereign, meaning He is the supreme power with autonomy and the controlling influence in everything that happens in this world. But along with this sovereignty, He has also given humans free choice. I often think of God's will as a perfectly straight line on a map from A to B. As we live our lives, we make choices every day that either stay on that line, leading us toward God and His righteousness, or moving us off the line on our own path (sin), leading away from God. Detours can eventually still lead to God's will in our lives, but they may take a little longer and acquire some baggage (maybe even some consequences) along the way.

The story of Ruth is a great example of what staying on the line looks like. As you read these four chapters, notice how God brings pure joy and transformation to Naomi because of the character and choices of Ruth and Boaz.

Characteristics of Ruth

1. Loyal: Ruth was loyal to her grieving mother-in-law, Naomi.
2. Respectful: Ruth respected her deceased husband's family.
3. Patient: Ruth was patient for God to act.
4. Hardworking: Every day she would glean in the fields.
5. Grateful: Ruth did not complain about her lot in life.
6. Self-sacrificing: Ruth gave up her own desires for Naomi's.

Characteristics of Boaz

1. Generous: Boaz allowed Ruth to gather barley above and beyond.
2. Kind and respectful to women: Boaz showed gentleness toward Ruth.
3. Protector: Boaz instructed the men in the field not to harm Ruth.
4. Conscientious: Boaz took on the responsibility of the family redeemer.

Ruth's and Boaz's character and choices led them directly toward God's perfect will. Ultimately, Boaz married Ruth, she bore a son named Obed, and then straight down the line, they become the lineage through which Jesus our Messiah would come.

–Tammy

Believe and Not Doubt

1 Samuel 16; Luke 6:45; Ephesians 3:20; James 1:2–8

There's a correlation between what is in our hearts and what is played out in our life. What is deep in our soul usually gets executed in words or actions, intentional or not. The way we think, talk, and behave, it all points to who we are. In Luke 6:45, the author teaches us that the mouth speaks what is in a person's heart. And since 1 Samuel 16:7 recounts God's statement that man looks at the outward appearance and God looks at the heart, we know that when we approach God with requests for anything, He is paying attention to our heart. What is our motive in asking? Do we even believe God can answer *this* prayer?

As I read through the book of James, it's hard not to hear the tone of Jesus' words. James was Jesus' half-brother, so he probably spent a great deal of time around Jesus. As I read what James wrote, I often picture Jesus talking to James and James thinking to himself, *Wow, that's actually good stuff … I ought to write that down.*

In his opening chapter, he instructs his readers to take care in how we approach God. He reminds us that God gives to all without finding fault. That's huge. God isn't looking for reasons to keep His blessings from you. He's not hiding himself or holding back so that you and I will continue to wander aimlessly. God wants to be in relationship with you and me.

But James also gives a word of warning, "When you ask, you must believe and not doubt. For the one who doubts is like a wave of the sea, blown and tossed by the wind. That person should not expect to receive anything from the Lord" (James 1:6–8 NIV).

That's a big deal. God is God. He is omnipotent (all-powerful) and omniscient (all-knowing). In fact, God goes above and beyond to those who are truly seeking and trusting Him. Today, whatever requests you come to God with, believe and not doubt.

> Now all glory to God, who is able, through his mighty power at work within us, to accomplish infinitely more than we might ask or think. (Ephesians 3:20 NIV)

-Scott

Week 38 Reflections

1. After reviewing the Scriptures for each day, name three to four passages that jumped out at you this week.
2. How can you practically apply these verses to your life today and the upcoming week?
3. Depression can be devastating, either personally or in someone close to you. God is in that prison of depression. Take time to write a prayer for God to invade your prison or your loved one's prison and intercede on their behalf.
4. Can you think of a time when you praised God during turmoil? If so, what was the outcome?
5. What does standing on the solid rock of Jesus look like to you? Explain.
6. What big thing would you like to bring to God to find a solution, even if it seems impossible? How can you pray so that God reveals His will for you?
7. How have your choices drawn you closer to God's will or away from God's will?
8. Give an example of a time when you doubted God? James 1:2–8 gives specific instruction of how we should pray. What is it?
9. Do you trust God? Why or why not?

MONTH 10
World Views Will Challenge Our Beliefs and Stomp on Our Convictions

A FAITH THAT STANDS
Produces a Spirit-Centered Mindset

The Holy Spirit "Thing"
Acts 1:1–11; Galatians 5:20–24

I'll never forget hearing about the Trinity for the first time. I knew who God was, the Father God incarnate, Creator of the whole universe. I also knew that God sent His Son Jesus in human form to die for our sins as the ultimate sacrifice. But the Holy Spirit "thing" was something I hadn't thought much about.

Scripture tells us that when Jesus was resurrected and ascended into heaven, He left the Holy Spirit with us. Anyone who proclaims that Jesus is Lord of their life will receive the gift of the Holy Spirit. This is an extraordinary thing, as we no longer need to make animal sacrifices for our sin as they did in the Old Testament, but instead claim the gift of salvation so that God's spirit can dwell in us.

There is power in the name of Jesus and His Holy Spirit. He has the power to transform us and intercede for us. He gives us wisdom, guidance, strength, and comfort and convicts us when we are going down a wrong path. His Spirit provides unity among believers when sought out with humility and expectation, enabling us to live victoriously over sin by uniting us with Christ through His resurrection.

If you desire to lead a life led by the Holy Spirit, you will begin to see new fruit and develop new habits. As you pray by listening and talking with God, the Lord will fill you and guide you with His Spirit. When you make yourself available to God, you will see a relationship with Christ blossom, and you will become aware of opportunities to serve Him.

Remember the truths you have read in His Word. The Spirit of God is alive and active in you, speaking into your thoughts, language, and decisions you make. Perhaps you've taken a few steps backward and haven't had the discipline you want to have in maintaining this relationship. Now is the time to get back on track! Begin by confessing any sin in your heart, and ask the Holy Spirit to grow His fruit in you!

—Tammy

Those who belong to Christ Jesus have nailed the passions and desires of their sinful nature to his cross and crucified them there. (Galatians 5:20–24 NLT)

Are We in Tune?

John 14:15–41; Romans 12:2

The most magnificent gift I have ever received is the gift of the Holy Spirit. When I decided to follow Jesus in my early teens, I was all in on that decision. But before that decision was made, I wrestled with God for fear of being strapped down by a bunch of spiritual rules. I was strong-willed. I wasn't sure how following Jesus would affect my will, but I took the plunge, I repented of my sins, and the Holy Spirit came into my life.

> Do not be conformed to this world, but be transformed by the renewal of your mind, that by testing you may discern what is the will of God, what is good and acceptable and perfect. (Romans 12:2 NLT)

As a new believer, I knew that I still had a lot of baggage in my thinking to work through. I had been skeptical of stories in the Bible. I also didn't believe that God could heal, transform, and do miracles in this day in age. But the desire of my heart was clear. I wanted to trust God more and stand on my convictions, even if my questions were unanswered.

I began to name out loud specific areas in my life that I wanted the Holy Spirit to renew and reveal truth to me: skepticism, doubt, swearing, being critical, and disrespect. In turn, I asked God to fill me with more faith, self-control, discernment, and gentleness, and the list goes on. I knew that I could not muster up these things on my own. I had to let the Holy Spirit do His work in me. I needed to be in tune with Him every day.

Being in tune with the Holy Spirit became a steady prayer for me. I could understand this term well, being a pianist and violinist. There is nothing more cringing to me than to play on an instrument that is out of tune. I'm not only making an awful noise, but I can't play well with others. Likewise, our lives need to be in tune with the Holy Spirit, or we cannot reflect Him or play well with others.

May the desire and prayer of all of us as Christians be to be in tune with the Holy Spirit. Until we reach the grave, He will continue to do His work in us if we allow Him to!

—Tammy

Living a Spirit-Filled Life
1 Corinthians 6:18–20; Titus 3:1–6

I was watching a TV show not too long ago featuring people who could do unnatural things with their bodies: knees bending opposite ways, eyes popping out of their sockets, or bodies being tied into knots. You get the idea! I recall saying out loud, "That is just not natural!" When I think about it as it relates to our focus today, living by the Holy Spirit is not natural either!

Let's look at the two passages in 1 Corinthians and Titus. Although the focus of these two Scriptures is different, one focusing on self-control and sexuality and the other focusing on our response to our government and authorities, the concept is the same. In our human flesh, the natural thing to do would be to have sex whenever we want with whomever we want, disobey the government, quarrel with one another, slander people, and envy and hate each other whom we disagree with. However, through the Holy Spirit, the unnatural thing, we have the power to overcome those things and truly live by the Spirit instead of the flesh.

Living a Spirit-filled life comes from a heart of surrender and repentance to God, allowing His gift of Jesus to not only forgive our sins, but to fill us with His presence. The presence of God opens our eyes to our human, fleshly ways and desires, convicting us of areas in our lives that are not in line with Him. This is a lifelong process! We cannot do this in our own strength. He will help us battle that addiction and bad habits, so we don't do this alone! The Holy Spirit is a strong tower, and when we cling to His Spirit, He will give us strength to overcome the sin and stumbling blocks in our path.

—Tammy

Once we, too, were foolish and disobedient. We were misled and became slaves to many lusts and pleasures. Our lives were full of evil and envy, and we hated each other. But, when God our Savior revealed his kindness and love, he saved us, not because of the righteous things we had done, but because of his mercy. He washed away our sins, giving us a new birth and new life through the Holy Spirit. (Titus 3:3–5 NLT)

The Holy Spirit Over Mind
Romans 8:5–11

"Those who are dominated by the sinful nature think about sinful things, but those who are controlled by the Holy Spirit think about things that please the Spirit" (Romans 8:5 NLT).

Like so many people have experienced, I had a lot of turmoil at home in my growing-up years. I left for college with a suitcase full of emotional baggage I was not proud of, some of which reared its ugly head during a music class. I was in rehearsal with a large group, and the professor made a simple error. I'm confident she would have caught this error on her own, but I was quick to the draw, calling her out on it in front of the whole group. I was so wrong, and my actions of disrespect were uncalled for.

The pit in my stomach kept this incident at the forefront of my mind for quite some time, but I didn't know how to make things right. I was a Christian, so I questioned myself as to why I did this terrible thing. I hemmed and hawed over it, eventually sweeping it under the rug, hoping to never see that side of me again. I went on as if nothing had happened.

A few years later, after I was married, our pastor preached a sermon on Romans 8, which is our Scripture reading for today. Verses 5–6 hit me right between the eyes. The anxiety in my stomach told me that the Holy Spirit was speaking to me, but also spurring me to action. I quieted myself to listen. I owed my professor an apology from my actions years before and needed to get in touch with her. I hurried home, got out a pen and notepaper, and began writing a lengthy letter to my professor, apologizing to her, explaining to her what God had been teaching me, and asking her forgiveness for my pride and disrespect.

A few months later, I was a part of a wedding in Nashville, and my professor was there also. She came up to me, embraced me, and told me she forgave me. She said she had a new respect for me, and she was grateful that I acted on the Holy Spirit. When I made myself less, God became so much more, and forgiveness and reconciliation took place. If we have the Holy Spirit in us, let's not only listen to Him, let us act on it and obey Him when He nudges us. We will never regret it!

—Tammy

Beware of False Prophets
John 8:31–32; James 1:27; 1 John 4:1–6

My husband, Dale, and I both grew up in the church, both in the same denomination, so we grew up accepting it as truth. We didn't know anything different, and no one told us that there was more.

After being married for a few years and were raising two young daughters, we developed much stress in our relationship. I became very depressed and found myself at the end of what I thought I could handle. I remember thinking, *Is this all there is? Can't someone help us?*

I talked to the minister, thinking he could direct me to some help, but that was no use. Then one day, a family from Florida moved to New York and visited the church we attended. The wife, Sharon, was unique. She glowed with the love of Jesus, and I was drawn to her. Sharon soon started and taught a small Bible study in a nearby bank, and there, I trusted Christ as my Savior. What a life-changing experience that was! For the first time in my life, my eyes were opened to God's truth, and I began understanding the Bible. My life was transformed, and so was my family's. I found a new church, as did Sharon and her family.

False prophets are all around. We need to be discerning. From my own experience, I learned that there are questions one needs to ask when choosing a place of worship:

1. Does the pastor clearly present the gospel, communicating the need for a personal relationship with Christ versus earning our way to heaven through works?
2. Is Scripture watered down (or very limited)?
3. Are missions well-supported?
4. Are the pastor and set of leaders building their own empire, doing everything in their power to protect their own ideas instead of addressing truth?
5. Are important biblical principles and standards being upheld?

Beware of false prophets and teaching! The Holy Spirit will give you discernment when you ask for it.

—*Sharon*

Hoarding the Gift
Luke 2

I have known families through the years who have adopted children from orphanages in extremely poor countries. Because of the scarcity of food available to the orphanages, many children only eat one meal a day and oftentimes not even that much. As a result, many of the children are malnourished or dehydrated, even having lead poisoning from the water. When families have brought a child home from one these countries, they have witnessed the child hoarding food. Hoarding is a survival instinct that kicks in after living without food consistently. When food is finally available, the children store it away, saving food for later in case they don't get fed again for a while.

This concept of hoarding can correlate with Christians and the gift of Jesus. Before knowing Jesus and making Him a part of our daily lives, we are much like the orphans, searching for spiritual food, redemption, peace, forgiveness, and significance. We are looking for daily bread. Then when we find Jesus and begin to build a relationship with Him, we sometimes fall into a trap of hoarding Jesus if we are not careful. We begin to keep Him to ourselves, afraid to share Him for fear we will offend someone or be politically incorrect. We want Jesus, but we want our reputations intact, making Jesus a private perk in our lives. The irony is, if no one had ever told us about Jesus, where would we be?

We read the Christmas story in Luke 2, telling us about the miraculous birth of Jesus our Messiah, our King of Kings and Lord of Lords. We then learn that in order to receive the gift of Jesus, we need to accept the gift. Finally, once we are adopted into God's family as His child, God wants us to share His gift with others. He never intended us to keep Jesus all to ourselves.

I don't want to be a Jesus hoarder, even though I admit I sometimes am. The first step is recognizing this tendency in our own lives, but then confessing it and praying for opportunities throughout the day where we can share Jesus with others. The Holy Spirit will lead you. You only need to be ready and willing!

−Tammy

Week 39 Reflections

1. After reviewing the Scriptures for each day, name three to four passages that jumped out at you this week.
2. How can you practically apply these verses to your life today and the upcoming week?
3. What is the role of the Holy Spirit in our lives?
4. Are you spiritually in tune? Are you playing well with others?
5. What does living a Spirit-filled life mean to you? Be specific.
6. What are some of the signs of false prophets?
7. When have you experienced or seen false teaching? Have you ever believed it, or do you now?
8. In what circumstances are you most tempted to hoard the gift of Jesus? What are some of the signs of hoarding Jesus?
9. What is God teaching you this week?

Perseverance

Matthew 25:31–46; James 1:2–4

The year 2020 will never be forgotten as our world was plagued with the COVID-19 epidemic and political havoc, shaking up every bit of normalcy we had ever known. This dark period of, now history, affected our health, jobs, schools, churches, sports, shopping, and mental health. Yes, it was tough, and some are still reaping the consequences.

COVID certainly challenged us to prioritize our lives differently, to reevaluate our family time and our approaches to education, work, church, and events. Yet it also gave opportunities for Christians to persevere, soldier up, and pray. For many Americans, this period was one of the first times we experienced daily discomfort doing without things we had grown accustomed to having. On a worldwide scale, life was out of our control.

On the flip side, I believe that the year 2020 was the year that God showed Himself to an extraordinary amount of people across the globe. With the number of churches closed at the initial onset, God particularly showed His power by providing a way for even more people to hear the gospel message through online technology. Persevering through 2020 taught me about my own faith. I learned that I am too comfortable and too busy. I learned that nothing is in my control. I learned that I am spoiled, for I was saddened by not being able to go out to dinner or do group activities as I was accustomed to. There is a dying world out there spiritually, and God used this time to challenge me to reevaluate my priorities.

James 1:2–4 challenges us to allow God to test our faith by going through trials with joy, His joy, seeking maturity in our faith so it stands the test of time and trials. I want to be a soldier for Christ, to stand on a rock, and to persevere when times get tough. When the next challenge comes, I long to be ready to persevere for a greater purpose!

—Tammy

> When the Son of Man comes in his glory, and all the angels with him, he will sit on his glorious throne. All the nations will be gathered before him, and he will separate the people one from another as a shepherd separates the sheep from the goats … (Matthew 25:31–33 NLT)

Are You Blown and Tossed?

James 1:5–8

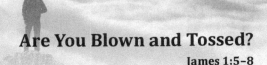

One of the most sensational sites we saw on the island of Maui were the sea turtles that had come to rest and lay their eggs on the beach. The turtles are magnificent creatures coming and going with the ebb and flow of the tide. Not far from that little beach was another beach, one with giant rocks and crosses marking tombstones of the many surfers who had reached their fate on the high tides. The number of crosses were staggering, about equal to the number of sea turtles. With the image of the crosses in mind, read on to the passage in James.

> If you need wisdom, ask our generous God, and he will give it to you …
> But when you ask him, be sure that your faith is in God alone. Do not waver, for a person with divided loyalty is as unsettled as a wave of the sea that is blown and tossed by the wind. Such people should not expect to receive anything from the Lord. Their loyalty is divided between God and the world, and they are unstable in everything they do. (James 1:5–8 NLT)

These words carry an amazing promise attached to a strong warning. The promise is that God will give us wisdom whenever we ask. The warning, however, is to not waver in our faith, having one foot in and one foot out of the world. If we do, we are like one of those surfers in Hawaii, blown and tossed by the crashing waves.

There have been moments in my life when my loyalty has been divided between God and the world. I would think that if I said the right things like a Christian does, then I was a Christ-follower. The act of prayer was something I would do as a last resort just to see if it worked, but my faith was weak. I had more disbelief than I was even aware.

We may be able to hide our hearts from others, but never from God. He longs for both of our feet to be all in. Today, as you spend time with the Lord, ask Him to reveal any areas of unbelief in your life. Ask Him for a stronger faith, and then plant both feet on the ground!

-Tammy

Are We Like Sheep?
Psalm 119:175–176

Why are sheep mentioned over five hundred times in the Bible? More than any other animal, Jesus directly parallels humans with sheep in order to teach and explain our relationship with God. In learning more about sheep, we learn more about ourselves. Here are some fun facts about sheep:

- Sheep are defenseless, and if they are scared, they will run away in groups to protect themselves.
- Sheep cannot get up by themselves if they find themselves on their back.
- Sheep are emotional (yes, they feel emotions) and can recognize the shepherd's voice.
- Sheep are said to be not very smart, but they just have no sense of direction.
- Sheep are not able to carry burdens. You will never see a sheep with a load on its back.
- Sheep will settle for less and drink out of a dirty mud puddle right in front of them when there is a clean water hole nearby.
- Sheep cannot care for themselves when they are wounded like other animals can. They need a shepherd.
- Lastly, sheep were valuable in Bible times, as they provided wool, milk, and meat. A shepherd would make sacrifices in order to protect the sheep, which was often their livelihood.

Our need for a shepherd is great, and our need for a Savior to rescue us is undeniable. How often do we need God to come and find us because we have lost our way and need Him to guide us back to the fold, heal us, carry our load, and help us up? He designed us to need Him. Our tendency is to be a little too independent, but He wants us to lean on Him and to rely on Him for everything! Are we like sheep? I hope so! We have a shepherd who desperately wants to care for us.

—Tammy

> I have wandered away like a lost sheep; come and find me, for I have not forgotten your commands. (Psalm 119:176 NLT)

Bold in Suffering

Acts 7; 1 Peter 2:20–22

I have a morbid interest when I am studying a person from the Bible. I look up when and how they died. I do this because the suffering that person endured for following Jesus is often a check to my own spirit. Am I too willing to boldly suffer for Christ? I currently think of our brothers and sisters around the world who are suffering torture and painful deaths because of their belief in Jesus. I am impressed to pray daily for them that they would stand strong and be bold in their suffering until the very end.

Three martyrs in the Bible that stand out to me because of how they died are Isaiah, Stephen, and Peter. Isaiah was a Hebrew prophet who lived approximately seven hundred years before the birth of Jesus. He was born in Jerusalem and was called to be a prophet in the year 739 BC (Isaiah 6). Isaiah prophesized the coming of the Messiah, and he spoke up for the powerless under unjust rulers. How did he die? Jewish tradition says that he was sawed in half under the orders of the evil king, Manasseh.

Stephen was the first Christian martyr whose story is found in Acts 7. He testified before the Sanhedrin because he had the Spirit of God, performing many wonders and signs and feeding the widows and orphans. Opposition arose, but it was no match for Stephen's God-given wisdom, so they falsely accused him of blasphemy. To the leaders, he boldly declared his belief in Jesus and gave a full account of Israel's history and how they had turned against the Lord. He was then taken to a place where he was stoned to death.

Following Jesus' death and resurrection, Peter continued to preach to the Jews, becoming the first bishop in Rome. Under the orders of Emperor Nero, Peter was put to death in AD 64. He was to be crucified like Jesus, but Peter asked to be crucified upside down, as he did not feel worthy to die like his Savior.

Choosing to follow Jesus may cost us everything we have, including our family, our jobs, our friends, or even our lives. The important thing is that God will give us the strength and endurance to be bold in our suffering. Hopefully, we will not have to be sawed in half, stoned, or crucified upside down, but the question is, are we willing?

-Tammy

Little Reminders

Psalm 44:21; Proverbs 3:5–6

I never realized that I had a cross hanging in every room of my house until someone came to my house one day and made a comment about it. She asked if they had significance for me, and I explained how I love and need little reminders in my life that prompt me to focus on God. I also told her that sometimes I put little Scripture verses on sticky notes and place them around the house as reminders that God is here and wants to be a part of everything I do and say.

How easily I can get distracted and begin to worry or stress over life! As I age, some days are harder than others. Whether it's my health, my low energy level, or the tasks I have before me or doing things for others, these little reminders around the house cause me to stop, pray, and be still before the Lord until a peace and calm wash over me. The Lord is with me. He sees me, and I can start moving forward again with a new focus. "Trust in the Lord with all your heart; lean not on your own understanding. In all your ways, acknowledge Him, and He will direct your paths" (Proverbs 3:5–6 NIV).

Whether it is a cross or a sticky note with a Scripture on it, placing one in every room is a reminder that God wants to be in every room of my own heart. I need to ask myself, "Have I invited the Lord into every room of my heart, or are some areas too private to enter?"

Guess what? We need to be brutally honest with God because He knows every detail of our lives anyway. Jesus wants to be Lord of every room in our lives, including our successes, relationships, and struggles. You can trust Him. He's the best friend you'll ever have! "For God knows the secrets of every heart" (Psalm 44:21b NIV).

—Sharon

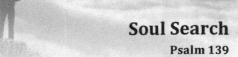

Soul Search
Psalm 139

I've been to a handful of professional baseball games, each time having my purse searched by the security team. The first time, I wasn't prepared for it, so there were some things in my purse I didn't want exposed. The second time, although I didn't have anything to hide, I still didn't care for the invasion of my privacy.

That's how I feel when I reflect on what God might find deep in the core of my heart when He searches it, a little embarrassed. What is He finding in there? Pride? Lust? Bitterness? I cringe just reflecting on all my shortcomings. The truth is, no matter how much I may want to hide things from God, I can't.

The God I know is full of compassion and slow to anger. He also desires for me to repent of my sin and turn away from it. In Psalm 139, David, the author, expresses his full desire for God to not only search his heart, but to reveal anything that would be contradictory to God's will for him. God does that for David and shows him how much he is thought of by God, how much he is loved, and that David can trust Him with his life!

Have you ever cried out to God like David did? Have you ever sat alone in a room and fallen flat on your face, begging God to search your heart and your thoughts? I know I have. Even though He knows my thoughts anyway, I might as well come clean!

> For the word of God is alive and active. Sharper than any double-edged sword, it penetrates even to dividing soul and spirit, joints and marrow; it judges the thoughts and attitudes of the heart. (Hebrews 4:12 NIV)

God's Word shows us certain aspects of our lives that He would still like to transform. But He also wants to encourage our souls and give us His wisdom and strength. As you spend time with God today, ask God to search your heart. He is not there waiting to condemn you. He loves you and values you as His child.

—Tammy

Week 40 Reflections

1. After reviewing the Scriptures for each day, name three to four passages that jumped out at you this week.
2. How can you practically apply these verses to your life today and the upcoming week?
3. What is God teaching you about what perseverance looks like?
4. When you pray, is your natural bent to believe or doubt what you are asking for?
5. Are you like a sheep who needs his shepherd or an independent person, only needing a shepherd when you are lost?
6. How can you be bold in suffering?
7. What daily reminders do you put in place that draw you toward God?
8. Write out a prayer asking God to search your soul. Take time and allow God to reveal not only sin in your heart, but more of who He is.
9. David cried out to God in anguish. He needed God so much. Write a prayer that cries out to God and expects Him to move on your behalf.

Spiritual Boundaries

Titus 2:11–12

I asked a group of high school students to name some things in everyday life that start small but can quickly grow out of control. Their answers included a house fire, weeds in a garden, clutter in a locker, financial debt, and physical attraction. These are great examples. All of these have the potential to grow quickly if not attended to right away.

In our spiritual lives, there are certain temptation areas that we battle, which, if not nipped in the bud immediately, can grow to a point of major consequence. Without proactively placing boundaries for ourselves ahead of time, things can get dangerous in a hurry.

Boundaries protect us from harm. When my parents were first married in the 1960s, they went camping in Albany, New York. They took a long walk around the secluded campground, coming across an open field with golden grass surrounded by maples. Even though there was a fence, a large section was trampled to the ground and overgrown with weeds. The fence appeared to be old and not in use anymore. Thinking it was ok, my parents walked through the field until they saw the bull staring them in the face, ready to charge. Fortunately, my dad knew that if you come across a wild animal, you should stay as still and calm as you can, even if it charges at you. Reluctantly my parents stood still. The bull came running and fortunately stopped ten feet in front of them. A clear boundary would have protected them and kept them out of the area completely.

The purpose of a spiritual boundary is to promote godly discipline, keeping us within the parameters that God intends for us. It also serves to protect us from harm when we least expect it. As a mentor to younger women, I know how important it is to have accountability in the area of temptations. If identified ahead of time, proper spiritual boundaries will protect us before temptation even has a chance to take hold!

> For the grace of God has appeared that offers salvation to all people.
> It teaches us to say "No" to ungodliness and worldly passions, and
> to live self-controlled, upright and godly lives in this present age.
> (Titus 2:11–12 NLT)

—Tammy

Temptation
1 Corinthians 10:1–13; 1 Peter 5:8; James 1:12–18

The Christian life would certainly be easier without dealing with temptation. Temptation will often confront us when we are most vulnerable, so having a plan of defense is a must. Jesus knows all about this, for He Himself was tempted by Satan after a time of not eating for forty days. Satan doesn't play fair, and he will often kick us when we are down.

Be encouraged! Jesus has given us a plan to deal with temptation well and be victorious through it. When Satan strikes, we must stand firm in prayer and communication with God, ready to guard against the traps that can so easily entangle us. We must be honest and transparent with God so He can strengthen us to withstand the devil's schemes! "If you think you are standing strong, be careful not to fall. The temptations in your life are no different from what others experience" (1 Corinthians 10:12–13 NLT).

> God blesses those who patiently endure testing and temptation. Afterward they will receive the crown of life that God has promised to those who love him. And remember, when you are being tempted, do not say, "God is tempting me." God is never tempted to do wrong, and he never tempts anyone else. Temptation comes from our own desires, which entice us and drag us away. These desires give birth to sinful actions. And when sin is allowed to grow, it gives birth to death. (James 1:12–15 NLT)

What are some of the temptations that plague you today? I would encourage you to write each one down, commit to praying through each one, and ask God to help you. Remember, temptation cannot destroy a person, but sinful actions that transpire from those temptations can.

Satan can seem scary, but we have a God who has already defeated him, and God is much more powerful than any evil that may come our way. God is ready for victory over your temptations if you allow Him to help you overcome them and kick that Satan right behind you!

—Tammy

Identify Your Temptations
Mark 7:20–22

Do you ever rank sins from bad to worse? For example, someone might say that murder is worse than lying and sexual immorality worse than pride. But another person might say lying is worse than pride and greed is worse than sexual immorality. What is the truth? The spiritual truth is that all sin is equal in God's eyes, and we should take caution to all the red flags of temptations, big and small, so we can nip them in the bud. "For the person who keeps all of the laws except one is as guilty as a person who has broken all of God's laws" (James 2:10 NLT).

People are good at keeping things private from others, especially when it comes to admitting temptations that torment them. I know I can easily diminish the effects of certain temptations in my life, holding them at bay until I find myself in a vulnerable situation. I may be able to hide things from others, but I can never hide what is in my heart from God.

> For from within, out of a person's heart, come evil thoughts, sexual immorality, theft, murder, adultery, greed, wickedness, deceit, lustful desires, envy, slander, pride, and foolishness. (Mark 7:20–22 NLT)

In order to gain victory over the temptations in our lives, we need to be able to identify them without prejudice. This can be challenging, as some temptations can be easily dismissed as harmless. But in this sea of neutrality, danger lurks. Temptations lead to sin unless we have a plan in place to deal with them when they come.

—Tammy

> And God is faithful. He will not allow the temptation to be more than you can stand. When you are tempted, he will show you a way out so that you can endure. (1 Corinthians 10:13–14 NLT)

Don't Try to Hide

Psalm 44:21; Proverbs 15:10–12; Ephesians 4:20–24

Transparency about our own weaknesses makes us vulnerable, yet our deficiencies are a reality of our human condition. Fear of others seeing our faults and dysfunctions is scary. Because of our private nature, we create defenses for ourselves to protect us from anyone truly knowing our struggles. Yet, by hiding our weak sides, we may hinder ourselves from being real so we can grow in our relationships.

Sadly, the tendency toward privacy can affect our relationship with God. Openness with God in a thriving relationship can quickly turn stale if we stop being honest with God. We tell ourselves that we should know better by making better decisions. We grow ashamed from repeated mistakes, keeping the heavenly Father who loves us at arm's length. There is no need to put on a façade. With Jesus, we leave our shame at the door, pick up our feet, and go and talk with Him.

Living a Christian life is a journey that requires us to be forthright with our human nature and private thoughts with God. We cannot hide from Him. We cannot fool Him. We are completely exposed, whether we want to be or not! I encourage you to meditate on these Scriptures as you draw close to Him today.

> If we had forgotten the name of our God or spread our hands in prayer to foreign gods, God would surely have known it, for he knows the secrets of every heart. (Psalm 44:21 NLT)

> Even Death and Destruction hold no secrets from the Lord. How much more does he know the human heart! Mockers hate to be corrected, so they stay away from the wise. (Proverbs 15:11–12 NLT)

> … throw off your old sinful nature and your former way of life, which is corrupted by lust and deception. Instead, let the Spirit renew your thoughts and attitudes. Put on your new nature, created to be like God—truly righteous and holy. (Ephesians 4:22–24 NLT)

−Tammy

The Narrow Gate
John 3:16–18

"You can enter God's Kingdom only through the narrow gate. The highway to hell is broad, and its gate is wide for the many who choose that way. But the gateway to life is very narrow and the road is difficult, and only a few ever find it" (Matthew 7:13–14 NLT)

In this world, there are many roads to get to the same place. If the road is closed, we take a detour. If our child didn't get the grade we thought they deserved, we speak to the teacher in hopes to get it changed. If we want a certain job but don't have the credentials, we look for added experience to add to our résumé. We are goal-oriented people, and we pride ourselves on getting where we want to go, even if it means bending the rules a bit or taking a meandering way to get there.

I believe that this reality is why this lesson from Jesus' teaching in the Sermon on the Mount is a hard pill to swallow. He very clearly states that the way to heaven is a narrow gate and very difficult, while the way to hell is wide. There aren't any detours. There isn't any persuading. There's no roundabout way to get there. Plain and simple, there is only one way to heaven, and that is through the saving power of Jesus Christ. There's no rationalizing our sin. There's no adding our own opinions to what we think God could have meant. Jesus is clear, and every person has the same choice, to follow Him or not.

> For this is how God loved the world: He gave his one and only Son, so that everyone who believes in him will not perish but have eternal life. God sent his Son into the world not to judge the world, but to save the world through him. (John 3:16–17 NLT)

Scripture clearly says that the road to hell is broad, inviting many to go with the flow of procrastination, complacency, or uniformity. There is no substitution for living a life for Jesus Christ. Jesus is not narrow-minded. Rather He is the narrow gate! We must embrace it and go through it!

—Tammy

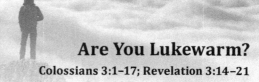

Are You Lukewarm?
Colossians 3:1–17; Revelation 3:14–21

Have you ever asked for a lukewarm cup of coffee from a coffee shop? Probably not. The choices are hot or iced, but not lukewarm. Revelation 3 instructs the church in Laodicea to either be hot or cold, but if they are lukewarm, God will spit them out of His mouth. Let's take a closer look at the context and history of this common paraphrase of Scripture I've heard all my life, "don't be a lukewarm Christian."

God would rather you be all in or all out. If you've heard that, you're probably like most modern Christians. But let's take a closer look at who and why John wrote that. First, John was writing to the church in Laodicea. Laodicea was known for its wealthy banks, a renowned medical school, and a fashion industry that was unmatched in its time. To the north was Hierapolis, known for their incredible hot springs, and to the south was Colossae, whose snow-melted runoffs provided crisp, cold water. Laodicea received its water from an aqueduct six miles to the south, so whenever the water finally reached them, it was lukewarm and quite undesirable. In fact, the water was nauseating.

The problem wasn't that Laodicea lacked passion for Christ. The issue was that the church wasn't doing anything. The city, including the Christians, were so comfortable with their amazing lifestyle that they felt no need to rely on God for anything. They professed a faith that, to them, simply meant they were granted access to heaven. But it didn't change anything about their earthly lives.

So when Jesus revealed these words to be written to this church, He was explaining that He wished they would either be like the beautiful hot springs of Hierapoli or the glistening cold water from the mountains in Colossae rather than the disgusting lukewarm water of their city.

While faith in Christ grants access to heaven, the more immediate purpose is to experience transformation through an active and committed relationship with Christ. I encourage and challenge you today to ask yourself if you are hot like the springs, cold like the melted snow, or dangerously lukewarm.

—Scott

Week 41 Reflections

1. After reviewing the Scriptures for each day, name three to four passages that jumped out at you this week.
2. How can you practically apply these verses to your life today and the upcoming week?
3. Name something that has started small in your life but quickly grew out of control.
4. Spiritual boundaries help with temptation in our lives. What are some boundaries you have now or need to put into place?
5. Name the various temptations that you are faced with every day.
6. What secrets are you keeping from God?
7. Describe the narrow gate. What are your thoughts about this? What does that mean to you?
8. Are you hot, cold, or lukewarm? What does God say about each of those?
9. Name specific areas in your faith that need to move away from being lukewarm?

Anger
Proverbs 15:1

"A gentle answer deflects anger, but harsh words make tempers flare" (Proverbs 15:1 NLT).

College was a time of soul-searching for me. I discovered I had an anger issue, and that bothered me. I had grown up in a family where anger was prevalent, causing a lot of hurt that affected my peace and sanctity of security. I was fearful of my father often. When I left for college, I never expected to see those traits rear their ugly head in me, as I had convinced myself that I would never follow in those footsteps of destructive anger.

I was wrong. I began to react with anger more often than I wanted to. I saw a counselor to work through some of these issues and thought I was fine to move forward. I did seem to be fine, until I had my second son, Matt. Matt was a strong-willed child, just like I had been, and there were times when an explosion occurred between us. I started a bad habit of yelling and found my temper flaring more often than it should have, causing my husband and me both concern.

I sought counseling once again for getting to the root of my anger issues. I wanted to be able to be angry without sinning, without hurting someone else in my anger. Through the help I received, I uncovered trigger points I had, such as not feeling protected, not feeling respected, and not feeling heard. Becoming aware of those things brought healing through the work of the Holy Spirit. I was able to catch the red flags as they occurred, which allowed me to be proactive with better responses.

From that point on, Mark and I taught the boys that they could express their anger by punching their bed pillows, crying, or writing down things they want to say and rip them up. However, they were not allowed to destroy property (e.g., throwing things or punching holes in the walls) or hurt people, either with words (e.g., "I hate you") or physical harm. If anyone did, they would face consequences for sinning in their anger (including me).

Self-control in my anger was key to changing the course for our whole family. There were times when I just needed to remove myself from the situation and pray. Overall, God stepped in to bring change and healing to my heart, and I am forever grateful.

—Tammy

Ahh, the Good Ol' Days!

Ecclesiastes 7:10, 13–14; John 16:33

Visiting my grandfather in North Carolina was, at the very least, free entertainment! He was the funniest and wittiest grandpa around, doing things like spitting out his false teeth and retelling stories from his youth. Grandpa's stories were not the normal Grandpa-type stories one would expect because they shocked us, revealing the hidden rascal he had been. Yet Grandpa was also a sensitive soul that was demonstrated in the way he loved my grandma. My grandparents had a great life together, and he often would refer to the good ol' days as treasured memories that he would always hold close.

We all long for what is familiar to us, especially the good things that have created the memories we now have. We miss the way church, government, social culture, and morals used to be. Unintentionally however, those longings for the past can cause negativity in one's thinking. The reality and truth is, God has not changed one bit! He is the same God that was back then, now, and in the future.

> Don't long for the good old days. This is not wise ... Accept the way God does things, for who can straighten what he has made crooked? Enjoy prosperity while you can, but when hard times strike, realize that both come from God ... nothing is certain in this life. (Ecclesiastes 7:10, 13–14 NLT)

If we are too hung up on longing for the past, we could easily miss God's call for us in the present. Yes, the moral fabric of society has deteriorated, but God's power has equipped Christ-followers with the same Holy Spirit that raised Jesus from the dead. God placed you and me in the here and now for a very specific purpose for such a time as this.

As Ecclesiastes says, we are to enjoy prosperity while we can, but, when hard times come, to recognize that God is working through both. Jesus told us that we will have trouble, but that He has overcome the world! (John 16:33). Someday down the road, today will be the good ol' days. Let us rejoice and make the most of today!

–Tammy

Righteous Anger
Matthew 21:12–17; John 2:13–22

"Jesus made a whip from some ropes and chased them all out of the Temple. He drove out the sheep and cattle, scattered the money changers' coins over the floor, and turned over their tables" (John 2:15 NLT).

Jesus lived to be thirty-three years old, while the last three years He spent preaching, teaching, performing miracles, and preparing the disciples for after His death and resurrection. The daily, practical, and eternal lessons we learn from Jesus are easy enough for a child to understand, yet deep enough to challenge the most knowledgeable. We learn about anger in the story about Jesus and the money-changers and are shown that not all anger is bad. Sometimes we can be justified in our anger if it pertains to defending God and His principles laid out for us in Scripture.

As the story is recounted, a week before Jesus was crucified, He and His disciples traveled to Jerusalem. When they got there, they entered the temple, where people were preparing for Passover. The problem was greedy merchants selling animals that the people needed for sacrifice, placing astronomical prices on the animals. To make matters worse, they were using God's temple to do so! The blatant actions of robbing the people and turning God's house into a den of thieves (Matthew 21:13) made Jesus angry. In his anger, He turned the tables over and raised his voice to them.

Did Jesus have a temper problem, making a scene in front of so many people? No. As it is with God, there is always a purpose and reason for every action. In this case, Jesus was purposefully rebuking the religious leaders for misguiding the people in their worship and their money, even cheating God with their sacrifices.

Righteous anger is that fire that burns inside of us that spurs us on to stand up for God and others. As we examine ourselves and our own tendency to get angry, what triggers us to righteous anger? This kind of anger leads us away from complacency and brings us forward to action. We are never to sin in our anger by hurting people with our words and actions, but God will use it to speak up for someone else or fight for right and wrong according to God's will.

–Tammy

Sinful Anger

Psalm 37:5–9; Ephesians 4:26–27

Violent anger was common in our home growing up. I vividly remember my dad throwing a bowl of tomato soup across the kitchen, breaking and splattering all over the wall, and almost hitting my mom. Why? Because he was angry. Years later, Dad changed because he came to know Jesus in a personal way. Forgiveness and healing took place, and our family celebrates that Dad is in heaven today.

Anger itself is not a sin, but when we take our anger out on other people, whether it be with words or actions, we sin against God. There are three examples in the Bible of men and women who sinned in their anger.

1. In Genesis 4, Cain despised his brother Abel. As the story goes, both brothers brought an offering to God, but God was only pleased by Abel's offering. God gave Cain the opportunity to make things right, but instead Cain blamed Abel for his own poor choices. He was angry, so he killed Abel.

2. In Numbers 20, Moses was at the end of his rope with the Israelites and their complaining. When they arrived in the wilderness of Zin, there was no water. God instructed Moses to speak to a rock and said water would gush out, but the people continued, making Moses very angry. Instead of speaking to the rock, he lost his temper and hit the rock twice. While the water still gushed, God expressed His disappointment in Moses for not trusting God enough to demonstrate His holiness to His people with a calm and trusting attitude. As a result, God told Moses he would not lead the people into the Promised Land.

3. In 1 Kings 21, King Ahab and his wife, Jezebel, wanted to purchase property of Naboth to add to the king's property. They were used to controlling others and getting what they wanted, so when Naboth refused because of a scriptural mandate, Ahab and Jezebel were very angry. Ahab went away to sulk, but Jezebel was vicious and ruthless, killing Naboth and taking his land.

The Word of God gives our closing words, "Stop being angry! Turn from your rage! Do not lose your temper—it only leads to harm" (Psalm 37:8 NLT).

–Tammy

The Lord Will Fight for You

Exodus 14:13–14

We read in Exodus that the Israelites were slaves in Egypt. After many years, Pharaoh freed them and let them go. Outlandishly, he changed his mind and sent his troops back to go after the Israelites, and so this is where the story picks up.

The Israelites knew that Pharaoh's armies were coming and had gotten as far as the Red Sea with no way over. Since God's favor was on the Israelites, God revealed to Moses again His power and mercy.

But Moses told the people, "Don't be afraid. Just stand still and watch the Lord rescue you today. The Egyptians you see today will never be seen again. The Lord himself will fight for you. Just stay calm." (Exodus 14:13–14 NLT)

Wow! Can you imagine hearing those words during utter panic, fearing for your life and your family's lives? Then God, making it known that He will fight for you, asks you to stand still and stay calm. I don't know about you, but "still and calm" might not be my first instinct when hundreds of people are charging me, possibly trampling, drowning, or killing me with a spear in a matter of hours! But this is how God works. He wants us to trust Him so much that we will believe the unbelievable.

God proceeded to instruct Moses to wave his staff over the sea. He did, and it parted in half, allowing the Israelites through on dry ground. When Pharaoh's armies came after them, God brought the waters back together, drowning all the king's men and their horses and chariots. "God then said, 'When my glory is displayed through them, all Egypt will see my glory and know that I am the Lord!'" (Exodus 14:18 NLT).

This week, when you find yourself facing an attack or being swallowed up by the sea, remember that you have a God that will fight for you, and He will be victorious if you just be still!

—Tammy

Slow to Anger
Numbers 14:17–19

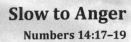

Though I never was taught this way, I used to think that whenever I sinned against God, He would be mad at me and stay mad! I'd allow myself to believe that He didn't even want to hear from me at all (like shunning me). I felt some sort of imaginary clock start from when I sinned to when I was allowed to talk to God again and make amends. It was such an isolating feeling. And while I had already begun separating myself from that false view of God, what solidified a proper view of God for me was a class I took in graduate school on the book of Numbers and the people of Israel.

Over and over, the children of Israel sinned against God, rebelled, and complained, yet God always had compassion on them. Certainly, there were clear punishments for their sins, but to read in Numbers 14 and see how God's heart could be moved by the passion of a human leader, Moses, is astounding to me. Instead of destroying the Israelites, which they probably deserved, God once again showed mercy and compassion. He chose to remain in a relationship with His people and continue His favor upon them.

Going through that class helped me to understand why God punishes sin, having the depth of love and compassion He has for us. I don't know about you, but sometimes I take a wrong turn in life, and I find deep comfort in knowing that my God is not just shaking His fist at me in anger, shunning me far, far away. Instead, He's holding out His hand with a gentle invitation for me to repent and come back to Him. God's love for me is unfathomable, and I must remember that He does not respond with human responses.

God loves you. God wants to be in relationship with you, just like the Israelites. There is not a sin God doesn't know about. He is slow to anger, and His grace is unbounding. God will never shun you, and you never need to worry whether He will forgive you. He loves you way too much.

–Scott

Week 42 Reflections

1. After reviewing the Scriptures for each day, name three to four passages that jumped out at you this week.
2. How can you practically apply these verses to your life today and the upcoming week?
3. How do you display anger? Explain.
4. Describe sinful anger and righteous anger. What are their effects on you and others?
5. Do you long for the past (the good ol' days)? Does that ever keep you in a negative state of mind because you miss what is familiar to you?
6. Name a time when you have been hesitant to come to God after you knew you had gone against His will. Explain.
7. When has God fought for you? Think carefully.
8. Have people ever shunned you? Explain. Will God ever shun you?
9. Write a prayer asking God to fight for you now. Name the situation and ask Him to take it on.

MONTH 11

Distractions and Busy Schedules
Can Hinder Our Time with God

A FAITH THAT STANDS
Produces a Life of Worship

Practice His Presence
Romans 13:14

"Instead, clothe yourself with the presence of the Lord Jesus Christ. And don't let yourself think about ways to indulge your evil desires" (Romans 13:14 NLT).

Nicholas Herman was born in 1614 in the eastern part of France. When he was sixteen years old, he came to know Jesus Christ after a vision he had of a leafless tree in the middle of a battlefield. Realizing that the tree would be in full leaf and flower in a few months, he saw the tree as a symbol of God's ability to transform the human heart.

Growing up as a poor pauper boy, he decided to become a soldier in the Thirty Years' War in order to feed himself, as meals were guaranteed. In 1635 he fought against the Swedes and the French, but was taken captive by the Germans, who treated him like a spy. They planned to hang him, but the courage he displayed in disputing this accusation changed their minds, and they let him go free. He went back to fight and was soon injured, resulting in being permanently lame. The slaughter of people that he witnessed during the war left him to rely heavily on his faith, and at the age of twenty-six, Nicholas became a lay brother in a monastery community in Paris. His religious name became Brother Lawrence of the Resurrection.

As part of his service, he became cook of the monastery until his leg became ulcerated and he was given an easier task of sandal-maker. Although his lowly position prevented him from doing anything beyond these two things, his deep relationship with God gave him wisdom, grace, and a prayer life that was constant and full of God's presence. The humility and character of Brother Lawrence attracted many people to him who were seeking spiritual guidance in hopes to experience the kind of peace he had. He often told people that God was the Lord over his pots and pans and over the sandals that he made, even though he personally would never walk again.

Brother Lawrence wrote many prayers and believed that in the mundane of life, one can practice the presence of the Lord, being in constant communication with God. May we too learn from his example and practice God's presence!

—Tammy

Take a Bow

Genesis 41:42–43; Psalm 95:6–7; Daniel 3

"Come, let us worship and bow down. Let us kneel before the Lord our maker, for he is our God. We are the people he watches over, the flock under his care. If only you would listen to his voice today!" (Psalm 95:6–7 NLT).

I just finished watching a TV series on historical European royalty in the 1600s to 1800s. If the series is anything like the reality of the times, I am taken back by the culture where the gestures of bowing or kneeling in the presence of the king, queen, or even the king's mother were the expected sign of respect. In twenty-first-century America, this is a foreign concept to us; hence we don't see much of that at all. However, Scripture refers to bowing as an act of reverence, respect, and humility.

One of the first examples we see of the act of bowing in biblical history is in Genesis 18:2 when Abraham was visited by three heavenly beings. He recognized them to be of God, and so he bowed to the ground in respect.

Years later, King Pharaoh of Egypt ordered all Egyptians to bow down to Joseph as a sign of respect because he had been promoted to the second-in-command from a slave (Genesis 41:42–43). So, early on in human history, the act of bowing or kneeling came to portray humility before someone of greater importance.

In the story of Shadrach, Meshach, and Abednego in Daniel 3, King Nebuchadnezzar decreed that everyone should bow to the golden statue that he had just created to be his own "god." Well, God has no tolerance for other gods, and the three men refused to worship any other god but the one true God. They would not bow. Bowing meant worship, and they wanted nothing to do with false gods. The three men knew they would face death, and sure enough, they were thrown into the blazing furnace to die. But guess what? God honored their reverence for Him and stood in the fire with them, not singeing a single hair on their heads!

The next time you are in a quiet place of worship, try something different, bowing in God's holy presence. Allow your body posture to honor Him while you exude reverence, humility, and worship to Him.

—Tammy

Lay Down Your Crown

James 1:12; Revelation 4:9–11

The book of Revelation is a difficult book of the Bible to understand, but a fascinating study. The content is bizarre but intricate with symbolism that communicates and prophesies what is to come. Christians expectantly wait for God to unfold His divine plan that lies in the pages of this book. The words are like a picture, so let's try to visualize the image these verses are painting:

> ... the twenty-four elders fall down before him who sits on the throne and worship him who lives for ever and ever. They lay their crowns before the throne and say: "You are worthy, our Lord and God, to receive glory and honor and power, for you created all things, and by your will they were created and have their being." (Revelation 4:9–11 NLT)

Here we have twenty-four elders with crowns on, entering the throne room of Jesus. They immediately recognize their humble position of simply being in His presence, that it was by grace that they were there in the first place. As an act of worship, they relinquish their crowns, knowing that the true glory comes from the one who gives life true meaning.

Throughout history, crowns have been the primary image for authority and honor, symbolizing power and dignity for the ones who wear them. Crowns also represent our successes, our identity, our service, and the control we have over our lives. Surrendering our crowns is one of the purest forms of worship, saying to Jesus, "Not my will, but Yours." "Not my control, but Yours." "Not my recognition, but Yours."

A crown could also represent the Crown of Life that Jesus promises in James, "Afterward they will receive the crown of life that God has promised to those who love him" (James 1:12 NLT).

When we lay down our own crown in exchange for the Crown of Life, Jesus becomes Lord over our lives, forgiving us and giving us salvation through Jesus. Therefore, we worship Him, laying down not only our crowns, but ourselves at the feet of Jesus.

—Tammy

No Other Gods
Exodus 20:2–4; Psalm 81:8–10

The Ten Commandments start with telling us to have no other gods before God, followed by not creating or making any image to bow to or serve. For me, the second commandment has never really been a temptation. But as I think upon the first commandment, it has not been quite as easy.

In the Old Testament, we have examples where the people are drawn to serve the gods of foreign nations. Sometimes this is after being conquered in war or during a time of duress in their lives where they did not feel God was taking care of them generally as a people. In this direct context again, I have not had this as an area of strong temptation.

But Jesus clarified and broadened this concept. Jesus made it clear that idols in our lives might not be just idols from foreign countries or statues we create with our own hands. He pointed out that these might include our time, status, or job. That changes everything for me.

Do I truly put God first in my life each day? Some days I can be rushed in the mornings, and my prayer and Bible reading are shortened or missed altogether so I might be on time for my work meetings. It might be my job that is taking the top spot over God, or maybe it is my desire for sleep. Clearly having a job or sleeping are not bad; however, we must be sure to put them in their proper place.

We don't always prioritize our time with God, and yet we make sure we don't miss getting our kids to their event, being on time for a dinner out, or watching our favorite team. These too are not bad things by themselves; however, if they take priority and crowd out our time with God, this becomes the problem.

Each of us is likely to have different activities that can become gods in our lives. Some will seem odd or insignificant to the other person, but we must be honest with ourselves and God and assure that we are always putting Him first. The world will offer up to us many other options, which we must prioritize properly. Our God is a jealous God, and for that I am very thankful.

My Soul Yearns and Even Faints

Psalm 84:1–3

The depth of our worship coincides directly with the yearning for God in our hearts. If we long for Jesus more than anything else in this world, our soul will faint with the anticipation of being with Him. "I long, yes, I faint with longing to enter the courts of the Lord. With my whole being, body and soul, I will shout joyfully to the living God" (Psalm 84:1–2 NLT).

Years ago, our family took a week's vacation to Washington DC, where we spent one of our days at the Holocaust Museum. This sorrowful place of remembrance realizes the depth of pure evil that took place during the reign of Hitler, while millions of Jews were slaughtered. We saw the well-known room of over four thousand shoes once worn by victims of the Holocaust, a memorial representing each life that was lost.

We journeyed upstairs to find one of the Holocaust survivors sharing his story to those who visited. He told of the capture of his family in Poland and their executions in Treblinka, but mostly his miraculous escape to freedom through a narrow opening in a fence. He had snuck away unnoticed during a death march to the gas chamber, but for everyone else, their fates were sealed.

I can only imagine what it would have been like to have been a prisoner in the Nazi Auschwitz concentration camp and then receive a "get out of jail free" card through a narrow opening in a fence. Spiritually, this is where we all are, in chains because of our sin until we know the saving grace of Jesus Christ. He is the only way out, the narrow gate.

But the yearning for God in our hearts comes from the reality that only Jesus can offer freedom. Only Jesus can wipe our sins away and give us a new start. When we yearn for Jesus to the point where our soul faints for Him, we are in a place of worship. As lasting survivors recount their stories to hundreds of people a day, may we recount our story of freedom from hopeless bondage to everlasting life through Jesus. Let us worship Him with gratefulness and in reverence.

–Tammy

Where Do I Start?

1 Thessalonians 5:16–18; Psalm 105:4–5, 138

My daughter has been encouraging me to write some devotionals for this book. I can give her every reason imaginable why not to, "I have so much else to do. I don't know where to start or what to say." It's not that I'm biblically illiterate. I read and study the Bible continually. I lead Bible studies and worship. But write devotionals? I don't know where to begin.

As I sat down to write, I took a deep breath, focused on God, and asked Him, "How shall I begin?" Then I picked up God's Word to look for answers, and God led me to a psalm. "Search for the Lord and for his strength; continually seek him. Remember the wonders he has performed" (Psalm 105:4–5 NIV)

I knew I needed to stop and worship Him, so I turned my thoughts and heart to God, praising and thanking Him for what He was going to do through or even in spite of me. I sought His wisdom and His strength, and then the words began flowing. I continued to reflect on who God is and how He has never failed me, for I have learned to seek God in everything I do, whether a big or small thing. When I have sought Him first, I have been repeatedly and expectantly grateful. How much better my day goes when I remain in Him!

> I give thanks to Your Holy Name, for Your steadfast love and Your faithfulness; for You have exalted above all things Your Name and Your Word. On the day I called, You answered me; my strength of soul You increased. (Psalm 138:1–3 NIV)

So to answer my own question, "Where do I start?" I need to begin with worshiping my God. This will open the channel for Him to work through me. May you also begin your tasks today by worship and praise.

—Sharon

Week 43 Reflections

1. After reviewing the Scriptures for each day, name three to four passages that jumped out at you this week.
2. How can you practically apply these verses to your life today and the upcoming week?
3. What do you learn from the life of Brother Lawrence?
4. Our body posture is an added response on our part to worship God. How can you physically show worship to God?
5. Crowns represent our successes, our identity, our service, and the control we have over our lives. What does it mean to you to "lay down your crown" at the feet of Jesus?
6. What are potential gods in your life if you are not careful?
7. Have you ever experienced yearning and fainting for Jesus? Explain. Write a prayer that seeks God from the depths of your soul, yearning for God in the deepest way.
8. With anything you face in life, when you don't know where to start or how to start, what should you do?
9. How can worshiping God first thing in the morning steer the course of your day?

Prayer

Matthew 6:9–13

I remember as a girl loving to camp at a running farm near Albany, New York. My sister and I would help milk the cows in the morning, gather eggs, go on hayrides, and catch frogs. At night, my mom challenged us to read or have quiet time in our bunks before we fell asleep. One night, she specifically suggested for me to memorize the Lord's Prayer.

> Our Father in heaven, may your name be kept holy. May your Kingdom come soon. May your will be done on earth, as it is in heaven. Give us today the food we need and forgive us our sins, as we have forgiven those who sin against us. And don't let us yield to temptation but rescue us from the evil one. (Matthew 6:9–13 NLT)

When it comes to prayer, Jesus wanted us to keep it simple. In the previous verses, He explains that God desires us to pray behind closed doors, as to not flaunt our prayers in public, but also not to babble on with repetition. If you are unsure how to pray or where to start, perhaps this simple guideline will help.

- **(P)** Praise God: Extol and honor the character of God (i.e., Holy, Redeemer, Provider, Healer, Forgiver, Peace, Transformer, Hope)
- **(R)** Repent of Sin: Run from sin by confession and renew your heart and mind through Jesus
- **(A)** Acknowledge and appreciate God for what He has done for you and others
- **(Y)** Yearn for God: Seek His will by presenting your requests to Him

We don't need to be fluffy with our prayers or hide things from Him. After all, He already knows before we even say a word. When you take the time to pray, you will quickly see how it will change your life!

–Tammy

Hebrew Praise

Psalms selected verses

One of the passions of my soul is to encourage others to express their praise to God. There isn't a whole lot that excites me more because when we praise God, He inhabits every part of our being and makes Himself known to us through our acts of praise! As we investigate the Hebrew, it will enable us to deepen our worship and praise to God, stretching our hearts and souls toward Him.

Praise is acknowledging God for who He is, His character, and His worthiness because He is the almighty God. Our one English word, *praise*, can mean one of seven different words in Hebrew, each having their own meaning. In looking through the book of Psalms, we see examples of these seven Hebrew words. Take the time to study these words and explore the various ways we are to praise!

1. **YADAH**: To revere or worship with lifted hands. "May the peoples praise (yâdâh) You, God." (Psalm 67:3 NIV)

2. **HALAL**: To boast, celebrate, be clamorously foolish. "Let them praise (hâlal) His name with dancing and make music to Him with timbres and harp." (Psalm 149:3 NIV)

3. **ZAMAR**: To make music with a musical instrument. "On a harp of ten strings, I will sing praises (Zâmar) …" (Psalm 144:9 NIV)

4. **TOWDAH**: Thanksgiving for the yet to come. "In God I have put my trust; I will render praises (tôwdâh) to You." (Psalm 56:11–12 NIV)

5. **BARAK**: To kneel, bow down with our eyes fixed on God. "Praise (bârak) the Lord, my soul; All my inmost being, praise his holy name." (Psalm 103:1–2 NIV)

6. **TEHILLA**: A new song of praise. A spontaneous song. "He put a new song in my mouth, a song of praise (tehillâh) to our God." (Psalm 40:3 NIV)

7. **SHABACH**: To shout. To glory, and triumph. "One generation shall praise (shâbach) Your works to another." (Psalm 145:4 NIV)

–Tammy

Repent, Lament, and Worship
2 Samuel 11–12; Matthew 4:17; James 5:15–16

Being in the wrong place at the wrong time can lead to temptations that instigate a snowball of sin and its consequences. 1 Samuel 11–12 recount the story of David and Bathsheba, when David started on a downward slope being in the wrong place at the wrong time. David was supposed to be out fighting on the battlefields with his troops, but being the king, he delegated the responsibilities to others while he stayed at his cozy palace. It was then that he couldn't sleep, roamed the rooftop, and saw beautiful Bathsheba bathing for all eyes to see. Before he knew it, the sinful path he went down included rape and adultery, an illegitimate pregnancy, lying, and eventually murder.

David knew better. He was a man after God's own heart. But he messed up, big time. He could have thrown in the towel, carrying the weight of shame on his shoulders and living the rest of his life with a cloud of failure looming over his head. But he didn't do that. Instead David owned up to his sin and confessed to the Lord.

He acted on that apology and lamented his sin by covering his body in sackcloth, laying on the ground and fasting for seven days, praying to God and pouring out his soul to Him. On the seventh day, the baby Bathsheba gave birth to died. David rose, and the first thing he did was worship the Lord. He put his sins behind him and moved forward in God's mercy and forgiveness, not looking back.

How often do we lament over our sin? I know I probably do not lament enough. But like David did, the first step is to confess our sin, lament and grieve, and worship God with a clean heart.

> And the prayer offered in faith will make the sick person well; the Lord will raise them up. If they have sinned, they will be forgiven. Therefore, confess your sins to each other and pray for each other so that you may be healed. The prayer of a righteous person is powerful and effective. (James 5:15–16 NIV)

—*Tammy*

I'm Staring at the Wall

Psalm 40:1–3; Romans 8:26–28

Tragedy has stricken. I sit here alone. I long to pray, but I have no idea where to begin. Grief and loss cripple my soul, paralyzing any thoughts or words I might form. The burden I carry is heavy, like a boulder crushing my head and lungs, suffocating the life and breath out of me. I'm staring at the wall. "Speak to me, Jesus" are the only words that come before my tears fall endlessly into a pit of despair.

> I cling to these verses, "And the Holy Spirit helps us in our weakness. For example, we don't know what God wants us to pray for. But the Holy Spirit prays for us with groanings that cannot be expressed in words. And the Father who knows all hearts knows what the Spirit is saying, for the Spirit pleads for us believers in harmony with God's own will." (Romans 8:26–27 NLT)

Why God? My heart is breaking. I know You are here. I feel Your presence washing over me like a warm blanket. I lift my hands for You to pick me up. I need the strength of Your loving arms to embrace me, holding me tightly until my tears run dry. The Holy Spirit speaks to You on my behalf. I sit quietly. I close my eyes and weep. I lean into the grief and allow Your Spirit to overwhelm me with peace. In Your presence, there is comfort. In Your presence, there is peace. In Your presence, I am safe. I won't give up. I won't lose hope. I will be still and know that You are God.

> I waited patiently for the Lord to help me, and he turned to me and heard my cry. He lifted me out of the pit of despair, out of the mud and the mire. He set my feet on solid ground and steadied me as I walked along. He has given me a new song to sing, a hymn of praise to our God. (Psalm 40:1–3 NLT)

Today, if you find yourself staring at the wall, you are not alone. The Holy Spirit is here. Lean into Him and let Him carry you.

—Tammy

Shh, I Think I Hear Something
1 Kings 19:9–13; Mark 4:22–24

"Be still and know that I am God" (Psalm 46:10 NIV).

Being a pianist and a violinist is a curse as well as a blessing. My ear is finely tuned to pitch, both in what I am playing and everyone else who is playing with me. If a note is missing or wrong, I notice, even among twenty other instruments and singers.

My husband, a sports lover, notices every play, every position, and every person on the team, fine-tuned to finite details of the game. He often tells me what is going on behind the scenes just before the announcer says almost verbatim the exact same thing he said! He can do this because he is watching and listening, totally engaged.

Whether music, sports, educational classes, or other things we employ our minds with, if we are not totally engaged, we may miss the discreet. When God speaks to us, it isn't always loud and obvious. He often waits until we are paying attention and quiet before Him; thus we might miss His soft, still voice. When God spoke to Elijah, it was not powerful! God told him,

> "Go out and stand before me on the mountain," ... And as Elijah stood there, the Lord passed by, and a mighty windstorm hit the mountain. It was such a terrible blast that the rocks were torn loose, but the Lord was not in the wind. After the wind there was an earthquake, but the Lord was not in the earthquake. And after the earthquake there was a fire, but the Lord was not in the fire. And after the fire there was the sound of a gentle whisper ... (1 Kings 19:9–13 NLT)

We may expect Him to speak strongly because of our own internal storm. The grief, worry, or panic seem all-consuming, and we believe He should feel the same way. But God is a patient God. When we finely listen with our ears tuned to hear Him, He will give us everything we need to move forward. Shh! Can you hear Him? I think I hear something.

—Tammy

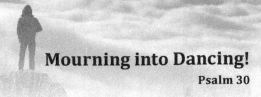

Mourning into Dancing!
Psalm 30

Grief is paralyzing. One minute, your life is the way you know it, and the next minute, you are faced with a loss you can't begin to wrap your mind around. I have visited old gravesites from two hundred years ago containing a whole household of children at once who passed away on the same date. Was it a house fire or other terrible accident? I've also seen individual gravestones with family members, all passing away within weeks and months from each other. Was it a disease that plagued the family?

No matter how deep the loss, mourning is a painful and lingering process. The loss of those we love leaves holes in our hearts that will always be there. The psalmist David experienced many seasons of mourning in his kingly life that are recorded in 1 and 2 Samuel.

- 1 Samuel 1:11–12. David mourned the loss of King Saul and his son, Jonathan, when they were killed in battle.
- 2 Samuel 12:13–25. David mourned the death of his newborn son consequently for his sins against God with Bathsheba.
- 2 Samuel 13:31–33. David mourned the death of his oldest son, Amnon. Absalom, David's other son, avenged his sister Tamar's rape by her half-brother, Amnon, by killing him.
- 2 Samuel 18:33–19:4. David mourned the death of his son, Absalom, his third and favorite son, whose arrogance and pride caused him to usurp David's authority and speak against him to the people.

Fifteen years ago, I suffered three miscarriages back to back. My body ached with grief. During that time of suffering, I clung to the words in Psalm 30, "You have turned my mourning into joyful dancing. You have taken away my clothes of mourning and clothed me with joy, that I might sing praises to you and not be silent. O Lord my God, I will give you thanks forever" (Psalm 30:11–12 NLT).

Years later, my faith in God has multiplied as I experienced His faithfulness to help me to live again, to lean on His strength, and to rest in His comforting arms. He does turn our mourning into dancing!

—Tammy

Week 44 Reflections

1. After reviewing the Scriptures for each day, name three to four passages that jumped out at you this week.
2. How can you practically apply these verses to your life today and the upcoming week?
3. Write out the PRAY template for prayer with personal application.
4. Which Hebrew words of praise do you find easy to demonstrate? What is difficult for you (or not natural)?
5. When have you ever been in the wrong place at the wrong time, leading you to a snowball of sin? How did David deal with his sin with Bathsheba?
6. Have you ever felt paralyzed by grief? What does God want us to do when we are in total despair?
7. God turns our mourning into dancing. What does that mean for you, whether it be from the past, present, or future hope?
8. Write your own song (psalm) to God, expressing your inmost thoughts. Include what God is teaching you and who you know Him to be.
9. How can you encourage someone who is grieving?

Where Can I Go?

Psalm 139:1–18

As you read today's passage, consider underlining or highlighting God's attributes and what He knows about you.

O Lord, you have examined my heart and know everything about me.
You know when I sit down or stand up. You know my thoughts even when
I'm far away. You see me when I travel and when I rest at home.
You know everything I do.
You know what I am going to say even before I say it, Lord.
You go before me and follow me. You place your hand of blessing on my head.
Such knowledge is too wonderful for me, too great for me to understand! I
can never escape from your Spirit! I can never get away from your presence!
If I go up to heaven, you are there; if I go down to the grave, you are there.
If I ride the wings of the morning, if I dwell by the farthest oceans,
even there your hand will guide me, and your strength will support me.
I could ask the darkness to hide me and the light around me to
become night—but even in darkness I cannot hide from you.
To you the night shines as bright as day. Darkness and light are the
same to you. You made all the delicate, inner parts of my body
and knit me together in my mother's womb.
Thank you for making me so wonderfully complex!
Your workmanship is marvelous—how well I know it.
You watched me as I was being formed in utter seclusion,
as I was woven together in the dark of the womb. You saw me before I was born.
Every day of my life was recorded in your book.
Every moment was laid out before a single day had passed.
How precious are your thoughts about me, O God.
They cannot be numbered!
I can't even count them; they outnumber the grains of sand!
And when I wake up, you are still with me!
(Psalm 139:1–18 NLT)

—Tammy

Not a Star Is Missing

Isaiah 40:25–26

The night was clear on the beach in Maui, and Mark and I gazed up at the bright celestial bodies from a hammock tied between two palm trees. We had seen the moon, stars, and planets many times before, but there was nothing like viewing them from this part of the world on a cloudless night. Brilliant heavenly twinkles lit up the sky with their splendor, some burning away and shooting across the sky. To interpret what we were looking at, we downloaded an app on our phones to identify the many stars, planets, and constellations that captivated us.

Our newfound evening habit brought about many discussions about the power of God, His majesty and unfathomable greatness. Of all the millions of stars that He created by name, He also created you and me, along with every animal, plant, and living thing under heaven. How could I ever doubt that there is a God when the tiny, glowing, little bright lights I was staring at were hanging in a galaxy millions of miles away? And to think of the billions of stars out there that we can't even see!

> "To whom will you compare me? Who is my equal?" asks the Holy One. Look up into the heavens. Who created all the stars? He brings them out like an army, one after another, calling each by its name. Because of his great power and incomparable strength, not a single one is missing." (Isaiah 40:15–26 NLT)

To think that God calls each star by name and that none are missing assures me that His attention to detail is like nothing you or I can wrap our heads around. He knows you by name. God does not make mistakes. He created you with a very distinct purpose in mind. Ask God to show you His divine purpose for your life. He will show you!

In those times when we are tempted to doubt our reason for living, we need to set our gaze on the majesty and holiness of God. What is God calling you to do? Ask Him! Every star has a glow, and there are not any mistakes or any missing things in all of His creation!

–Tammy

Sing and Proclaim
Psalm 96:1–3

"Sing a new song to the Lord! Let the whole earth sing to the Lord! Sing to the Lord; praise his name. Each day proclaim the good news that he saves. Publish his glorious deeds among the nations. Tell everyone about the amazing things he does" (Psalm 96:1–3 NLT).

Years ago, when Scott and Matt were toddlers, I was involved with a moms' playgroup. As a young mom, I looked forward to the weekly opportunities to talk with other moms about our children's development and their eating and sleeping habits, trying to learn from the experiences of others. Naïvely, as most new parents do, I remember the temptation I felt to brag about my boys for all their toddler accomplishments and outstanding cuteness (until the trying threes cropped up and some humility set in)!

This overwhelming feeling of wanting to boast in our children is the same idea in Psalm 96 about boasting in the Lord. We should feel like we would need to hold back for fear we will say too many wonderful things about our God! When we meditate on who God is and what He has done for us, we can't help but sing and proclaim it!

Sadly, we can grow accustomed to the gift of salvation that Jesus freely gave to us, and our fervor can grow dull. But God is the "Great I AM," our Provider, our Strength, our Hope, our Everything, our Healer, our Peace, and our Redeemer who is faithful to forgive and quick to show mercy. The very nature of God surpasses anything we experience here on earth, and that is worth singing about!

I had a poster on my closet door growing up that said, "Sing your praise to the Lord, even if you are a little off-key!" It doesn't matter what we sound like. To God, our singing and proclaiming His faithfulness is a symphony to His ears. The Psalms are full of songs that were written to sing not only praise, but lament and prayer as well.

As you spend time with God today, consider singing a song of praise! Then ask Him to give you fresh opportunities throughout your day to boast in the Lord, telling all who will listen the amazing things He has done!

–Tammy

Doubts When Leading
Nehemiah 2:4–5, 4:1–9

Early in my career I would observe key leaders and wonder how they reached the position they held. I would look for clues on what I might try to emulate so I too might reach a position of leadership. One of my false assumptions was that once you reached a certain level of leadership, your fears and doubts would somehow go away or at least greatly diminish. Now late in my career, I realize that fear and doubt don't necessarily go away as we move further up in leadership.

One leader in the Bible that gives us a great example of how to handle fears and doubts is Nehemiah. When Nehemiah gets the report that the walls of Jericho have been torn down and the gates burned, he is faced with a most difficult situation. As he mourns over this, he starts with what will be a pattern throughout the book. He goes to God in prayer. As he speaks to the king, the Bible tells us that Nehemiah is terrified. I love when the king asks Nehemiah how he can help. Nehemiah replies with a prayer to God (Nehemiah 2:4), and then he lays out his plan to the king.

While the king grants his request, the difficulties do not stop there. The people are ridiculed, and Nehemiah prays to God. The people are threatened, and Nehemiah prays to God, all of this while trying to lead the incredible task of rebuilding the wall around Jerusalem. After praying in every situation, Nehemiah also showed great skills in problem-solving as he laid out detailed plans, established teamwork, and clearly put in the personal effort to accomplish the task.

As I reflect on my life at every level, I have had some fear and doubt when faced with difficult tasks at work and even outside of work. Fear and doubt can be healthy as it raises our awareness of the situation. But when fear and doubt come upon us, we should not shrink back from the task at hand but rather follow in the wonderful leadership example of Nehemiah. Pray first. Then use the skills God has given you to lay out the detailed plans to accomplish the task.

When your fear and doubt have been overcome and the task is completed, take time to worship God.

–Mark

Tremble in Awe
Micah 7:15–17; Luke 8:40–48

Ten years ago, our family hosted a Japanese foreign exchange student. He lived with us for a year, and so we took him sightseeing to some of the hot spots in the United States, Niagara Falls being one of those places. I remember sitting on the ledge of the falls with the whole family, staring in awe at the thunderous water below. I could feel the rush of pounding water resonate through me. So much water. Such an amazing God.

Throughout history, God's creation and power never cease to amaze me. In the Old Testament, God showed Himself and His miraculous power through parting the Red Sea for the Israelites and protecting Shadrach, Meshach, and Abednego in the fiery furnace. Whenever God showed Himself, people trembled in fear, understanding His power and majesty on this earth.

> All the nations of the world will stand amazed at what the Lord will do for you. They will be embarrassed at their feeble power. They will cover their mouths in silent awe, deaf to everything around them. Like snakes crawling from their holes, they will come out to meet the Lord our God. They will fear him greatly, trembling in terror at his presence. (Micah 7:16–17 NLT)

God also showed Himself in the New Testament through Jesus, performing uncounted miracles of healing and transforming hearts of stone. Thousands of people followed Him because of what they had witnessed, including a woman in need of healing from constant bleeding in Luke 8:40–48. She pushed through the crowd to touch the robe of Jesus, and because of her faith, she was healed. She fell to the ground and trembled in awe from the extraordinary thing that had just happened.

God is the Healer of broken hearts, the Mender of relationships, and the Miracle Worker in situations we don't see a way forward in. Hang on to your faith and look for Him to do the impossible! Believe and not doubt. When you do, you too will tremble in awe!

–Tammy

A Blessing and a Curse

Psalm 139:13–14

For over seventy years, I have had a very creative mind. This can be a blessing and a curse in many ways. It is a blessing because I used to be a schoolteacher and am continually thinking about a myriad of things to do. In the mornings, my mind darts from "What's on my schedule this morning? I can't wait to get to my scrapbooking, I need to work on my puzzle, I have to make two new cards, and I haven't gotten my paints out in a long while." You get the picture." The curse part is that, as a retired widow, I simply drive myself bananas with my clutter! I even added a room onto my house so I would have a spare room for all these fun hobbies.

Ok, so now you know. My strength of creativity is also my weakness. I can be a messy person. As far back as I remember, there wasn't a time when I was neat. I used to think there was something wrong with me and that this trait was a bad thing. As a result, my life has been full of guilt. My mother was neat, so it was certainly not in her example!

Years went by living with the blessing of inspirational cleverness and the curse of disorder. Not too long ago, I read from Psalm 139, "for you formed my inward parts; you knitted me together in my mother's womb. I praise you, for I am fearfully and wonderfully made" (Psalm 139:13–14 NIV).

It dawned on me that the two traits went hand in hand. God had given me a beautiful, interesting mind. But creativity is seldom tidy. He wants me to embrace my uniqueness so I can bless others and stop feeling guilty over the clutter it all makes. When life ends, it will be more important to have invested in others rather than to have had an immaculate house.

What strengths and weaknesses do you have that you believe to be both a blessing and a curse? Now think about how God designed you uniquely with those qualities! Embrace who God made you. God is all about using the gifts He's given you to bless Him and bless others. A blessing and a curse? Maybe, but God wants to focus on the blessing!

-Sharon

Week 45 Reflections

1. After reviewing the Scriptures for each day, name three to four passages that jumped out at you this week.
2. How can you practically apply these verses to your life today and the upcoming week?
3. What does God say about you in Psalm 139?
4. Describe God's majesty in Isaiah 40.
5. Nehemiah prayed to God every time he made a decision, every time he felt doubt, and every time he faced a task. What do you need to pray about today?
6. When have you experienced trembling in awe? Write down all the ways that make you in awe of who God is.
7. What strengths and weaknesses do you have that you believe to be both a blessing and a curse?
8. What strengths has God given to you that He wants to focus on?
9. What is God calling you to be obedient in?

Audience of One
Matthew 6:1–18

I am a purist when it comes to corporate worship. Worshiping God stands alone for what it is, the gathering of voices in praise, reading Scripture, praying, testifying, singing worship songs, all with the unified engagement of the congregation. Serving as a worship leader, I used to feel less effective when the congregation wasn't participating or was smaller than I had hoped for. But God showed me through the years what my focus needed to be and who my real audience is and always has been.

I have led worship for some very large and some very small crowds. As I have matured in my faith, I can tell you today that it matters none the size of the crowd for me to put 110 percent into worshiping the Highest God, the Creator of the Universe, my Redeemer, Provider, and my Comfort. When I reflect on all that God has done for me and where I would be without Him, I have no choice but to worship God and God alone, an audience of one.

Romans 12 talks about living our lives as living sacrifices, holy and pleasing to God, and that this is our spiritual act of worship. When we serve behind the scenes or give anonymously to a family in need, we are worshiping an audience of one. Likewise, if we find ourselves serving by ministering on stage to seek recognition for our efforts, that can be a slippery slope to pride.

I have had some of the most spiritually anointed moments of worship in my living room, just me and the piano, singing, playing, and crying out to God, heard by only Him. These have been some of the sweetest moments that I have tried to adapt and incorporate into corporate worship by keeping my eyes on Jesus, singing and playing only to Him, knowing that if every person left and I was left there alone, my worship would be the same. My intensity would be the same. My fervor would be the same, all for an audience of one!

—Tammy

Lord of My Aspirations

1 Peter 5:5–6

"I want to be rich and famous when I grow up!" I told my mom at an early age. I had lots and lots of dreams, such as being Miss America, a famous pianist and songwriter, and the wife of the president. My mom used to tell me that I should probably have a plan B since those dreams were most likely going to go unrealized.

Being known was important to me, especially in my teens. I observed famous athletes, musicians, and speakers, and I desired what they had. I think I felt like being known would give me worth in others' eyes. God revealed to me through a handful of circumstances that my purpose was far deeper than what can be seen on a platform or camera. I didn't need a title to be worth something in God's or others' eyes. What I did need was a heart of surrender that would allow God to be the Lord of my aspirations.

I began asking God to dissect my heart by showing me where I needed to become less so that He could become more.

> Fear of the Lord teaches wisdom; humility precedes honor. (Proverbs 15:33 NLT)

> For those who exalt themselves will be humbled, and those who humble themselves will be exalted. (Luke 14:11 NLT)

> Don't be selfish; don't try to impress others. Be humble, thinking of others as better than yourselves. (Philippians 2:3 NLT)

Putting the Lord over my aspirations meant that He was Lord over every talent, every gift (big or small), and every element of my personality. It meant that I could heartfully rejoice with others when they succeeded and give of myself in ways that may have in the past seemed beneath me. My prayer today is that God will always be the Lord of my aspirations and that my speech and actions will be coated with surrender to Him.

—Tammy

If My People

2 Chronicles 7:14; 2 Timothy 3:1–5, 4:1–22; Revelation 3:16

In 1989, our youth group saw a movie about the end times and the rapture found in the book of Revelation. I won't lie. The movie scared me, not because I didn't know Jesus, but because I knew so many people who did not. The reality is sober. Everybody has a choice, to follow Jesus Christ or live life without Him. There is no in-between.

When Paul wrote to the young pastor Timothy in 67 AD, he was sitting in a Roman dungeon waiting to be beheaded. Paul was giving Timothy final thoughts on fighting the good fight and carrying on where Paul left off. The world is in chaos. (This is not a new thing.) People turn to other gods in their lives, seeking out teaching that their itchy ears are wanting to hear. Truth is being watered down, and those who claim Christianity are living somewhere in the middle of truth and lies.

> So, because you are lukewarm—neither hot nor cold—I am about to spit you out of my mouth. (Revelation 3:16 NLT)

> But mark this: There will be terrible times in the last days. People will be lovers of themselves, lovers of money, boastful, proud, abusive, disobedient to their parents, ungrateful, unholy, without love, unforgiving, slanderous, without self-control, brutal, not lovers of the good, treacherous, rash, conceited, lovers of pleasure rather than lovers of God—having a form of godliness but denying its power. (2 Timothy 3:1–5 NLT)

Spiritual warfare is raging all around us. The only way to combat spiritual warfare is through prayer.

> If my people, who are called by my name, will humble themselves and pray and seek my face and turn from their wicked ways, then I will hear from heaven, and I will forgive their sin and will heal their land. (2 Chronicles 7:14 NLT)

—Tammy

Fasting and Prayer
Matthew 6:16–18

"And when you fast, don't make it obvious, as the hypocrites do, for they try to look miserable and disheveled so people will admire them for their fasting ..." (Matthew 6:16 NLT).

The spiritual discipline of fasting is one of the most challenging acts of our Christian faith. Although seen as optional by many who are Jesus followers, Jesus Himself instructed his apostles to fast. Fasting is giving up something in your life that you depend on and replacing that thing with prayer. The purpose of fasting is not to suffer, but to take the opportunity to reprioritize God in our life. Fasting can be a powerful act to bring us closer to Jesus and must always be accompanied by abundant prayer.

I remember years ago I chose to fast coffee during the Lenten season. I did this because I had profoundly become aware that every morning, I would crave what many of us crave, coffee. Yet when it came to spiritual disciplines, such as Bible reading and prayer, let's just say I could easily omit them from my day. The Holy Spirit convicted me of my sin of putting something as a higher priority than Himself, and I knew I needed to reprioritize.

During that month, I was often asked to go out for coffee, but in aligning with this Scripture passage, I did not want to tell others I was fasting for their sympathy or to make myself look like a spiritual hero. I would go and visit, but order something else with no explanation. I replaced my coffee time with Scripture reading and prayer. The aromas about killed me when coffee brewed at work, at church, or in coffee shops, but they were all reminders that I was renewing my mind to crave prayer and spending time in God's Word.

Years later, I remember that special time of fasting with gratefulness and reverence. Now, while I am drinking my coffee each morning, I open His Word and have a lengthy prayer time on my knees. Yes, of course there are days when I fall short, but the habit is there now, and I owe that habit to the time I fasted specifically for that purpose.

—Tammy

So Distracted
Luke 10:38–42

Cockroaches are a nuisance! Mark and I were talking with Matt and Hannah, our son and daughter-in-law, the other day when they informed us about the cockroach problem they had in their apartment in Phoenix. Both are very neat people, so understandably, seeing these dirty creatures crawling around in their home was very bothersome.

The next morning, I called Matt, but he was right in the middle of tackling the cockroach problem and it was hard for him to focus on our conversation. I knew he needed to make a few calls, so we ended our conversation so he could do so. This made me think of how often little things in life, good or even necessary, can totally distract us from what we set out to do in our day initially, taking us away from the more important things we would do normally.

In the story of Mary and Martha in Luke 10:38–42, we learn that Jesus came to their house for a visit. The two sisters were siblings of Lazarus, whom Jesus had raised from the dead not long before, and they were all friends. While Martha busily made food preparations, Mary chose to sit with Jesus, listening to His teaching and spending time with Him. Martha was doing an honorable thing by being a good hostess, which is why she wasn't thrilled with Mary's complacency. She responded,

> "Lord, doesn't it seem unfair to you that my sister just sits here while I do all the work? Tell her to come and help me." But the Lord said to her, "My dear Martha, you are worried and upset over all these details! There is only one thing worth being concerned about. Mary has discovered it, and it will not be taken away from her." (Luke 10:40–42 NLT)

Notice that Jesus didn't tell Martha that she was wrong, just that Mary had chosen what is better. Yes, food prep is necessary, but in the scheme of eternity, spending time with Jesus is more important. We can have good intentions to spend time with Jesus until we get a flat tire, our furnace breaks, or we find cockroaches in the kitchen. The key is to make Jesus a priority so when distractions arise, we can still find time for what is best!

—Tammy

Faith with Doubt?

2 Corinthians 5:7; Mark 9:24

As humans, we naturally think a lot about life and the things that are important to us. As Christians, we often think about our faith. Sometimes these thoughts turn into skepticism and doubt about God, which often turns into guilt from having these thoughts. Is it bad for a Christian to doubt their faith? What should we do when we have moments of doubt? "For we live by faith, not by sight" (2 Corinthians 5:7 NIV).

When we are going through moments of doubt, we don't often like to hear this verse, as it seems to magnify the root of our doubt. We can't just go and physically see Jesus any time we want, and that can be frustrating knowing that we must rely on our faith to trust and believe in God. But to the same effect, it takes faith to believe in any alternative, which renders knowing with full human certainty what is true. Ultimately, as Tim Keller said, "it is not the strength of your faith but the object of your faith that actually saves you." All Christians will and should experience doubt throughout their faith journey, as it is what ignites deep and critical thought into the reason behind our belief. A Christian who never has questions or doubts has possibly turned their brain off.

The critical next step for a Christian is what we do with this doubt. We can brood over this doubt and become increasingly discouraged and disbelieving, or we can act and use this doubt to strengthen our faith! Write down your doubts and questions. Study what the Word says about those topics regarding your doubt. Research what scholars who have spent decades studying these questions have said. Pray. A simple, yet powerful prayer we can say to God during moments of doubt comes from the book of Mark 9:24 (NIV), "I do believe; help me overcome by unbelief!"

It is absolutely critical to make the effort to look into the answers you crave to overcome your doubt. And remember, you aren't guaranteed to find every answer you're looking for here on earth, and that's what requires the next step, a leap of faith.

-Matt

Week 46 Reflections

1. After reviewing the Scriptures for each day, name three to four passages that jumped out at you this week.
2. How can you practically apply these verses to your life today and the upcoming week?
3. What are your reflections on worshiping an audience of one?
4. What aspirations do you have? Write them down with a prayer that asks God to be Lord over those aspirations.
5. Prayer is powerful because there is power in the name of Jesus. Paraphrase 2 Chronicles 7:14 and write it out.
6. What does God do through our fasting and praying? Have you ever fasted? Why or why not?
7. Distractions can keep us from God. What distractions are you dealing with right now that take you away from what is best?
8. Have you ever been skeptical about the Bible and faith? Explain.
9. What is God asking you to focus on to help build your faith?

Celebrate What God Has Done!

1 Samuel 7:1–17

I grew up singing the old hymn, "Come Thou Fount of Every Blessing" (words by Robert Robinson, 1758). The second verse intrigued me.

> *Here I raise my Ebenezer*
> *Here by Thy great help I've come*
> *And I hope by Thy good pleasure*
> *Safely to arrive at home*

What in the world is an Ebenezer? The only Ebenezer I had ever heard of was Ebenezer Scrooge from *A Christmas Carol* (Charles Dickens, 1843). It was years later as a teen when I took the time to look up the meaning of this verse, particularly the word *Ebenezer*.

The story is found in 1 Samuel 7:1–17. In this chapter, the Israelites were feeling abandoned by God, but they had actually abandoned Him, not the other way around! Samuel instructed them to turn back to the Lord, destroying their foreign gods and images of Baal and Ashtoreth. They did so and began to worship God. Samuel then gathered them at Mizpah to pray for them, and they fasted and confessed their sins to the Lord.

When the Philistines, their enemies, heard that the Israelites were together at Mizpah, they gathered troops to engage in battle. The Israelites asked Samuel to pray on their behalf, and God heard their prayer. God spoke with a thunderous voice and confused the Philistines, ultimately leading to their defeat. "Then Samuel took a stone and set it up between Mizpah and Shen. He named it Ebenezer, saying, 'Thus far the Lord has helped us'" (1 Samuel 7:12 NIV).

The stone was a reminder of God's faithfulness! Sometimes we too neglect to remember all that God has done for us. We pray for His intervention in our lives, but then what? Do we write down or tell others what He has done? Let us do what Samuel did and "raise our Ebenezer" in victory!

—Tammy

Take Time to Praise
Nehemiah 9

We are people in a hurry. We pack as much as we can into a twenty-four hour period and often wish we had more time. But when it comes to praising God, how many of those hours do we offer Him in praise? As we mature and grow in our faith, our yearning for praising God grows. When time restraints are lifted, we are then freed up to focus on who God is with a praise that is uninhibited.

In Nehemiah 9, the people did exactly this. They took an undefined amount of time to praise God. Yes, this chapter is a very long chapter, but I encourage you to read the whole thing. It is a thorough verbal account to the people of all that God had done for them.

> They remained standing in place for three hours while the Book of the Law of the Lord their God was read aloud to them. Then for three more hours they confessed their sins and worshiped the Lord their God. (Nehemiah 9:3 NLT)

Have you ever experienced a time when the praise to God was a verbal account of all He has done? If so, what was it like? Now imagine standing in one place, recounting everything God has done for you in your life, followed by three more hours confessing your sins and the sins of your ancestors and your country? When I read Nehemiah 9, I am reminded of how short I fall in taking the time to praise and for prayer.

The verses go on to say that the leaders of the Levites shouted to the Lord with loud voices and urged all the people to do the same! Talk about uninhibited! Do you think anyone said, "I don't think I can do that because I'm an introvert"? I doubt it. Do you think people were keeping track of the time because they had somewhere else to be? Probably not. The people worshiped Him and spent six hours in praise, worship, and confession, making sure that their hearts were right with God. Wow. I hope that sinks in.

Yes, we are busy people, but Father, help us! Help us to be more cognizant of our need to praise You with uninhibited praise. May we tell our kids, our neighbors, and our coworkers of all You have done and make Your presence known.

–Tammy

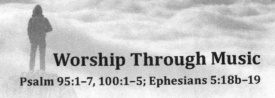

Worship Through Music

Psalm 95:1–7, 100:1–5; Ephesians 5:18b–19

Music has always played a vital role in my life because for me, music is the highest form of praise that I can offer. I feel that I touch heaven when I sing praises to my God.

> O come, let us sing unto the Lord; let us shout for joy to the Rock of our salvation! Let us come into His presence with thanksgiving; let us make a joyful noise to Him with songs of praise! (Psalm 95:1–2 NIV)

My love for music started when I was very young. My grandfather and my aunt sang to me from infancy on. My Baby Book says, "By the time Sharon was 3 years old she could recite and sing 18 nursery rhymes." I have always loved to sing, and I know that it was a gift to me from God.

Singing became even more precious when I became a Christian at age thirty-three. I now had a reason to sing. God had redeemed me and given me new life through His Son. The psalms resonated with me as I read them, and my soul praised God for all He had done for me.

Before my two daughters were born, I had prayed that I might have a child that would grow up to love music as much as I did. I encouraged music in my daughters because I wanted them to know the passion of worship that comes through song. Music goes deep and speaks the words we don't know how to say. It affects our perspective by offering hope and a oneness with God. Singing and playing instruments is scriptural and one of the most intimate ways we can express our praise! " ... be filled with the Spirit, addressing one another in psalms and hymns and spiritual songs, singing and making melody to the Lord with your heart" (Ephesians 5:18b–19 NIV).

When we sing a spiritual hymn or song, we let the Holy Spirit into our inner being, a very sacred moment when it often brings tears.

–Sharon

When I Am Alone

Joshua 1:9; Isaiah 41:10

My sweetest moments with God have been when I feel utterly alone. I have often felt this way when we have had to move out of state. The last move we made to Wisconsin, I found myself depressed like nothing I had experienced before. I wanted to give up, and I felt completely alone, even though I was surrounded by a family that loved me.

Depression is a hard thing to go through, and before experiencing it myself, I never understood the depth of impact. God taught me a lot through that period in my life. I learned to lean on Him for everything, to seek Him and His strength, and to worship Him in the pit of despair. Two verses that helped me out of the black hole were:

> This is my command—be strong and courageous! Do not be afraid or discouraged. For the Lord your God is with you wherever you go. (Joshua 1:9 NLT)

> Don't be afraid, for I am with you. Don't be discouraged, for I am your God. I will strengthen you and help you. I will hold you up with my victorious right hand. (Isaiah 41:10 NLT)

In times of loneliness, I have read these verses aloud, claiming them as promises. He is a loving Father and hears the cries of His people. He commands me not to be afraid! He is right here, right now, dwelling in my heart. He knows me inside and out. He promises to give me strength and holds me up with His victorious hands. The question is, do I trust Him to do what He promised amid how I feel? "God is our refuge and strength, an ever-present help in trouble" (Psalm 46:1 NIV).

He is my lifeline. He is a shield around me, my Protector and Strength. He is faithful to pull me out of the pit of despair. I may feel alone, but He is always with me … always.

—Tammy

The Spirit Leads

Psalm 119:105, 139:23–24; Acts 2:25–28

I resigned from my job. When I have stepped away from an assignment in the past, it was because of a move or I was moving to a larger opportunity. This time, however, I didn't have anything else lined up. I only knew that God had released me and I needed to step out in faith. This was unfamiliar territory for me. But when the Holy Spirit leads, I know I need to follow, even when I can't see what is up ahead. "Your word is a lamp to guide my feet and a light for my path" (Psalm 119:105 NLT).

How do we know when God is leading us? First, we can decipher God's will based on what we know already to be God's will for us. For example, do our goals or desires reflect God? Or are we being self-centered? Greedy? Unforgiving?

Second, is God asking us to confess or surrender anything, such as hidden motives or pride? I have found that once I totally confess my sin and surrender my will to His, I can hear Him. My spirit is aligned with His, and I can trust Him to lead me with peace, confidence, and joy.

God has always been faithful to me. Every time I lean into the Holy Spirit with expectation, I add one more faith notch to my belt. Remember, God is not trying to hide His will from us. He wants us to pursue Him so He can pour out Himself upon us and lead us to a stronger faith in Himself.

> Search me, O God, and know my heart; test me and know my anxious thoughts. Point out anything in me that offends you, and lead me along the path of everlasting life. (Psalm 139:23–24 NLT)

—Tammy

Persistence in Prayer
Luke 18:1–8; 1 Thessalonians 5:17

Since living in Wisconsin, I have been exposed to an array of wildlife, especially birds like sandhill cranes, blue herons, Baltimore orioles, blue buntings, and others. But there is one bird that likes to build an unusual nest over our front door. Mud swallows build nests similar to a hornet's nest and lay their eggs inside. We like the birds, but not the nests. When the mud swallows attempted to build this summer, we knocked their nest down immediately. On the next day, it was the same thing. Third day, we washed the area well and placed a piece of taped paper over the area. They kept building. This went on for several more days. These persistent little birds didn't take no for an answer.

This persistence reminds me of the parable that Jesus taught in Luke 18:1–8 about the persistent widow. The unjust judge in this story ignored a woman who came to him for justice against her enemy. In the end, the judge, even though he didn't fear God or care about people, gave her what she asked for because she was wearing him out! Jesus concludes the story by explaining how if an unjust judge could give justice to someone who wouldn't stop asking, how much more our heavenly Father cares about us when we cry out to Him with consistent prayer!

I long to have the persistence of a mud swallow. It sounds so simplistic, but I don't want to doubt God just because my nest keeps getting knocked down. I don't want to doubt Him because I have to wait for Him to answer. I don't want to give up too quickly or stop praying just because I can't see the answer in front of me. God is always faithful!

Our persistence isn't nagging. It tells God how much we trust in Him. The reality is, if we completely trust God, we will be tenacious in our prayers! He's not playing games with us, but He is working all things, all people, and all situations out for the good of those who love Him and are called according to His purpose (Romans 8:28).

Remember, if the widow in this parable trusted and persisted to a judge who did not even respond to her, how much more does your God love you and hear you? He is always working, so trust Him. Be persistent. "Never stop praying" (1 Thessalonians 5:17 NLT).

–Tammy

Week 47 Reflections

1. After reviewing the Scriptures for each day, name three to four passages that jumped out at you this week.
2. How can you practically apply these verses to your life today and the upcoming week?
3. What does the book of Psalms teach us about worship? How is music used to worship God in a unique and meaningful way?
4. I have many Ebenezers (accounts of God's faithfulness). Write out your Ebenezers and take time to thank God for each one.
5. Have you or someone you know experienced depression? How can God meet you where you are and draw close to you, even though you may feel numb emotionally?
6. Describe a time when you have followed the Holy Spirit's leading but had absolutely no idea what was next. How did you feel? What did you learn from that experience?
7. How persistent are you when it comes to prayer? What do you glean from the parable of the persistent widow?
8. Name one thing you could incorporate or add to your personal time with God that you would like to develop and grow in.
9. How can you incorporate more time for praise into your day? What does uninhibited praise look like for you?

MONTH 12
Our Lives Pursue a Journey in Relationship with God

A FAITH THAT STANDS
Will Never Be Shaken

A Burr Under Your Saddle

Matthew 18:21–35

I was watching a TV show not too long ago about a racehorse that had gone missing. Unlike this wild-at-heart champion, the horse's identical twin had a calmer demeanor, not precipitating many wins on the track. Gamblers sought to take the champion racehorse out of contention, so they stole the horse and killed it. To cover it up, they put a burr under the twin horse's saddle to make it act wild like his champion brother.

That made me ponder that if a burr can affect a horse's behavior, even misrepresent the identity of the horse, could a burr affect human behavior as well? Maybe not a physical burr, but a burr such as a constant agitation from someone difficult to love? Yes! And I know firsthand that the constant irritation can evoke a poor response from me, igniting a flame of a bad attitude. If I'm not careful, the flame will grow out of control, ready to explode at any moment. Has this ever happened to you?

The story in Matthew 18 jabs me right in the heart because it is so convicting. How easy it is for me to desire the forgiveness of others, but then not forgive someone else who has wronged me! There is no softness in this parable, so brace yourself.

> "You evil servant! I forgave you that tremendous debt because you pleaded with me. Shouldn't you have mercy on your fellow servant, just as I had mercy on you?" Then the angry king sent the man to prison to be tortured until he had paid his entire debt. (Matthew 18:32–35 NLT)

Forgiving someone seventy-seven times as Jesus commands seems doable until you have someone in your family, a coworker, a boss, or a friend whose behavior becomes the burr under your saddle. Let the burr go. Remember, the burr is changing you and keeping you from experiencing God's forgiveness. Sometimes we just need to saddle up and face the ugliness so we can forgive those who have wronged us. Then we can move on with peace and maturity in the Lord. It's hard, but so worth it!

—Tammy

Faithful in the Little Things
Luke 16:10–13

I worked in the construction industry for most of my life. When I became a general contractor building houses, I quickly found out that there are many crafts involved with multiple steps along the way. Sometimes I found that if workers thought their part in the building process were a small and insignificant part of the project, they might not be faithful in giving their best.

As the general contractor, I realized that just about everything that one worker did affected the next worker that followed in the process. If the concrete workers did not pour the footers level, the bricklayers had trouble and became unhappy. If the bricklayers did not get the foundation wall square, the carpenters had trouble and became unhappy. If the framing walls were not plumb, the drywallers had trouble and were unhappy. And so it went on and on from start to finish.

In Luke, Jesus teaches that if we are faithful in little things, we will be faithful in large ones. But if we are dishonest in little things, we won't be honest with greater responsibilities. The focus here is on money and how we handle that in our lives. This concept can be applied to many parts of our lives, including our work or our roles within our family.

If we want to advance in our jobs, we need to be certain that we are taking care of the little things and that we can be trusted with whatever we have been given responsibility for at that time. In my own time in construction, I saw firsthand those who did their job poorly or cheated in their efforts were looked over when it was time for a promotion. Some were even let go entirely. However, those who did a good job and could be trusted with little were given bigger and better jobs.

Jesus gave practical advice that if we are untrustworthy about worldly wealth, who will trust us with the true riches of heaven? And if we are not faithful with other people's things, why should we be trusted with things of our own? As we go through our day-to-day lives, let us remember not to let money deceive us but rather show ourselves to be honest and trustworthy. Our investments on earth can bring an eternal reward.

–Dean

Safer on the Sidelines
Matthew 25:14–30

I used to spectate at both the boys' baseball and basketball games, and I occasionally witnessed broken bones, broken teeth, bloody noses, or concussions. Being sensitive in nature, this bothered me, but I was very glad that I wasn't out there playing! If the physical injuries weren't disturbing enough, some of the parents were shouting at the refs for calls they made, and the tension could be cut with a knife. As I sat in my seat, I remember thinking that it was certainly safer on the sidelines. No one was breaking my nose or calling me names.

This analogy sets the tone for today's passage in Matthew 25:14–30, the parable of the talents. God has entrusted all of us with talents, which, broadly interpreted from this parable, refer to all types of gifts God has given to us for our use. This includes our natural, spiritual, and material gifts, as well as our health, money, and education.

But what happens when God has given us gifts, but we are afraid to put ourselves out there for fear of being rejected or overlooked? What if someone hurts us by making a comment that stings? It's easy to compare our gifts and resources to others. Sadly, when we do, we are inclined to talk ourselves out of serving, thinking that someone else can do it better. This is where we need to stop in our tracks, for that is never what God had in mind!

Yes, it is often easier on the sidelines because we feel safer. When we put ourselves out there, we are opening ourselves up for criticism and injury. Even cheerleaders on the field can get hit by a ball or fall prey to an occasional derogative comment. Being all in is a vulnerable place to be. Leaders particularly are subject to criticism and hurt, but we need leaders! We need workers! We need those to serve on the front lines.

Jesus taught us in this parable to work hard and serve Him according to the gifts He has bestowed upon us. As children of God, our lives are not about us. Let us be encouraged when we are beaten down and battered, for it is during these times we can enter a deeper understanding of Christ and His sufferings. Safer on the sidelines? Maybe, but not what God intended.

–Tammy

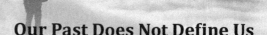

Our Past Does Not Define Us

Romans 8:1; Philippians 3:13–14

I can be obsessive when it comes to reliving wrong things I've done or spoken. Before I know it, I find myself dwelling on the past, unable to shake off the things I wish I could redo. A longtime friend told me years ago that I had a mean streak, and she was right. I have been personally horrified at my ability to throw verbal darts right between someone's eyes, making them feel an inch tall! It's not something I'm very proud of. Even when I have been obedient to God by apologizing to someone and God, I find myself stuck in the mud, feeling defined by my past outbursts. I know in my mind that God has forgiven me, but I'm keeping a "record of wrongs" (1 Corinthians 13) for myself, creating a new identity of failure.

God has been so patient with me through the years. He has shown Himself to me through this verse, "So now there is no condemnation for those who belong to Christ Jesus" (Romans 8:1 NLT). He has taught me that when I ask His forgiveness and genuinely repent, He forgives me. Period. The slate is clean.

What do you feel condemned about? We all have faults and sinful tendencies because we are human, but Satan will loom over us with shame. When we hold on to past mistakes, we are stealing energy that God wants to use for us to move forward. We may expect more from ourselves, but life is a journey, and this journey is not over until we breathe our last breath. The key is being aware of where we are weak and continually allow God to show Himself through those weaknesses.

We are not defined by our past when we are forgiven children of the Most Holy God! He is our identity. He renews us and sets our feet on a rock and a new path, creating new ways for us to move forward.

> No, dear brothers and sisters, I have not achieved it, but I focus on this one thing: Forgetting the past and looking forward to what lies ahead, I press on to reach the end of the race and receive the heavenly prize for which God, through Christ Jesus, is calling us. (Philippians 3:13–14 NLT)

—Tammy

We'll Never Know the Impact

Psalm 145; Proverbs 22:6

"Direct your children onto the right path, and when they are older, they will not leave it" (Proverbs 22:6 NIV).

Like others that have had a loved one pass, I have many memories of my mom. Some of these memories are of a specific event in time, but one that has grown in significance was repeated so many times throughout my years living with my parents. Many mornings I would get up, and like most young boys, I would be ready to eat. In my case, that would mean Mom making something for me. So first I would have to find my mom.

Understand that without her hearing aids in, my mom had very little hearing. My search generally took me to the living room, where I would find my mom kneeling at the couch reading the family Bible and praying. As a young boy, I was more interested in getting her to the kitchen than what she was doing there. As I got older, I remember being more interested in the Bible itself, not for the words yet, but for the fact that many of the pages had come loose from the binding.

Eventually I would come to realize that these pages were tattered and pulled out based on the frequency of use. Better yet would be the time when Mom would begin reading the Bible to me and helping me to understand its meaning.

Psalm 145 is a wonderful psalm of praise. Just as my mom had a time of devotion with the Lord every day, David also spent time with and praised God every day. David reminds us that the Lord is close to all who call on Him. My mom clearly wanted and needed the Lord to be close to her, and she understood setting aside time each day was critical.

As I reflect on my time with my mom, the way she lived her life each day has had such an important impact on my life and decision to accept and follow Jesus. I am not sure if she ever knew it all started by observing her in the living room as a young boy. Each one of us has this opportunity each day with those around us. Stay close to God and love those around you. You may never know the impact.

— Mark

Seek the Lord and His Counsel

1 Kings 22:4-6; 1 Chronicles 16:8–12

"Seek the Kingdom of God above all else, and live righteously, and he will give you everything you need" (Matthew 6:33–34 NLT).

How large does a decision you are making need to be before you will consult another person for their input or advice? What about God? How big does a decision need to be before you consult God and His guidance and direction? If you are like me, my initial tendency in the small decisions is to figure things out myself, and if they are a little more important, maybe ask a friend. But if they are life-changing (like moving or figuring out where to go to college or who to marry), I will naturally seek God first and foremost. But what does God say in His Word about this?

Whether you find yourself considerably self-sufficient or intuitively talking to God about every little thing in your day, God's desire is for us to come for Him for everything. God wants to be our main source of counsel, no matter how big or small the matter is. He will never get exhausted by us coming to Him repeatedly. In my experience, my independence has caused me to be knocked down a few notches by relying on my own expertise. For instance, I used to neglect asking for God's help if I felt totally prepared to perform, lead worship, speak, or teach a lesson of some sort. I was self-sufficient, relying on my natural abilities, my personal preparation, and leadership. Therefore, *I had this covered!* Or so I thought. My lack of asking God for His guidance, wisdom, and Holy Spirit to come upon me caused me to lead in my own efforts, forget important material, or lack flow or passion. I have learned my lesson. I need God. I now find myself asking God for His counsel for anything I must do, no matter how small or insignificant. "Search for the Lord and for his strength; *continually* seek him" (1 Chronicles 16:11 NLT).

Mark and I have a picture hanging above our fireplace with this verse on it. May we continually seek the Lord and His counsel, and be dependent on Him for everything.

—Tammy

Week 48 Reflections

1. After reviewing the Scriptures for each day, name three to four passages that jumped out at you this week.
2. How can you practically apply these verses to your life today and the upcoming week?
3. Do you have a burr under your saddle (an irritant you can't shake)? How does God want you to handle life when you get a burr?
4. Are you faithful in the little things? How do you respond to the little things compared to the bigger things in life? What does God say about this in His Word?
5. We can get bogged down by our past mistakes. What, if anything, in your past creeps up now and then affects the present?
6. Who in your life has made an impact? Who do you think you are impacting?
7. Does your insecurity or fear keep you on the sidelines serving Jesus? Explain.
8. God wants us to come to Him with the big things and the little things. What little things should you pray about that you hadn't thought about until now?
9. What is one action item God has given you for this next week?

Out of Our Control

John 16:33; 1 Peter 5:7

"Give all your worries and cares to God for He cares for you" (1 Peter 5:7 NLT).

My dear friend Lori passed away on Christmas Day at age forty-five from a seven-year battle with breast cancer. When she first was told that she had cancer, her world was turned upside down. A disease that seemed to silently creep up on her squashed any long-term hope, as the cancer had already spread. With a husband and two young children, Lori grieved the loss of a normal life going forward and chose to live in the eternal rather than the temporary. Everything she had energy to do, she did with a purpose, making sure that her time was not wasted with unimportant things, and treated every relationship with clear intentions. When Lori finally succumbed to the cancer, her funeral service was a worship service, thanking God for the gift of life and offering the hope of salvation to all who had not yet heard. The celebration of her life was an eternally focused remembrance, and God was glorified!

We do not have control of our lives. We anticipate there will be a tomorrow, but truly, all we have is today. So when life crumbles around us and the security of all the things we hold dear turns into the impossible and disheartening, how do we respond?

Jesus tells us that we will suffer. We will have trials and struggles. However, Jesus also tells us that when we choose the path of following Him and living a holy life, we are putting our hope in the eternal, not the temporary. He has overcome the world, which simply means that this world is not our home. Our faith alone has overcome and will overcome anything that comes our way.

Yes, we will grieve. Yes, we will experience loss, evil, and hardship. Yes, people will disappoint us. But being a Jesus-follower is an eternal calling, and I would so much rather go through this life with Jesus than without. Evil lurks around us. Potential diseases await. Grief and loss are inevitable. But let us remember that eternity is forever. What happens to us on earth is out of our control, but we do control the choice to follow Jesus or not. Choosing Jesus chooses eternity!

—Tammy

Questioning God
Isaiah 45:9–12; John 16:33

Have you ever taught a three-year-old?

Teacher: "The sky is blue."

Child: "Why?"

Teacher: "Because that's how God made it."

Child: "Why?"

Teacher: "Because God wanted a variety of pretty colors."

Child: "Why?"

Teacher: "Because God thought blue was prettier than black."

You get the picture. Humans are ingrained to want to know why things are the way they are. Sure, knowing why can allow us to learn from our mistakes or accept the facts of the situation better. However, even when we place God in control of our lives, we may never know the whys behind life's events.

Knowing in John 16:33 that He says that we will have trouble in this life helps me know that God is not punishing me when a tornado hits my house. On the other hand, if I sin against God and that leads to a sea of hardship, then I know why. It was my sin that led to those results.

God is not afraid of our questions. Ultimately, we need to rest in knowing that God is sovereign. This means that God has the supreme power and the authority to all that happens. God never chooses evil things to happen to us, but He allows the evils of this fallen world to play out in His sovereignty. Why? Because in the end, He will have the last word.

> This is what the Lord says ... "Do you question what I do for my children? Do you give me orders about the work of my hands? I am the one who made the earth and created people to live on it. With my hands I stretched out the heavens. All the stars are at my command." (Isaiah 45:11–12 NLT)

—Tammy

Close to the Brokenhearted

Psalm 34:15–20

No one gets too far in this life without knowing heartbreak. Our hearts can be broken over many things as we walk this earth, from small to big things. We know the end of relationships, the death of dreams, the loss of loved ones, health concerns, and betrayals. There are times we feel so much pain it can feel like our hearts might physically break in two.

Sometimes all it takes is one sentence or one phone call for life to forever feel completely different. My husband and I experienced this right after our second daughter was born. I was young and healthy, had a great pregnancy with no complications, and had the picture of what life would look like when this new daughter joined us and her big sister. However, soon after she was born, the sentence that changed it all came from a doctor saying, "We believe your daughter was born with Down syndrome." There are too many moments to describe that come along with receiving a lifelong diagnosis that will change your life. For me, it was months filled with fear of what her life would look like and sadness over all the ways the future I had in mind now felt different from the reality we were given. It was these days where I experienced for myself the truth of Psalm 34, the "Lord is close to the brokenhearted" (Psalm 34:18 NLT). As I woke up in the night crying, the Lord was close. As scary doctors' appointments came, the Lord was close. As some dreams died and the Lord began to replace them with new ones, He was close.

We grieve countless things as we walk through this life. Being given a child with Down syndrome started out with grieving, and the Lord has replaced it with great joy in the gift of this precious daughter. However, He knows us and sees us and has compassion for the way our hearts break when we don't understand and when we are surprised. He is always at work and holding our hearts as we walk through things that knock the breath out of us. If you have a broken heart today or if you are crushed in spirit today, there is a promise straight from God's Word to you. He is close to you, and He will rescue you. You can count on that.

–Shari

Think on These Things
Philippians 4:7–9

I have always been someone who thinks deeply. My thoughts can become either uplifting or discouraging. The mornings are a rare moment of quiet time in our household. When I am able to wake early and spend time in quiet prayer, my thoughts tend to align with His. However, eventually the busyness of the day kicks in, and I forget to keep my mind focused on what He outlines for us in Philippians 4:7–9. Whenever I sense myself getting overwhelmed, these verses provide a practical tool to getting back on track. His truth provides a peace that surpasses all understanding.

Thinking on any one of these things takes intentional effort. Take truth, for example. It is easy to believe the lies of this world. As a woman, I am constantly told how I am supposed to look, how I should be spending my time, how I am supposed to act, and where my worth lies. However, the real truth lies in who God made me. He defines my worth. This doesn't stop other thoughts from entering my mind. I am bombarded with somebody else's opinion of me almost daily. Each time I have to step back and ask myself "Is this true?" Without taking the time to discover the truth, seemingly harmless comments can ruin my entire day. Or I can choose to live in the peace that His truth provides.

Meditating on these things is important, along with pausing to reflect and spending quiet time thinking and praying over them. However, the verses do not command us to stop thinking of these things. Verse 9 also commands us to practice them in our lives. Both are equally important. If we are not careful, our own thoughts can turn negative. We might start putting ourselves down, judging our own decisions or worrying about our insecurities.

One practical way to combat negative self-talk is to memorize Scripture. Whatever we continuously feed our thoughts will slowly become the lens through which we view the world, how we see ourselves, and how much, or how little, we empathize with others. With more and more distractions so readily available, it is even more important to intentionally consume His truth.

-Ashley

Who God Says I Am

Romans 3:24; 2 Corinthians 3:12; 1 John 3:1

"And then there were three ..." Ever heard that phrase before? It's usually a quip after someone leaves the room and then someone states the obvious of how many are left. What if we took the humor out of it for a moment and turn the phrase onto myself?

"Three" describes how many "Mes" there were in middle school and even partly into high school. Yes, that's right. I was trying to be three different people, someone at home who was different than the one at school, who was also different than the one at church. I lived an exhausting lifestyle, always trying to remember who knew what about me and in what context. I carefully maintained this web of who-knew-which-me and wouldn't hang out with certain people when other certain people were around in case something accidentally got said in front of someone who shouldn't know what they shouldn't know.

Whew! Confused yet? Eventually I was too. I got to college, and life smacked me in the face. Just in the first semester, I missed more Sunday services than I had in my whole life and then landed a C- in Old Testament of all things! I literally passed the class with the lowest possible point accumulation allowed. I had horrible study habits, meaning I didn't study ever. But there was a deeper issue. I knew I was called to be a pastor, and yet suddenly it became clear in just a couple short months that I knew far less about Scripture than I thought I did. Pride and arrogance had grown rampant in my heart, and I wasn't even aware.

I had gotten so used to trying to be someone else that I had never really found myself. I didn't understand what an identity in Christ looked like because I never asked God, "Who do You say I am?" If you're like the younger me, you question yourself constantly, you doubt your abilities, and you seek approval from others. I know that feeling. You're not alone.

But there is hope! Scripture speaks. May these verses speak to you like they have spoken to me in the past. You are *Wonderfully made* (Psalm 139:14), *Child of God* (1 John 3:1), *Redeemed* (Romans 3:24), and *Hope* (2 Corinthians 3:12). Who does God say you are?

-Scott

No Excuses

John 1:1, 14:6; 1 Timothy 2:5

"Jesus told him, 'I am the way, the truth, and the life. No one can come to the Father except through me'" (John 14:6 NLT).

The road to salvation is a narrow road. Jesus Christ is the narrow road. We may have trouble with this concept of narrow because we live in a time when if the road is too narrow, we make it wider to suit us. If the Bible is too rigid, we adapt it to make it more politically correct for our liking. If we want to live a certain lifestyle contrary to the will of God, we fall on the knowledge that Jesus loves us and made us this way, ignoring the whole character of God in order to rationalize the sin in our lives. We hear it preached, "I'm broken, you're broken, we're all broken, let's just embrace our brokenness!" But let's call it what it is. Brokenness is sin. No excuses.

Sin is sin, and we are all in need of repenting and turning to Jesus. Repenting means turning and running 180 degrees the opposite direction! Is this easy for us to do? Of course not! Let's admit: sin can be a lot of fun and feel good for the moment. But we must recognize, a life of justifying our sin can falsely exempt us from any accountability. Sin is of the evil one, and in the end, everyone is accountable to God.

> Obviously, the law applies to those to whom it was given, for its purpose is to keep people from having excuses, and to show that the entire world is accountable before God. (Romans 3:19 NLT)

Are we making excuses? Remember, life is short, but eternity is forever. Yes, the road is narrow. Yes, it may seem harsh, but God will not compete with any other god in our lives. God will not bait us or woo us to choose the narrow road. He will not compromise, and He will not change. God is a loving, merciful, and compassionate God, but He also is a jealous God, and His justice and mercy go hand in hand. No excuses.

—Tammy

> For, there is one God and one Mediator who can reconcile God and humanity—the man Christ Jesus. (1 Timothy 2:5 NLT)

Week 49 Reflections

1. After reviewing the Scriptures for each day, name three to four passages that jumped out at you this week.
2. How can you practically apply these verses to your life today and the upcoming week?
3. Choosing Jesus means choosing eternity with Him. What does that mean to you?
4. Sometimes we question God and ask Him why something happens to us or someone else. What does He say about that?
5. Name a time when your heart has been broken and you have grieved over a loss. What has God shown you about Himself?
6. God wants us to think about things that are pure, lovely, admirable, and good. Make a list of things that God wants you to think about when you are tempted to dwell on the negative.
7. Who does God say you are?
8. We all have given excuses why we don't do something we know we should. What is something God is impressing on you to do or change, but you are coming up with excuses?
9. Write out a prayer asking God to draw close to you.

Holy Living
1 Peter 1:13–15

My husband and I have a lot of fun in our marriage. He is the CEO/engineer person in the relationship, while I am the creative, spontaneous one, opening doors to many humorous conversations. For instance, Mark has an amazing gift of finding a home for everything in the house! In our twenty-seven years of marriage, I have learned that the whole house is not a shoe closet (ha)! I've also learned that there is a home for keys and purses, which could benefit one like me who misplaces those things at least once a week.

Believe me, my desire has been to improve in this area of putting things away. This may seem unbelievable to those of you who relate to Mark, but I decided to try a new habit, which was to hang my bathrobe instead of throwing it over a chair. I had heard that habits develop if you stick to them for sixty days, and I can tell you that it worked! To this day (over ten years later), I am still hanging my robe!

Some disciplines come easy for certain people, while others are a little more difficult. Peter writes, "prepare your minds for action and exercise self-control" (1 Peter 1:13 NLT). Preparation and exercise take lots of discipline, often requiring the need to form new habits. We all have bad habits. Unfortunately we sometimes accept the way that we are rather than strive to improve on personal weak areas, probably because it takes time, discipline, and hard work.

> Don't slip back into your old ways of living to satisfy your own desires. You didn't know any better then. But now you must be holy in everything you do, just as God who chose you is holy. (1 Peter 1:14 NLT)

God instructs us to be holy because He is holy. This means we can't get lazy. We need to be constantly striving to be more like Jesus and continually develop good habits for ourselves. What new habits might you consider today? As we spend time with the Lord today, let's ask Him what holy habits will glorify Him and set us apart as Christ-followers.

—Tammy

Spirit Living

Joshua 1:8; Isaiah 55:11; Psalm 119:27, 52

The term *study* has not always been a fun or motivating word for me. Although I was a good student in school, I hated to study. I am a type-A person, on the go and action-focused, so the thought of sitting down to go over material that didn't interest me often resulted in procrastination.

As Christians, we are instructed to study God's Word, to meditate on it, and to apply it to our lives. Yes, this too can seem overwhelming when we open the Bible, not sure where to start.

> Study this Book of Instruction continually. Meditate on it day and
> night so you will be sure to obey everything written in it. Only then
> will you prosper and succeed in all you do. (Joshua 1:8 NLT)

I'd like to shed a little bit of perspective and encouragement if you find yourself avoiding God's Word or even scrambling to know where to start. Unlike studying for a test in school, pouring into the Bible and applying it to our lives comes with the promise that we will prosper and succeed in all that we do. God's Word is clear that there are ways to prosper in godliness, yet there are ways to falter in living contrarily to God's will.

As it applies to reading God's Word, instead of using the term *study*, how about we use the phrase "opportunity to grow"? When I began to look at reading God's Word with a mindset of gaining an opportunity to grow, I stopped seeing it as a chore and more as a life-changing experience. I began to apply what I read and made significant changes in my daily life. I began to put time with God at the top of my list, even if it meant waking thirty minutes earlier. I limited the busyness in my life to accommodate more time for others and mentor younger women.

Spiritual living is not putting a straitjacket on. Rather it is fruitfully living in the freedom in Christ so that we may be victorious over our human nature.

—Tammy

Emotional Hijacking
Philippians 2:12–13, 4:6–9

We don't all wear our emotions on our sleeves. That doesn't mean we don't have emotions. Being a musician, I lean toward the high emotional spectrum, occasionally losing all sense of sane reasoning. When stress, pressure, anger, or panic come over me, I refer to it as "emotional hijacking" because, if I'm not careful, my emotions take over and affect my sense of reasoning.

From a scientific standpoint, strong emotions can trigger an emotional hijack when a situation causes your amygdala to take over control of your response. The amygdala disables the frontal lobes and activates the fight-or-flight response. Without the frontal lobes, you can't think clearly, make rational decisions, or control your responses. But even knowing that, I believe that God can help those of us who may struggle with overactive emotional responses and show us steps forward.

> Don't worry about anything; instead, pray about everything. Tell God what you need and thank him for all he has done. Then you will experience God's peace, which exceeds anything we can understand. His peace will guard your hearts and minds as you live in Christ Jesus. (Philippians 4:6–7 NLT)

What is Paul's command in these verses? Not to worry. To pray. To lay your heart out before the Lord and tell Him what you need. In turn, He promises to give you a peace that exceeds anything you can understand, and that is the peace that will guard your heart and your mind.

That is good news! We are not on our own! We can trust God to do what He says, and when we seek Him for His help, He will give it to us. The Holy Spirit will help us to control our emotions and establish a new pattern of responding from an area of peace rather than a place of stress, anger, or fear. Don't let emotional hijacking consume you. Instead, allow God to make His way into your mind and heart, instilling His peace and the desire within to please Him.

–Tammy

Physical Self-Control
1 Corinthians 3:16–17, 6:15–20

As a sophomore in high school, I attended a church retreat with my youth group. Each morning and evening, we gathered in the large living space of the retreat center to hear messages from our youth pastor and then broke out into smaller discussion groups. One of the messages changed my life. The youth pastor spoke boldly on the physical self-control of our bodies, both in the care for our bodies and in our sexuality.

The first part of his message focused on how low self-esteem can lead to injuring our bodies, like drugs, alcohol, and cutting. He used the verses in 1 Corinthians, "Don't you realize that all of you together are the temple of God and that the Spirit of God lives in you? God will destroy anyone who destroys this temple. For God's temple is holy, and you are that temple" (1 Corinthians 3:16–17 NLT).

The second part pertained to our sexuality through the will of God. He not only stressed that sexual relations were between a man and woman in the context of marriage, but he also reiterated that God assigned our sex at birth and He does not make mistakes.

> Run from sexual sin! No other sin so clearly affects the body as this one does. For sexual immorality is a sin against your own body. Don't you realize that your body is the temple of the Holy Spirit, who lives in you and was given to you by God? You do not belong to yourself, for God bought you with a high price. So, you must honor God with your body. (1 Corinthians 6:18–20 NLT)

At the end of one of the retreat, the youth pastor gave an invitation for anyone who wanted to commit their physical bodies to the Lord. While the words to the closing song were sung, I stood up, went forward, and committed my whole physical being at the feet of Jesus. I wanted to let the Holy Spirit guide my mouth, mind, eyes, ears, sexuality, and hands and feet. I accepted that His regulations were for my protection. I never want to hold anything back from God again. He deserves all of me.

—Tammy

Discipline

Hebrews 12:1–12

"And have you forgotten the encouraging words God spoke to you as his children? He said, "My child don't make light of the Lord's discipline, and don't give up when he corrects you. For the Lord disciplines those he loves, and he punishes each one he accepts as his child" (Hebrews 12:5–6 NLT)

My husband and I were relaxing on the couch watching the 2020 Summer Olympics in Tokyo. I was, once again, reminded of the type of discipline required to not only make it to the Olympics, but to stand on the podium to represent one's country. These athletes have sacrificed years of their lives to train their bodies and minds for a competition where the whole world is watching. I admire this type of training and discipline, for it inspires me in my own life, especially in my spiritual walk.

What if my spiritual fruits and spiritual discipline were on display for the whole world to see? What would people say about me? Would they see through to my motives and hidden thoughts, gaining insight into the priorities I have placed in my life? I would like to think of myself as a disciplined person. However, there are times I have struggled with making reading my Bible a priority. I have put off serving others at certain seasons of my life to seek my own pleasures and achievements.

Like an Olympian, we all need training and discipline when it comes to our spiritual walk. Bible studies, corporate worship, accountability groups, prayer partners, and a dedicated time every day for Scripture study and reflection are a great place to start. I may not end up at the spiritual Olympics, but God has given me a fervor to run this race as best I can and strive for excellence in my faith journey! If the world is looking (and they are), I want them to see the fruits of my discipline with Jesus working in me!

–Tammy

And let us run with endurance the race God has set before us.
(Hebrews 12:1 NLT)

The Old Way Shed

Romans 8:1–2; 2 Corinthians 12:9; Colossians 3:1–17

While humans shed millions of skin cells every day, a snake sheds its skin in one single, continuous piece between four and twelve times a year. The process is called *ecdysis*, and this happens because a snake's skin does not grow with the snake. It simply outgrows its skin! Another reason they shed their skin is to remove parasites and other bacteria that may harm the snake. Interesting creatures!

Colossians 3 teaches us about how we can shed our skin, or our old way. It's called repentance.

> So put to death the sinful, earthly things lurking within you. Have nothing to do with sexual immorality, impurity, lust, and evil desires. Don't be greedy, for a greedy person is an idolater, worshiping the things of this world … But now is the time to get rid of anger, rage, malicious behavior, slander, and dirty language. Don't lie to each other, for you have stripped off your old sinful nature and all its wicked deeds. Put on your new nature, and be renewed as you learn to know your Creator and become like him. (Colossians 3:5, 8–9 NLT)

Every time we shed our skin, this takes time, and we need to be patient with ourselves. Old habits are hard to break. Bad language, lust, greed, or whatever our old way includes, this is a daily process. Don't get discouraged if it takes some time. As we are diligent in prayer with a surrendered heart, we will begin to shed our old way and see the powerful transformation of Jesus at hand in our lives.

> My grace is all you need. My power works best in weakness. So now I am glad to boast about my weaknesses, so that the power of Christ can work through me. (2 Corinthians 12:9 NLT)

—Tammy

Week 50 Reflections

1. After reviewing the Scriptures for each day, name three to four passages that jumped out at you this week.
2. How can you practically apply these verses to your life today and the upcoming week?
3. What holy habits are God asking you to develop that set you apart as a Christ-follower?
4. What does meditating on God's Word look like to you? What is the importance of meditating on His Word?
5. Emotions can get the best of us at times. How do your emotions hijack the responses you want to have, but don't? How can God help?
6. What physical temptations are you facing right now? What do you need to do to stay on a straight and narrow path?
7. Where are you on the Christian racetrack? What do you need from God to help you finish the race well?
8. What old way needs to be shed? How can that be achieved? Explain.
9. What is God teaching you this week?

Scripture Speaks
Psalm 19:7–14

Scripture is God-breathed and stands alone. No writings have ever had any greater impact and meaning than the Word of God. When you read His Word, it is alive and active, which means God speaks to us through it. Our reading today is Psalm 19, written by the psalmist David. Respectfully consider all the phrases that exemplify God and the power of His Word. What do you take from this today and apply to your life?

> The instructions of the Lord are **perfect**,
> **reviving** the soul.
> The decrees of the Lord are **trustworthy**,
> making wise the simple.
> The commandments of the Lord **are right**,
> **bringing joy** to the heart.
> The commands of the Lord are **clear**,
> giving **insight** for living.
> Reverence for the Lord is **pure**, lasting forever.
> The laws of the Lord are **true**; each one **is fair.**
> They are more **desirable** than gold,
> even the finest gold.
> They are **sweeter than honey**,
> even honey dripping from the comb.
> They are a **warning** to your servant,
> a **great reward** for those who obey them.
> How can I know all the sins lurking in my heart?
> **Cleanse** me from these hidden faults.
> Keep your servant from deliberate sins! Don't let them control me.
> Then I will be free of guilt and innocent of great sin.
> May the words of my mouth
> and the meditation of my heart
> be pleasing to you,
> O Lord, my **rock** and my **redeemer**.
> Psalm 19:7–14 (NLT)

—Tammy

Applying God's Word

2 Timothy 3:16–17

"All Scripture is inspired by God and is useful to teach us what is true and to make us realize what is wrong in our lives. It corrects us when we are wrong and teaches us to do what is right. God uses it to prepare and equip his people to do every good work" (2 Timothy 3:16–17 NLT).

I have not always been a Bible reader, mostly because I never knew where to begin or what to read. I was the one that would often look for an à la carte answer to a question without knowing the context of the Scripture as a whole. It's probably not the best approach to studying the Bible! For this reason, I joined a Bible study years ago, to dig into the Bible and glean applications I could use forever. The Bible, as a whole, gives a very clear picture of God's story and is a fascinating journey to experience.

The more we know God's Word, the more we know God. From my perspective being a contemporary pianist who improvises, I often refer to my bag of tricks when embellishing a song. Knowing music inside and out allows me the freedom to play from what I know intimately and innately. Likewise, knowing the Bible allows us to draw from what we learn and apply those learnings at appropriate times. If you are ready to begin the adventure, here are some simple guidelines:

1. Start small. It is better to read and apply one verse than to read a whole chapter and not apply anything at all. Highlight key words!

2. The four Gospels (Matthew, Mark, Luke, and John) are a great place to start. Read a chapter a day. The book of Acts will capture your attention with the first churches and pioneers of Christianity.

3. The New Testament epistles by Paul should individually be read in their entirety, as that is how they were meant to be read. They are inspirational and encouraging to the Christian.

4. Try using Bible reading apps on your phone that have plans for understanding Scripture. Join a Bible study group or a small group that is going through the Bible together.

5. Worship God by reading through the psalms.

God speaks to us through His Word. He empowers us. He strengthens us. He delivers us. He heals us. God's Word with application is alive and active, and it will never return to us void!

–Tammy

Remain on the Vine
John 15:1–17

Mark and I planted bushes on the side of our house, but they have quickly gotten out of control, taking over the entire planting area. One might drive by and think the bushes look healthy and strong, but what they are is invasive and overgrown if not tended to. Every fall we aggressively chop them back to almost nothing! Then in the spring, the bushes fill out and look healthy, vibrant, and full once again.

Pruning is necessary for those who have a relationship with Jesus and follow him with their lives. Others may look at us and think that things are going well, and often they are. But God has other plans for our growth. God never wants us to grow wild and out of His control. He notices when branches are neglecting to produce the best kind of fruit that they could be. He knows how quickly pride, selfishness, dishonesty, gossip, and lust can grow in our hearts if we are not remaining on the vine of Christ. "Remain in me, and I will remain in you. For a branch cannot produce fruit if it is severed from the vine, and you cannot be fruitful unless you remain in me" (John 15:4 NLT).

The word *remain* means to live. Jesus is the vine, and He wants us to attach ourselves to Him, no one else. "No one can serve two masters. For you will hate one and love the other; you will be devoted to one and despise the other" (Matthew 6:34 NLT).

What kinds of fruit has God been growing in you? A peach cannot grow from an apple tree or vice versa. Likewise, gossiping about someone or using bad language are not fruits that come from the vine of Jesus. Having unforgiveness, selfish motives, or jealousy toward others are not fruit that are produced by the Holy Spirit. As Christ followers, let us welcome the pruning from the Master Gardener, making our fruit the sweetest it can be.

—Tammy

New Habits = New Vision
John 14:15; 2 Corinthians 5:17

My wife and I decided to become minimalists a few years ago, to become more intentional with our purchases, to think more before acquiring anything new, and to step back and answer all the what-if questions that often drive us to keep things we don't need. We eventually purged most of our possessions. Some things were easy, reducing clothes or discarding junk. Other things took more willpower like getting rid of our television, becoming a one-vehicle family, or photographing anything with sentimental value to avoid keeping an item out of nostalgia.

Beforehand we did not think too much of our possessions, the space to store them, the time and money to maintain them, and so forth. Now we are much more intentional. And almost everybody in our lives noticed the difference. Something had clearly changed in us. We had decided to live differently. There was us before minimalism and us after minimalism. The same thing should be true for Christ-followers. When we truly know Christ, we are called to live differently; to love like He loved; to see other people through the eyes of Jesus; to humble our perceptions, our instincts, our motives, or our opinions before God; and to love other people as Jesus loves.

Once we decide to follow Jesus, our lives should be noticeably different. We are commanded to love God and our neighbors. Are we putting our trust in God? Or are we continuously trying to control things ourselves? Are we treating people differently? Do we judge people for their actions or try to understand their hurt? Do we use people as a stepping-stone in our career or lift other people up along the way? Do we love other people like Jesus, or do we only say we are following Him? If we're not sure, we can ask the people around us. They should notice a difference.

—John

This means that anyone who belongs to Christ has become a new person. The old life is gone; a new life has begun! (2 Corinthians 5:17 NLT)

Victory Over Bad Habits

Romans 12:2; James 4:7

Habits are hard to break. As a teenager, I had a rather foul mouth until I made the decision to follow Jesus, allowing Him to search my heart and to cleanse it from all unrighteousness. I remember a Wednesday evening youth service in ninth grade when I felt the strong tug of the Holy Spirit convict me of my swearing and taking God's name in vain. The conviction was strong, yet I had sworn for so long, foul words were a normality for me in school or at home, especially when I was angry. Yes, I was a follower of Jesus at that point. However, the habits I had developed began way before my relationship with Christ did, so there was a lot to tackle. "Don't copy the behavior and customs of this world, but let God transform you into a new person by changing the way you think" (Romans 12:2 NLT).

Bad habits can be minor or very noticeable, imposing a life-changing effect on our lives. All in all, just like Romans 12:2 teaches us, God has the power and authority to renew our thinking and develop new habits that are pleasing and glorifying to Him. I knew I needed to get rid of this ugly habit, for it contradicted my faith in Christ. I hoped God would lead me to victory in this area.

I prayed, found other words to substitute the bad ones, and put an accountability partner in place. I consciously and diligently prayed for purity in my mouth. When I did mess up and swear, I challenged myself to apologize to whomever I swore to or with at the time. I'll admit, this felt a little vulnerable, especially with my school friends who also swore, but I disciplined myself to confess, even if the other person didn't care.

I write this today to let you know that in time I found victory over this bad habit because God transformed my thinking. He answered my prayer for purity and self-control. What seemed difficult or impossible at the time is now a testimony to God's faithfulness that He does give victory over bad habits!

—Tammy

Close the Sale

1 Peter 3:15

I've spent the last fifteen months working bi-vocationally as an assistant pastor and a car salesman. Following six years of biblical studies and a residency for a year, I believe God has taught me even more about being a pastor through being a car salesman. I may not have said that in the first few weeks of selling cars, for I didn't do very well at all. I remember thinking, *How hard can this be?* I wanted to grow as a salesman and was determined to figure out what I was doing wrong. After months of seeking guidance and learning some new skills, I rose to being the top salesman one month. Why? Because I learned how to close a sale.

There were three principles that helped me to close the sale.

1. I needed to know everything I could about the cars I was selling.
2. I needed to be friendly and respect each person, following up with them by taking the time to answer questions and setting appointments.
3. I needed to be honest with them and, with conviction, ask them in the end if they were ready to buy.

My hopes were that they wouldn't just look at the car, touch the car, or drive the car. I wanted them to buy the car and to be confident of their choice.

I got to thinking, *What if I were to sell the Christian life through Jesus? Would others want to buy Him from me? Would they see the fruits of God's love radiating from me, even under pressure? More importantly, do I capitalize on key opportunities to implement the same principles I do with cars to people and their faith?*

I needed to ask myself some questions. Do I personally know Jesus and actively live a life demonstrating the fruits of God's transformation in my life? Do I take time for people, loving them where they are at, following up with them during the week? Most importantly, do I close the sale? Do I help them consider Jesus by making a personal choice?

My prayer is that my life will reflect God's love and grace so much that people don't just hear about Jesus, dabble with the idea of knowing Jesus, or come to church, but that they have a genuine relationship with Jesus. I want to close the sale!

—Scott

Week 51 Reflections

1. After reviewing the Scriptures for each day, name three to four passages that jumped out at you this week.
2. How can you practically apply these verses to your life today and the upcoming week?
3. Write down as many words from Psalm 19 that exemplify the power of God and His Word. Which words resonate with you specifically?
4. What has been the hardest thing for you to do to apply Scripture to your life? What can you begin to do differently that will make a difference in your walk with the Lord?
5. Is it easy or difficult for you to stay on the vine? Explain.
6. We all have bad habits. Some last even into our new life through Christ. What bad habits are you still holding on to? Write down a plan for working toward breaking those habits.
7. Bad habits can prevent us from being all in on the Christian faith. Have you experienced this, or are you experiencing this now? What needs to happen for you to be all in?
8. Christ-followers are a light in this world of darkness. How can we close the sale when we share Jesus with others? What does that specifically look like for you?
9. What new habit would you like to develop?

A Something New
Isaiah 43:18–20

Let's talk about dirt, the dirty kind outside! Did you know that there are seventy thousand different types of dirt in the United States and that one tablespoon of soil has more organisms in it than there are people on the earth? Dirt is essential to our existence. If it weren't for dirt, we wouldn't have wood, vegetables or fruit. Farmers are skilled at knowing the importance of soil preparation, when to till, plant, and water their crops. Nursery farmers can determine when a plant should be transplanted for furthering its growth. Likewise, God is always doing something new in our lives, sometimes even transplanting us to a new thing. We need to be ready for it, making sure that we have prepared and watered our soil. "See, I am doing a new thing! Now it springs up; do you not perceive it?" (Isaiah 43:19 NIV).

I can't say I have always perceived when God has done a new thing. In fact, there are seasons in my life when I have dug in my heels for change, choosing not to embrace God's leading. Hindsight is 20/20, and when I look back at those seasons, I now am aware of what God was doing. He was shaping me, leading me, and transplanting me into a larger pot. I didn't always appreciate His moving and challenging me at the time, having to find new schools, new church, new job, and new friends. But I wouldn't change those seasons of transition and change for anything. I have learned to pay attention to God's gentle voice, anticipating the new thing He is about to do.

—Tammy

> But forget all that—
> it is nothing compared to what I am going to do.
> For I am about to do something new.
> See, I have already begun! Do you not see it?
> I will make a pathway through the wilderness.
> I will create rivers in the dry wasteland.
> Isaiah 43:18–19 NLT

Don't Look Back

Genesis 19:1–29

The story in Genesis 19 disturbs me. Sodom and Gomorrah were evil places, filled with flagrant sin. We learn that Abraham had a nephew named Lot who had backslidden in his faith and moved to Sodom with his wife and two daughters. The cries against these towns were heard by God, and He planned to destroy them because of the evil, but Abraham pleaded that Lot would be safe.

In the form of men, God sent two angels to destroy the two towns, but they were first instructed to rescue Lot, his wife, and his family. When the angels approached Lot, he invited them into his home as guests. That evening several evil men surrounded Lot's home, yelling for him to send out the men so they could have sexual relations with them. In efforts to protect his guests only, Lot offered his two virgin daughters to them, a heartless proposition. The angels overruled Lot (in God's mercy) and barred the door and blinded the entourage of men so they couldn't get in. Then the angels firmly instructed Lot and his family to run as fast as they could to Zoar and warned them not to look back, symbolizing their repentance in turning away from their sinful life. Lot's wife (we don't know her name) stopped to look back, and she sadly became a pillar of salt.

Quite a story, huh? I sadly can relate to Lot's wife. When God in His mercy rescued me from a situation I was going through, I knew God was taking me to a new thing. However, I kept looking back at the horrible situation I had been in, still pondering the way things used to be. Why did I do that? I struggled with letting go because I had grown used to the abuse. My faith needed to be exercised and put it into practice. God was doing a new thing, and once I was able to perceive that, I was able to let go and allow God to move me forward.

A wise friend told me that as you pick up the new thing in front of you, you have to drop something already in your hand. You can't hold on to both. The lesson? Don't look back! Look forward and keep your eyes on what's ahead. Your eyes will be opened to see God's new path He has set before you!

—Tammy

Where Do You Dwell?

Psalm 91:1–3

"Those who live in the shelter of the Most High will find rest in the shadow of the Almighty. This I declare about the Lord: He alone is my refuge, my place of safety; he is my God, and I trust him. For he will rescue you from every trap and protect you from deadly disease" (Psalm 91:1–3 NLT).

Have you ever rented a car? If so, you have probably exited the car lot by passing through the checkpoint and driving over a spike strip, a mechanism designed to pop your tires if you go over it the wrong way. Car rental companies must install spike strips on all their entrances to prevent car theft by those who bypass the checkpoint and exit out the wrong way.

Sometimes I wish I had a spike strip in my thought life so I don't turn back into the past. Every now and then, I need something to jolt me from dwelling on the what-ifs and how-comes, replaying events and conversations in my mind. The more I dwell in the past, the more anxiety overwhelms me.

How can I prevent myself from dwelling on the past so I can move forward? The first step is to recognize the right way out of the lot and stop at the feet of Jesus, my checkpoint. I need to then turn the engine off and commune with God first and foremost, as He promises He will lead me to the shelter where I need to dwell.

God is my security, and He desires for me to find true healing and peace. He wants to lead me to exit the lot into the arms of Jesus and rest in the shadow of the Most High. My God is my refuge, my protector, and my safety. When I have a raging battle in my mind, I must put every effort in place to keep from popping my tires on the spike strip by reentering the past. The past is done. I learn from it and move on, choosing to close the door on what was and focus on what is next.

Overall, I want the verses in Psalm 91 to serve as that *spike strip* in my thought life. I want the words to metaphorically remind me that when I *exit the lot*, I cannot turn back into it. I need to trust God to take me to that dwelling place of rest and shelter so I can be reenergized and prepared for what is next.

—Tammy

Prepare and Soldier Up!
Ephesians 6:10–20; 1 Peter 5:8

Hurricanes are one of the most frightening natural disasters that can turn states, cities, or individual homes upside down. Fortunately, modern weather devices give people a substantial heads-up when the storm will strike. Boarding up windows, gathering emergency supplies, and securing possessions are all part of the necessary preparations many people will make before they evacuate. Preparation is everything. "Stay alert! Watch out for your great enemy, the devil. He prowls around like a roaring lion, looking for someone to devour" (1 Peter 5:8 NLT).

Staying alert is everything to a believer in Christ. The metaphor of Satan being a prowling lion is an image we all can imagine. Stealthily hunting their prey through tall grasses of the African plains, they fatally pounce on the unsuspecting. Given that, how do we stay alert? We may have our eyes open, but does that mean we will see Satan in the tall grass?

> Stand your ground, putting on the belt of truth and the body armor of God's righteousness. For shoes, put on the peace that comes from the Good News so that you will be fully prepared ... hold up the shield of faith to stop the fiery arrows of the devil. Put on salvation as your helmet, and take the sword of the Spirit, which is the word of God. (Ephesians 6:10–20 NLT)

Now imagine a knight in shining armor, ready for battle, and every piece fit together with an intended purpose to protect. We are in a battle. According to this passage, God's armor allows us to see and stand for truth and put on peace that only comes from the Word of God. We encounter evil every day, but as we use the sword, which is the Word of God, let's prepare for battle and soldier up! His armor is all we need to withstand the spiritual war that is waging.

—Tammy

Burn the Ships
Philippians 3:13–14

History is full of fascinating stories. I was drawn to a particular action that was first demonstrated by Julius Caesar in his battle to take Britain. It again happens when Alexander the Great takes on the Persian empire and one more time as Hernan Cortez takes on the Aztec empire in what is now Mexico. What is it that intrigues me? In each case when the leader and his army landed by sea on the soil of the empire to be conquered, he ordered that his army burn the ships! The sailing itself was alone difficult but the upcoming battles were likely to be even more so. A quote credited to Alexander the Great puts things in perspective as he stated, "We will either return home in Persian ships or we will die here."

Each of these great leaders recognized that they would need the full support of every man, and by burning the ships, it was clear that there was no turning back. The only option was to press on for the victory. In the case of Cortez, there was a portion of the task to spread his faith to the people of this new land, but in most of these, the mission was to build a stronger empire for the leader of the conquering army. Paul tells a similar story but with a different purpose.

> But I focus on one thing: Forgetting the past and looking forward
> to what lies ahead. I press on to reach the end of the race to receive
> the heavenly prize for which God, through Christ Jesus, is calling
> us. (Philippians 3:13–14 NIV)

The men of these armies certainly had family back home and many other good reasons to return. The leaders made sure by burning the ships that going back to the past was not an option. In Paul's case, he had reasons to forget the past based on his life as Saul. But in the case of the army leaders and Paul, they all knew looking forward was the only option.

Regardless of what is in your past, Paul reminds us that our hope is in Christ. Because of this hope, we can burn the ships and put all our concentration on looking forward to the heavenly prize.

-Mark

A Faith That Stands

Hebrews 10:23; James 1:6–8

Authenticity and transparency are very important to me. I have learned abundantly from others who have shared their stories about how they came to know Jesus, how they wrestled with their faith at times, and how they are now in their nineties with faith that has stood the test of time. I stand in awe of God's faithfulness to them, and their struggles and celebrations inspire me to continue my own faith journey as a Christian.

We all have a faith story to tell. But sometimes the people in our lives that are closest to us, like our parents, children, nieces, nephews, or grandchildren, seem to get overlooked when it comes to sharing our own personal faith stories. We assume they already know.

Before the age of modern technology, families would pass faith stories down from generation to generation, recording God experiences for future generations to read. Nowadays, I think we neglect a major opportunity to share our faith, our faith struggles, and faithfulness of God with the people that we love most. Our kids and their children need to see unwavering faith lived out to encourage the ownership of their own faith. Those who are watching us need to see that conflicts can be resolved, self-control and purity are attainable, and forgiveness can be lived out. Unity can be gained, addictions overcome, new habits formed, and spiritual fruit realized.

Our life's example speaks louder than our words do, but our personal testimony puts the exclamation point on our actions. I ask God every day to search my heart to be sure that I am starting the day with a clean slate. I have learned to worship Him in the pit of despair and yet gratefully sit still in His presence and listen. I want to surrender everything God desires for me to surrender. Most importantly, I want to have a faith that stands and is unwavering, leaving a legacy for generations to come, standing the test of time, never to be shaken.

And finally, "Let us hold tightly without wavering to the hope we affirm, for God can be trusted to keep his promise" (Hebrews 10:23 NLT).

—Tammy

Week 52 Reflections

1. After reviewing the Scriptures for each day, name three to four passages that jumped out at you this week.
2. How can you practically apply these verses to your life today and the upcoming week?
3. We can live in the past if we aren't careful. What is something new that God is doing in your life right now?
4. Bad decisions and regret can paralyze us, keeping us from moving forward. When have you experienced this, and how does God want you to move on?
5. Where do you dwell (past, present, future, etc.)? What does that look like for you?
6. How does Paul say to dress for battle in the spiritual war we all are in?
7. To move forward, we need to burn the ships of the past. What ships are still there, needing to be burned?
8. Our life's example speaks louder than words. What does a faith that stands on Jesus look like?
9. What example is your faith to the world around you?

Family Authors That Contributed

Mark Thurman (Tammy's husband)
Mark is CEO of a private equity-owned company while serving in leadership roles in the local church. Mark and Tammy have been married for twenty-seven years, having raised two sons, Scott and Matt. Mark has served as a small group teacher to adults and teens and enjoys speaking to men about the art of sharing their faith in the workplace. Mark loves all sports and enjoys vacationing with family.

Scott Thurman (Mark and Tammy's oldest son)
Scott is a pastor, serving now in a bi-vocational role as an assistant pastor and car salesman in Missoula, Montana. Scott's role in this growing church plant allows him to utilize his gifts of speaking, leading worship, and serving the people around him. Scott has his bachelor's and master's degrees from Indiana Wesleyan University.

Matt and Hannah Thurman (Mark and Tammy's younger son and daughter-in-law)
Matt and Hannah met at Ohio State and have been married for three years. They are both engineers in Phoenix and, in their spare time, love being outside and trying new foods! They also host events in their apartment complex as a part of a ministry called Apartment Life. Together, they're bringing the gospel to the places they live, work, study, and play.

Dean Thurman (Mark's dad)
Dean is a retired homebuilder, bricklayer, and lay pastor who was married for fifty-six years before God called Mary home in 2006. Dean lives in Ohio and is a gifted wood craftsman. He loves people and has always been very active in serving in his church. He has three children, six grandchildren, and eight great-grandchildren.

Sharon Dellmore (Tammy's mom)
Sharon was married for forty-seven years until God called Dale home in 2013. Sharon is a retired schoolteacher and library aide, but also directed choirs and children's choirs for many years. Sharon resides in Syracuse, New York, serving in music and Bible study ministries. She has two daughters, four grandchildren, and one great-granddaughter.

Shari Hochstetler (Mark and Tammy's niece)
Shari lives in Indiana with her husband of twenty years and their four children. She spends her days running a household, caring for her family, and happily being a taxi driver for her kids. Shari loves connecting with friends, being with her husband and family, cooking, cheering her kids on in all they do, and serving in her community and the local church.

Kara Meza (Mark and Tammy's niece)
Kara lives in Shawnee, Kansas, with her husband of ten years. She works as an executive assistant at an established insurance company in Kansas City. Kara loves rooting for her favorite sports teams, walking the trails near her home, and enjoying Kansas City barbecue. Kara also loves spending time with family and friends and serving at her local church.

John and Ashley MacAdam (Mark and Tammy's niece and husband)

John and Ashley started as high school sweethearts and have been married for over fifteen years with two wonderful kiddos. John is a professional engineer, mobile app developer (appsbyjohn.com), and minimalist. Ashley loves raising the kids, hiking in nature, and spending time with her adopted dog. Together they are building an intentional life, rooted in faith.

Karissa Lyyski (Mark and Tammy's niece)

Karissa grew up in Syracuse, New York, and has been married to Joe for four years and a mom to River for one year. She stays at home with her new daughter while Joe works. Karissa waitresses on the weekends and enjoys spending time with family, particularly at outdoor events. One day at a time she's deepening her walk with God, putting that relationship to action.